Kind Revelations

On My Path to No Path

Christa Phillips

And the Spirit and the Bride say,

Come;

and he who is hearing—let him say,

Come;

and he who is thirsting—let him come;

and he who is willing—

let him take the water of life freely.

Revelation 22:17

(Young's Literal Translation)

Kind Revelations

On My Path to No Path

by Christa Phillips

English edition published July 2022 by Amazon

Copyright © Christa Phillips

Author and Translator: Christa Phillips

Cover design: Kim Erickson

ISBN: 978-0-9852910-1-3 (paperback)

Also available as e-book

The German edition was published July 1997

under the title *Gütige Offenbarungen* by Christa Phillips

Context Verlag, Postfach 10 08 50, D-33508 Bielefeld

ISBN: 3-926257-33-4

Acknowledgments

I am very grateful to *all* that have accompanied and supported me on my path.

My special thanks go to all those individuals who, just by being who they are, brought me into my frustrations and crises. They contributed to and tremendously intensified my longing for truth and liberation. I am thinking here of all those who bored, rejected, slandered, and challenged me; of all those who confined and limited me; "pruned" and reprimanded me; of all those who were given power over me and used it. I am deeply grateful! You "ruined" the fallacies and illusions I had lived by—making room for integrity and truth.

With deep gratitude I remember the men I loved and who ventured into relationship with me. They all contributed with their exceptional courage and friendship to my disillusionment. They also contributed significantly to my awakening awareness that love remains when nothing else is left! I am so grateful to every one of you!

Special thanks and loving gratitude go to my three sons, Adrian, Oliver (Dawa Tarchin), and Courtney (Ganapati), for their strength and courage to remain open to a loving and truthfully sincere relationship with me despite all that I have asked of them.

Thinking of my sister Ruth, I feel especially blessed by her long and selfless support in many ways for which I am forever grateful. The same holds true for her family, who accepted and sheltered my children and me for a few years at a very critical time.

Special thanks go to my friends and path companions Gabriele Wieching, Gabriele Ramsbrock, Anke Hagerisch, and Christiane Brellocks, for their loving companionship during the many painful processes that came along with the visions. I am especially grateful to Klaus Hagerisch for his friendship and his generous heart, and to all the many friends who took upon themselves to read early editions of the manuscript, gave feedback, and asked challenging questions.

With loving warmth in my heart, I remember Wilma Waag, without whose tortuous path and entanglements with me it would have taken much longer to write down these experiences. To her I owe overcoming my aversion to computers, which seemed insurmountable; her encouragement led to the great relief I experienced when I began working with it on the text.

For the German edition: Many thanks go to Andreas Runge, as much for his amicable support in looking for the "right" publisher as for his financial support that made the first published edition possible. I wish to express my deep gratitude to my publisher, Joachim Kamphausen, for receiving me and my experiences with valued acknowledgment and for his supportive critique. My sincere appreciation goes to my lector, Martina Klose, for her great patience and effort to undo my inadvertencies in the text and for her challenging and testing questions.

For the publication in English: I am deeply grateful to all those who read preliminary translated chapters and gave feedback and encouraged me to also publish the book in English. Special thanks go to Michelle Clement for the arduous task of a first editing of a manuscript by a non-native writer, to Lee Ann of First Editing.com for editing and feedback. Kim Erickson of Big Horn Signs took upon herself the challenge of the book cover—great job! . . and last but not least my heart full of grateful appreciation goes to Elisabeth Drumm, friend, final editor, encourager, and publisher. Thank you, Elisabeth for your willingness, your patience, and your support. I couldn't have done it without you.

THANK YOU, GOD, IN EVERYONE AND EVERYTHING.

Index

Preface for the English edition in 2022

The book was originally published in German in 1997. I have finally translated it into English after various failed attempts to have it professionally translated. It grieves me that it has taken me so long. Of course, the journey had continued after 1997 and had led me further and further away from belonging anywhere——neither to family, nor country——but in my spiritual home and in the physical place where guidance placed me. Yet, the teachings I am passing on are timeless and as much needed today as they were then.

The word "kind" in the title may have you wondering, for much of what I learned and speak about here was extremely painful and devastatingly true. I realized early on, even though I was brought into the pits, that the guidance was always filled with Love. And I was aware despite my fierce resistance that the truth being imparted was solely for my wellbeing. Eventually, I had to admit that only my resistance had caused my suffering during those years, if not all my life.

May this English addition reach those who may need it.

Preface for the German edition in 1999

Our times are afflicted. They are filled with the urgency of change, with the awakening from the dreams of memories and pictures of a future that have removed us from experiencing the moment and our responsibility for it. The voices of those who remind and warn have become louder and non—ignorable as our physical reality confirms the prophecies of old – and of more recent times that went unheeded by the ears and eyes of most people. Many of us recognize (perhaps!) that the signs of our times point to the consequences of our "sleep", as well as our lack of consciousness. They call us to pause, to question, to ponder, to seek anew or rediscover the meaning of our life; to wake up.

You may belong to those who seek new answers to old questions, after the "old" no longer holds what it seemed to promise before. What else could have made you take this book into your hands, or what else would have placed it into them?

One day, I no longer felt good with the explanations I had used for my life, with the concepts and beliefs by which I had arranged it. I did not feel well in my own "skin", the skin I had put on and around myself like a shield to protect against changes and pain. I no longer felt well with the face I wore, trying to be, or at least look, agreeable to everyone. To *conform* to a God of my perception, to a church or religion, the government, my family, my children, my partner, my employer, and even to myself and the expectations I had of myself.

Admitting to the naked truth about myself led me into a deep crisis, and also led to the collapsing of all the scaffolds that I had called "my life". Because of that, I lost all orientation at first. It took me a while to recognize that the total sense of lost-ness within was actually *the* precondition for a beginning that led me into an unknown newness. Today I can say that letting it all break down was not only worth it, but it was necessary in order for me to get up and walk into uncertainty.

The experiences other individuals have shared have greatly encouraged and supported me. It is because of this that I feel called to also share *mine*. The inner processes that are described in this book played an important part in my journey into life. They led me into depths and heights and brought me to where I am today and where I am not; they made me into who I am today and who I am not. Only thus can I describe this time sufficiently. Only thus can I adequately, and with not too many words, express how little alive I felt at the time the visions began and how much I conceived myself as a mute participant despite the many words I was speaking then and despite all my activities. I fulfilled expectations rather than being willing to yield to the expression of myself. And more than anything, I felt an inner strife. How clearly these experiences showed me not only my dilemma, but also the dilemma of humanity per se.

For publishing, I chose only *those* visions and mystical experiences I believe to be more of a general interest and consequence. It is a relatively small part of a wealth of holy instances I experienced as graceful teaching and healing.

When I spoke to people in the past, either privately, during their therapy sessions, or during public lectures, again and again I felt called upon to share some of these experiences. Thereby I learned that what I had benefited from was also beneficial to others.

However, the book would still not have been written had not a particular event happened with my ring. It was this event that finally pushed me to see my visionary experiences in a totally new light and to find myself willing to make them available to an unknown readership. Because this experience bears the same handwriting of the Spirit as all other experiences in this book, by which I feel affected and supported, I would like to share it.

First, there is some history. In 1956, when I was fourteen years old, I received a beautiful, 14-karat-gold ring with a coral from my favorite godmother (we all had three godparents) for Confirmation. I was very proud of it. No one in my family——neither my mother, nor any of my three sisters——owned such a gorgeous piece of jewelry. I felt rich in the face of the depressing poverty and lack experienced during the war and post-war years. Yet I did not wear this ring during my younger years, but kept it as a treasure in a small, red velvet box together with the memories of my beloved godmother. Relatively late, I developed a desire to "adorn" myself (besides makeup, which I started to use sooner), but even then, I kept this particular ring boxed in the drawer. Only in my late thirties did I begin to wear the ring. I loved to wear it, admired it on my hand, and received much admiration for it from others.

In 1991, a young woman was living with me in Virginia Beach. She had grown up under simple, very dysfunctional, and very poor circumstances, and had never learned to hold or appreciate any personal belongings. Even with the things she did love, she behaved as though they meant little or nothing to her. She gave them away, forgot them, lost them, or destroyed them to make something else out of them. She was often in a desolate emotional state—— but she loved my ring. Her eyes often rested on it, and she also mentioned how much she liked it.

One day I heard a voice, which almost demanded: "GIVE HER THE RING!"

3

I immediately resisted this request and felt sick. Just the thought of having to let go of this ring called forth an enormous inner protest and an equally strong feeling of frustration. Up to this moment, I had had no clue as to how much I was attached to this piece of jewelry. But I was yet to experience to what extent this attachment went.

After I had refused this "assignment" for the time being, it was repeated four weeks later with the same clarity and without any further explanation. I knew of the resistance I had felt until now and regretted it. To ensure I wouldn't fall again for the lure of resistance, I got up immediately from where I sat, went for the ring, and gave it to the young woman. I doubt that I mustered even a small degree of *willingness*! This gift ripped a noticeable hole in my heart, which nothing in the world would heal again. I could feel the presence of this hole like an open wound in my chest for weeks, without truly recognizing why. I also cried, but my feeling of a great loss did not leave me with the tears.

It was only a few months thereafter that my entire jewelry collection was stolen during a trip to Germany. While this was also a very enlightening experience in and of itself, it was nevertheless painful, and newly touched that deep wound in my heart the gifted ring had left. In the days that followed, I pondered the loss of the jewelry, the thief who took it, and the "thief" within me. Despite the loss, I felt greatly rewarded by the deep awareness that I gained from my pondering.

Up until this time, I had seen and experienced thieves only outside of me, had recognized theft only in connection with the taking of material and physically visible things, and because of that, had never considered myself a thief. How shocked was I about the manifold thievish expressions within myself that were revealed by guidance *and the closer looks I had to take*. Deeply moved, I recognized the many disguised ways the inner thief uses to not be discovered.

A few days after the jewelry was taken, I traveled on a train through Germany. During the trip I tried to read, but the coral ring kept appearing in front of my eyes. It was embedded in a strong light, which radiated beyond it and was so bright that I felt forced to put the book aside and bring all my attention there. When I did, I heard a voice: "THIS IS A CARRIER OF LOVE. YOU HOLD ONTO THE CARRIERS OF LOVE. PASS THEM ON AND LET THEM GO. THEY HAVE NOT BEEN GIVEN TO YOU TO BE HOARDED."

I had not perceived the ring as a carrier of love, but as my possession. Now I saw how it had indeed always been a carrier of love for me and how it could have become one for the young woman, too——had I not been so attached. I asked myself whether I had held onto the ring as an ode to the love that connected me with my godmother——as if her love would leave me if I gave the ring away. I had barely asked myself that question when I heard:

"YOU ARE THE THIEF! YOU WANT TO HAVE WHAT DOES NOT BELONG TO YOU!"

That was the truth. I was told that all love carriers have to be passed on; also, every evidence of divine love in the teachings and visions I had been given. That they had not been given for me to delight in or to "adorn" myself with them but to share my joy, to speak of the love of GOD and of all that is beyond all things.

"ONLY BY DOING THIS WILL LOVE REMAIN IN ITS FLOW; BY THIS YOU WILL NOT LOSE YOUR LOVE STORY WITH GOD BUT FULFILL IT."

I felt an immediate healing of the hole in my heart. It came along with my decision to write down the visions, messages, and experiences for publishing as soon as possible. What a gift that was! It led me to pay close attention once again to all the revelations I had been given. My awareness became yet more clear and steadfast, bringing joy.

My gratitude is endless for the awakening and for the opportunity to share my experiences with you. My wish is that my notes and thoughts touch you and address you in your heart. That they speak to you of the glory of God, the love of His Spirit, and of the convincing life of His Son, who came to remind us of our Sonship and to show us the path "out" from where we are stuck. I also wish that questions will form in you (more than the ones I have put to you here)——questions that bring you closer to yourself, to God, and to your relationship with HIM.

Introduction

In the following chapters, I not only share individual visions, but I also attempt to clarify what I have come to learn and understand through them, and how healing occurs through the revelation of truth. It has not always been easy for me to formulate and express what I became conscious of. My most difficult challenge has been to find words to convey experiences, some of which are difficult if not impossible to describe, and for which our language has hardly sufficient vocabulary.

It will not be easier for you, the reader. It is required of you to have an open mind and that you put aside your own ideas and perceptions, at least for a while, so that you may share in someone else's mystical experiences and make use of them. There may be the danger that you will place a person on a pedestal who has had these or similar experiences, and that you will conclude that these experiences are only valid for this particular individual. By doing this, you would hold the gift at a distance and reject what the Holy Spirit brought to Earth through this person. Only the love of GOD and the power of HIS Spirit should be worshipped. HIS Spirit will move when and where it sees fit. In doing so, IT can also draw near to you, if you choose to be receptive.

Some of the concepts in this book, or my definition of them, may seem foreign or unknown to you. Perhaps you feel at home in the Christian tradition and have never heard of such things as karma or reincarnation, or you find no link between these concepts and the teachings of the Church. On the other hand, you may still be furious with a church that, in your opinion, has been unable to represent its God to you adequately and credibly or has been unable to bring HIM close enough so that you can truly trust HIM and dare to experience yourself in HIS presence. Your longing may not have been fulfilled. Christian history may have left you with a sense of despair, and you may have filed this history away, as it did not correspond with what *you* believed the *message* was about or what you were longing for. I have been there and can well understand this; otherwise, I could not have chosen these words. However, do not let this prevent you from receiving, experiencing, and examining the essence of what has been written here.

Should you recognize yourself in what I share because you have had similar experiences and realizations in your search for GOD and the meaning of life, then they may have caused you to feel closer to GOD but further away from the people around you. I know while the journey is a lively one, it feels quite lonely at first. Rest assured that you are supported.

It seems advisable to *define* some of the terms I use because there is not always a consensus about what is meant by them and what they contain. This is why in Part II, I try to contribute to a better understanding of vision versus imagination. Since some of my experiences are related to memories from past lives, whereas others show that energy processes are at work in the body during every healing, I have provided essential information about the chakras, the ethereal bodies, and reincarnation.

If you are not familiar with energy work, these clarifications may provide you with a better understanding of the connection between body and soul. However, if you are already familiar with it, it is important to me that you grasp what *my* understanding of these energies and energy bodies is. I would like to offer some basic aid and will substantiate this with personal experiences. From my standpoint, there is probably still a lot more to be said about each of these topics. However, you can avail yourself of a wide range of specialized books if there is a particular area you wish to explore in more depth.

In Part III there are some guidelines for meditation and prayer. The appendix contains additional questions with reference to the experiences and lessons, which I hope you can use on *your own* journey.

At this point, I would like to mention the names I use when speaking of the HOLY ESSENCE of life. I refer to it as GOD and HE, and the Essence within me I call HIS SON or CHRIST. I have often been criticized when, during conversations and lectures, I used the masculine pronoun in connection with the name of GOD, thereby appearing to endorse the traditional notion of a masculine God. Personally, I see GOD as being both masculine and feminine, mother and father conjoint, and also beyond, neither form nor name. I do not know of any other terms that would do more justice to *my* experience of GOD, nor do I experience any lack. Therefore, I will continue to use the language with which I am familiar.

I experience a growing feeling of exhaustion with reference to this issue, and I would like to say to everyone who takes issue with me: Let go of the polemics and engage in GOD. Don't waste time on destroying old images of God, only to replace them with new ones. Seek to *experience* GOD. In your experience, all images will become invalid anyway, for eventually, GOD will take all of them from you.

It should be noted here that the Bible passages cited in the text have been taken from different versions of the Bible.[1] I chose to do this because the various translations differ in what are for me *essential nuances*. This is why I prefer to use one edition in some cases, and another for others.

PART I

The visions and teachings

1

The Human Dilemma

This vision appeared a few years ago during one of my own therapy sessions. I was confronted with my struggle of having to be aware of while being unable to do something about humanity's suffering. After I had cried and expressed my willingness, this vision appeared in front of my open eyes.

Ahead, I see the planet Earth formed entirely of human bodies. The people who form this globe have their faces and body fronts turned toward the Earth. They kneel, their knees pulled under their bodies (embryonic) with their arms held closely as well. Each body is closely huddled to the next body and thus they form the globe.

A deep sadness overcomes me. With an equally deep compassion forming, it dawns on me that humanity, glued to the Earth this way, will remain in an unredeemed condition forever. Upon this thought, something suddenly changes in front of me. I now see the entire Earth surrounded by a layer of light, like a very bright fog. Filled with awe, I ask from where this light appeared. I assume it comes from an inexhaustible source that is hidden from me as I see neither beginning nor end.

At the same time, I become aware that I am standing among the people and the ray of this light shines through me. Now I notice other beings standing, singularly isolated here and there; through them, too, light is flowing. This light is the same that surrounds the Earth and originates from the same source. I am deeply touched, and a very strong desire forms in me to raise the people so they may see the light that is present. However, turned away as they are, they can't see the light. Neither can they receive it.

But here I am stopped in my thinking. I am being told that I *cannot* help anyone who has not sat up, moved by his own query and desire. Only to those who have taken that first step can I offer my hand; only they can become aware of the presence of light, see my hand and accept it.

Ahhh! How painfully aware of my sorrow I become about humanity's condition. It is such a deep ache that fills me in view of the unredeemed Earth and unredeemed humanity, its turning its back blindly away from the Source of life and from the path that would lead back to it. I am also deeply aggrieved by the clear impossibility of such encounters between helpers and the distressed, when the latter are not aware of the misery they are in or if aware, not conscious of possible help; and the former do not realize this and yet insists.

Encounter becomes impossible when the individual in need cannot let go of his own idea of what would help, when his eyes are not lifted, when seeking is not awakened, when remaining stuck in complaints and self-pity hinders the necessary seeking; when self-answering the questions about life ends in hopeless platitudes (something like, "such is life," "life is hard," "no one is given anything for nothing") that feed the hidden arrogance (one knows what's going on, right?), thereby ruining any hopeful perspective. Awakening then appears impossible.

During the vision, while contemplating the light that I see surrounding the Earth, I remember Rudolf Steiner, a mystic and the founder of anthroposophy who spoke and wrote extensively about the mystery of Golgotha that left us the CHRIST permanently as the way and offer of redemption, the CHRIST who fulfilled Itself through the crucifixion of Jesus and remained for all of us as an accessible, attainable presence. I see that Light as present and unlimited, the bridge to healing, to consciousness and restoration, unrecognized by most. Joy about ITS presence unfolds and slowly increases in me; it ends up completely filling my heart.

In my astonishment about my obvious participation, I become aware that any participation or any possibility of being of help depends solely on my willingness to offer my hand *to the one who lifts his head*, to support him in standing and finding his own life, his own CHRIST-communion. I now feel

10

certain that this is my purpose for being on Earth and with it, I fulfill my calling. My willingness to follow is strong, and so are readiness and empathy.

It is only much later that I realize that the Earth has its specific and essential place in the macrocosm, just as much as in the microcosm, and that it awaits its redemption in both. For in the macrocosm, the Earth represents the root chakra of our solar system; in the microcosm, it is reflected and represented by the first chakra at the root of the spine in our body (see also chapter on chakras). Here, in the root or first chakra, where many of our personality aspects, especially expressions of physical neediness, are ethereally (by energy) attached, addiction and sense of lost-ness are also present. Here is reflected what binds us to Earth and keeps us in the karmic wheel of reincarnation and under its law (what man sows, he shall reap). In other words: earthbound, which will physically incarnate us again and again until we finally overcome.

Here is also our fear of non-existence, and as a result, the continuous search for self-images and their confirmation through external sources. Here rests the longing for the power self-images seem to offer as well as the fear of losing this power——namely, to die. Without developing the willingness to lift the head and to search for fulfillment and deliverance, we risk being stuck in the karmic cycle, even though we continue being part of creation and remain subjected to its evolutionary laws and motion.

In this vision, it becomes obvious to stop seeking deliverance and rescue through the external (earthbound) gratification of our senses. We are invited to recognize that our suffering will not end through the short-lived gratification of our senses. Only in awakening to that particular truth is a first step taken toward seeking and finding.

This awakening seems hardly possible without becoming painfully aware of the bygone, never-ending, unfulfilled longing, a kind of homesickness for our true home and our previously futile efforts to get there. This can be much easier grasped when you continue reading, as four years later, this vision returns in a healing process. I experience the condition of my own root chakra in relationship to the world of misunderstandings that has gathered there and is now being shattered.

11

The process was preceded by a conversation we had in our community in Virginia Beach about that part in us that believes to be of the Earth. One resident expressed the sorrow she experienced in that sense of separation and in the difficulty to overcome it. I am given an inner picture: I see her sitting in a meditative position in prayer to God with much light surrounding her. It looks as though her prayer has brought her close to the light or has attracted the light. It also looks as though it seems impossible for her to allow it inside and let it be there. She seems to remain stuck in a non-commitment, as though she knows of the light but isn't one with it; it seems her eyes are closed to the light. I see that it is not enough to know of the Light to rise. Belief alone is not enough. Something else has to happen. That's why at first, I relate this picture to myself and ask for clarification.

The picture of the terrestrial globe of human bodies comes back, but all the people now stand, screaming. I turn to my housemate and say, "All of Earth is screaming." I have barely spoken the words when I find myself immersed in pure light. The vision has disappeared and gone also is **the feeling** that connected me to the screaming earth. I know now what else has to be, what else has to happen: indispensable is the willingness to feel, to feel all and everything, every suffering, all of the lost-ness, all of the longing, and all of the fear.

A little while later, during meditation, I ask once more about the earth and its unredeemed condition within me. I feel a painful spasm at the end of my spine (root chakra). I hear a voice:

"HE CAME TO THAT WHICH WAS HIS OWN BUT HIS OWN DID NOT RECEIVE HIM".

I had always believed with "his own" were meant a nation, people in general, or maybe even a person. But now I see! I see there is an area in my life where I did not receive Him. I am still "worried". I put the word in quotes, as my worry hides from me and is not easily exposed. While I ponder deeper, further, I recognize that something else is underlying——not that which we commonly refer to as worrying. I feel a cause, an energy, which seems to exist as pure desire and expresses itself as such. It seems as though "worry" was a resulting thought or thought pattern by **which** this desire could be stilled. Out of these ideas are all forms of self-gratification born: The craving to get and to have, the craving for food, drink and sex, the craving for all forms of consuming without real joy, and particularly painful, without ever feeling truly satisfied or at peace.

The question arises in me: what keeps me so automatically tied to any self-gratification, and what causes me to do or look for what leaves me empty and dissatisfied in the end? This question isn't new; it has long been in me without finding an answer. Surely, one cause is that I have been in denial of this desire for too long and that it took quite a bit to learn to accept it and to actually enjoy the momentary satisfaction. Not in my dreams would I have assumed that one day I would have to give **it** up again or seriously question what had been acquired with such difficulty! But how could I——or anyone, for that matter——have overcome something I wasn't even aware of as present?

It is important at this point to understand that it is not about disallowing pleasure and enjoyment! It is more about the problem of **having to have things** in order to enjoy them. To feel pleasure and enjoy what I am given is gratitude; to want to have things in order to feel pleasure is addiction. This difference between gratitude and addiction, or better said, the misunderstanding that it harbors, is a great threshold to be crossed for all those on a path of transformation. I know that it is this threshold where many of us get stuck and initially fail. We seem to be torn between voluntary abstinence——a form of asceticism that no one demands of us——and the justifications for the satisfaction of our addictions that we call "self-love." Here I am reminded of the story of the rich young man in the New Testament. He approached Jesus and asked:

> 'Why do you ask me about what is good?'
>
> Jesus replied. 'There is only One who is good. If you would enter life, keep the commandments.'
>
> 'Which ones?' he inquired.
>
> Jesus replied, 'You shall not murder, you shall not commit adultery, you shall not steal, you shall not give false

witness, honor your father and mother, and you shall love your neighbor as yourself.'

'All these I have kept from my youth,' the young man said. 'What do I still lack?'

Jesus answered, 'If you want to be perfect, go, and sell what you have, and give to the poor, and you will have treasure in Heaven. And come, follow me.' When the young man heard this, he went away sad, because he had great wealth (Matt. 19:16–22 — ASV — American Standard version).

This is how it is with "my wealth" and to "grant myself something" as we call it, so smartly disguised, even when it no longer matters to us. So often I hear the sentence: "God cannot mean that I renounce everything." Who is God and who is I in that question? Our desire is not redeemed by asceticism, by suppression, or denial. But it is also not redeemed by seemingly justified self-gratification. HE desires to also dwell and live HIS fullness, *where this longing is*, on Earth and in Earth. Then it is fullness instead of longing, a change in direction by 180 degrees. If there, too, I accept HIM in, or if you take HIM in, is a matter of willingness and choice, which is continuously asked anew of you and me.

On a day in July of 1992, it became clearer yet! A dear friend who had just finished his training as a massage therapist was giving me a massage. I was his first official client. He had barely started when the vision of the Earth globe returned. I realized that this subject of Earth has now been with me for a long time. What continues to touch me deeply is the meaning of Earth within me. That's why on one hand I am surprised about the vision under these circumstances, while on the other I am unable to imagine a more appropriate one, since being on the massage table it is about my body, the Earth. But back to the vision.

I notice a lot of beings walking upright, laying around, sitting, crouching. Their bodies are not human the way we know them but are a mixture of human and animal bodies of different variations and forms. I begin to speak

14

to my friend about my current vision. I recognize the conditions the beings are in and that affects me profoundly: They seem to have incarnated on Earth without having a clue as to why; they are straying aimlessly in shock and lostness. They harbor a sense of being hopelessly caught in a trap. Simultaneously, they look desperately for ways to escape the feeling of having fallen into something, being in bondage. Shock and seeking seem energetically permeated by one another. These beings do not accept their condition but feel driven by patterns of refusal and denial and the subsequent seeking and addiction.

I can feel how much they are aware of having lost something, but they can't remember. They are filled with longing and a restless urgency to somehow recover what was lost. But instead of remembering (a backward movement——receiving) they seek outside (a forward movement——the addict) and try to fill the hole that they experience. I feel a growing need to call out to them. So, I do it right there on the massage table: "You do not need all these things you chase after. It is GOD you have left behind and your memory of HIM!" I yelled it and cried violently. I see how it dawns in their consciousness. "My God," I ask, "where are we, where have I been?"

I now register an empty space where those formerly unspoken words had been that I had carried inside and stored. I hadn't even been aware of them until just now when I shouted them out. They had been sitting firmly in my body, blocking the flow of energy. My lower body and my root chakra are relieved, feel free, and my body seems permeable. My friend, the massage therapist, has been surprised by my outburst and quite affected. He tells me that for the last few days he had been pondering his being on Earth and not wanting to be here. He admits that he knows this pain of feeling lost and not remembering. We are both deeply touched by what had just happened.

QUESTIONS FOR CONTEMPLATION

- Do you feel lost, without memory, and disconnected? How and with what do you try to overcome this pain?
- Do you have ideas about what you need and what would help you?
- Do you recognize that you are being forced by your suffering to get up and stop focusing on Earth and instead to turn towards the light and leave behind your illusions?

2

Divine Manifestation

One day in meditation, I had a question on my mind: How does God manifest in human form? I was shown this image and experienced what follows:

(Figure 1)

The graphic reminds me of the posture of a person standing firmly with both feet on the ground, his legs spread apart, his arms reaching up to the sky (or Heaven). Something about this makes me happy; it is familiar. I experienced it repeatedly in cognitive practices in meditation and physical exercises, and always believed it to be the manifestation of man between Heaven and Earth. So I ask: Is that the manifestation of man on Earth? The answer is:

"NO! THIS IS THE MANIFESTATION OF GOD!"

I am surprised, but right away another graphic follows, with the explanation following :

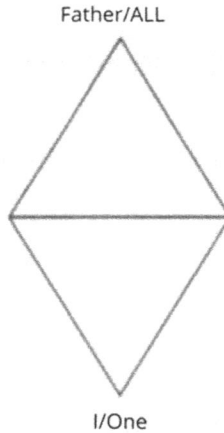

Father/ALL

I/One

(Figure 2) [2]

"THE UPPER TRIANGLE REPRESENTS MAN'S SPIRITUAL IDENTITY, THE LOWER TRIANGLE REPRESENTS HIS EARTHLY IDENTITY: ABOVE GOD AND ALL, BELOW I AND ONE——GOD AND I IS ALL-ONE."

At first, the word "Father" at the top of the upper triangle and the I at the tip of the lower triangle confirm a misunderstanding I have, which will only completely dissolve years later. Now I still understand the depiction and the explanation literally and recognize it as a dual, separated existence: spiritual being and earthly being as two and as such, distinguishable. Even though they correlate, they are seemingly connected and cooperative. I do not yet grasp how deeply rooted I am in polar perception and thought patterns, how much I have been taught, confirmed, and affected by the most common – if not only – interpretation of religious teaching. I am conditioned by this teaching that tells me there is a me *and* a father——an I/you relationship, yes——but two distinguishable, separate existences. The extent of this misunderstanding and the suffering caused by it becomes clear much later.

18

While the meaning of this is sinking in, I see how the chakra assignments relate to these identity levels and become immediately aware of what that implies. It looks like this:

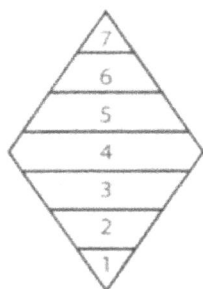

(Figure 3)

I remember now what I had read from Edgar Cayce, the well-known American clairvoyant and trance medium. I always valued his many references to the chakras themselves, as well as his answering of specific questions referring to them——his guidance in readings given to ill individuals seeking his help. However, more applicable here is his interpretation of the biblical book of Revelation. There, the seven seals and the seven churches are identified as chakras in the individual human, corresponding as much to the physical realm as to the emotional and mental realms. Fascinating![3]

Likewise, the chakras *also correspond* to the respective externalized expressions of culture, religion, zeitgeist, and the various levels of creation in Heaven and on Earth. They are to be recognized, integrated, and internalized by each of us.

Once I grasped the depiction of the Father/I relationship and recognized the context of the chakras, another graphic appears.

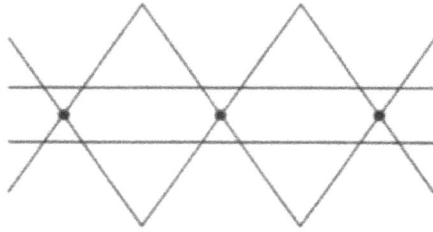

(Figure 4)

I immediately recognize *how* GOD manifests HIMSELF. The contact point between individual beings, I can clearly see, does not mean that humans connect here, but that here is the connection of humankind as if there were not many human beings but *only One Being, **The Being**.* And I slowly begin to understand that here, CHRIST manifests in interpersonal relationship as one Body and Wholeness. This manifestation can only come about through the heart, through the **Way, Love, and Truth** (see also John 14:6) in relationship and encounter. Or to word this differently: In breathing in as perceiving/receiving and breathing out as expressing and giving beingness.

The moment I understand this, yet another graphic follows. It leads to the cross as connection between both the spiritual triangle and the earthly triangle, as connection between Heaven and Earth, the "Holy" and "Hellish," the creating and the created——but also, as the connection between internal and external, between left and right, between the masculine and feminine aspects of expression, and between thought and feeling. This connection is the first indication that all these levels ought to and can be bridged, and that that is to be done.

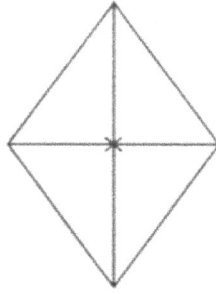

(Figure 5)

The symbol of the cross emphasizes our path as evolving consciousness. It becomes the bridge to unify and connect all separate, seemingly incompatible identities and forms of human expression and to integrate them. This path of growing awareness is as much an external journey as it is an inner one and leads not only to inner transformation but will also result in external transformation. Relating to this, many misunderstandings occur. Quite a few spiritual teachers and traditions focus solely on an inner path but fail to point out that this inner journey without the external expression is only a partial path. Breathing in and receiving what comes towards me, as well as breathing out and expressing what is inside, are part of relating to the external world. And that holds true as long as I do not journey to seek GOD for some self-gratification.

In this last graphic, you can see how a Being has this integrating function at the center. Man **is** this function, this centering and integrating all that is—in Heaven and on Earth. It is his one single purpose and meaning. To be in this center will eventually lead to the permeation of the earthly "part" by the spiritual "part," and thereby to transformation and Oneness.

The centric path manifests through the heart in love and truth——in deliverance from the unredeemed past and from clinging to the longing for a "better" future. It is neither an easy path nor are there any shortcuts. But there

21

are many and multifaceted steps possible and a phenomenal supply of divine intervention and assistance, if we are attentive and can recognize it.

The following graphic shows integration once achieved.

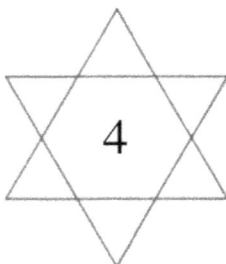

(Figure 6)

The center is the heart, the Four (heart chakra)——everything else orients itself around the heart and interrelates through IT. In the heart, "all" and "one" are united, and in this ALL-ONE (alone), GOD becomes Man. The trinity of heaven has merged with the trinity of earth. They permeate and determine one another. The world is overcome, HIS kingdom has come in heaven and earth (not only *on* earth as *all matter* is permeated).

That is why the Star of David symbolizes not only the completion of one individual being in his or her fully realized incarnation but also the entire humanity in its full realization and redemption as the body of CHRIST.

It is only now that I realize that the relationship between "Father and I" is not two-fold, but it is ONE-NESS. In this ONE-NESS the I is the expression of the Father on earth. HIS I is within and, therefore, I AM in HIS IMAGE, divine Being. HE expresses HIMSELF in human form. I AM in you, and you are in ME. All is and remains GOD. And finally: I AM in ME as HIS eternal PRESENCE.

During the process of integration many little deaths are to be died, and many small resurrections are experienced in the space that is freed by what has been left behind. It is this inner Spiritual Presence that assists in identifying the earthly "fallacy" and transforms it if we surrender to IT and ITS continuous Grace— a blessed, merciful, and redeeming way.

Quite incidentally, during these visions I gain insight into why I enjoyed geometry in school so immensely. So often I thought I encountered in it something, was awed, the full meaning of which remained mysteriously hidden, even though I already sensed its greatness and intangibility. How entwined and mysterious are HIS ways!

QUESTIONS FOR CONTEMPLATION

- Do you distinguish between GOD and yourself, between your spiritual and earthly home and existence, between Heaven and Earth?
- If you answered the first question with yes: What consequences do you experience from that? Are there times for GOD and times for you?
- What does it mean to you that GOD may be in you and you in HIM?

3

Via Crucis (Way of the Cross)

This experience came during a personal therapy session. While I was in a deep meditative state, my therapist asked me: "What does someone look like who has forgotten he is not 'of this world' and by contrast, what does someone look like who remembers it?" I tried to think about what they would look like but then stopped trying. The moment I did, an image appeared out of nowhere.

A human form kneels on the ground to my left (even though it is genderless, I will use the male gender here). He appears as a dark, dense mass without contour. On his back rests what looks like a heavy, dark, wooden cross. The burden of the cross seems to make it impossible for him to stand up, yet he has no idea how to free himself from his burden. His suffering is immense; *he has become* suffering itself. I feel the same within myself. His condition seems irrevocable, and he is caught in a fateful captivity to which he has to surrender——or so he believes.

To my right stands a Light Being. I am amazed and think: Jesus! The presence and quality, I always believed Jesus to have, are here manifested in this appearance. I am deeply touched and awed, especially by how utterly self-sufficient His identity is, securely resting in Himself. His walk, talk, standing, and doing is *at any moment* consistent with his inner being and truth. In Him there is no contradiction perceptible, no resistance, no denial. His appearance requires no explanation, no justification, and is autonomous and free of striving for any approval; it is pure BEINGNESS. Once I recognize this, something happens——my eyes are wide with wonder.

The Light Being turns and walks toward the dark human form. He takes the cross off his back and lays it on the ground. It seems so easy for him to do! I observe with great awe that by this mere action, the cross loses its dark appearance and turns white. The dark form sits up, and the Light Being extends his hand. The dark form accepts the hand and stands up aided thus. I see that the Light Being's approaching and offering his hand alone is helping the dark one to stand up. Nothing more is needed than that the suffering one became aware of and took the extended hand. Immediately, simply with the rising of the dark one, and without any steps in between, both beings now stand closely together on the cross.

I have barely grasped what I see, when I find myself inside the dark figure and become him. To my great joy, the presence of the Light Being becomes my support and hope. I sense the white cross under my feet and understand completely anew what is meant by "and take up his cross . . ." (Matthew. 16:24). My lifelong misunderstanding that I had to carry the cross, even if I were crushed under it, leaves me. It feels as though something has been adjusted, straightened out in me. Even my former belief has been taken that I would have to endure everything because of love or to "keep the peace" in order to not hurt anyone. I am now certain that this never was the truth and that I cannot avoid others painfully rubbing against me or feeling hurt because of me if I live the life I am given. The cross is to be walked. That is, I have to live, express who I am, and engage. And——*there are no shortcuts on this path.* With these thoughts entering my mind, the Light Being moves sideways partially into me, and I gladly accept and receive IT. IT is not yet totally integrated, but I can already feel ITS presence.

Now, the following words of Jesus in Matthew 16:24,25 (ASV) make much more sense to me, but differently: "Then said Jesus unto his disciples, if any man will come after me, let him deny himself, and take up his cross, and follow me. For whosoever will save his life shall lose it: and whosoever will lose his life for my sake shall find it."

To me, it now implies that I am to engage in life with every truth, also all momentary truth. It means to fully live and experience the life given, living it from inside out, expressing. Equally important is to allow external life, the life expressed by others, to fully reach me and engage with me. It requires the willingness to let all my illusions about life die, to be willing to experience the "crucifixion" of my fallacies and pride by GOD, by HIS appearances in the world (external) through Man. This also requires my willingness to FEEL every suffering simply by being and due to it, including what I perceive as the fallacies of others. I now know that walking with the cross under my feet, standing on that center point, represents life on Earth, represents the way GOD shows HIMSELF and manifests on Earth through me, the witness, at all times, in everlasting transformation and unpredictability. I have no clue where this path will lead me and into what IT will make me in the eyes of others.

Days after this vision, I had many wondrous experiences during meditation. I cried almost continually. During this time, I also listened repeatedly to Mozart's *Requiem Aeternam*. It helped me to stay in my deep sorrowful place, as I did not wish to escape any longer. Next to my meditation pillow I kept a vase with one fresh Easter Lily and a rose to remind me that this was about transformation——and to stick it out. The Light Being, whose presence I strongly felt integrating more into me daily——a separate body slowly taking over with each surrender. It settled in making my body Its home, a process to the degree that my willingness and openness grew to receive it. I slowly felt the connection to the Light, to God restored, even though I now knew less than ever. However, my trust to surrender to Him completely, no matter what happened, increased.

Once again, the story of Abraham came to mind and affects me deeply (Gen. 1:12), and I ask myself whether I am ready to follow this **being-called-by-God** and go like Abraham into a land that only GOD knows and wills to show me. Was I willing to leave behind my own plans, goals, directions, and needs for security? Would I let go of my own wishes and desires, and trust blindly?

QUESTIONS FOR CONTEMPLATION

- Which cross do **you** carry on your back; what cross are you suffering under?
- Where and how do you try to find and take shortcuts on your path (do you know what I mean by that question)?
- What prevents you from "walking" the cross? What keeps you from being clear, honest, visible, and vulnerable, and still remain on your path?

4

God's Altar

For quite some time, I have been struggling with memories of a past life in which I lived in France as a nun in a monastery under huge moral and religious fallacies that eventually shaped my entire life. Since I was painfully confronted by these errors——the obviously squandered life, the denial, the hypocrisy, and loneliness at the time the memories suddenly appeared——I have been in a continuous process of insight and healing. But something seems still to be unsolved; the memories keep coming back, hanging around as a restless presence, grumbling. They burden me, and today I have decided to make another effort to face what needs to be faced in order to uncover the full truth so I can be free of it. I lay down on the floor.

The moment I am in the memory, I know it is about the culpability for my actions towards people that I had met in that life. I incurred guilt by following conclusions and ideas created by my own unresolved suffering and its interpretation, which led me into a dogmatic religiousness. Furthermore, life itself had formed me into a "nun" who——self-righteously and stone-heartedly denying and judging her own problems——had not been able to care lovingly for the children who were entrusted to her or do any other beneficial work. I hated being a nun. Deep down, another truth had been buried inside of me in the shadows of denied feelings and unredeemed suffering. *Because I had not lived this inner truth*, I not only had felt a deep bitterness, but had also spread it around me.

The moment I become aware of this condition, I am back in the monastery in France at the time I was living there. I realistically feel being a nun in my former body; I am in my cell, can feel the tight, heavy habit in which I seem trapped. Feelings are coming up that almost choke me (literally), and I begin tearing off the nun habit and find myself screaming, "I am not who you think I am! My God, I am not who I thought I was!" Deep sobs shake me.

I experience profound contrition as the entire fallacy dawns on me——but also feel immediate forgiveness while I am still crying. It seems as though all the guilt is wiped out. A deep sense of grace and love fills me, and all pictures of that particular experience disappear. While they disappear, the monastery itself also disappears except for one corner of the foundation wall that still "sticks." I am surprised, and wonder what I may have overlooked, not faced, not understood. So, I look at this piece of wall and ask GOD to tell me, show me, what still remains concealed. And I hear a voice:

"TAKE THE PICTURE OFF THE WALL."

What? While acting surprised, I know exactly what picture the voice is speaking of. It hangs in my room: a wood carving of Mother Mary with the Child. I question the request and start arguing. Why should I take that picture off the wall? It is a holy example of spiritual experience; I know, for I have had visions and experiences with Mother Mary and know of her existence.

The voice repeats, now louder and more insistent,

"TAKE THE PICTURE OFF THE WALL."

And I tenaciously ask once more: "Can't I keep it for the sake of the people that come for therapy and spiritual guidance?"

And I hear: "NO!"

I reply, still feeling consternated but now also blindly believing that all of this must make sense somehow, even though I am far from understanding,

"Okay, fine!"——and the voice says:

"REMOVE THE ALTAR FROM YOUR ROOM."

I know again exactly what the voice is addressing. And again, I experience unchanged incomprehension and resistance. In my room, on the top of a small dresser are a small upright cross, a candle, healing stones and crystals, bird feathers, a Franciscan scapular, a rosary, and other small things I have come to cherish.

And again: "REMOVE THE ALTAR FROM YOUR ROOM."

I say, "Okay. Yes, yes, I will!" But I don't understand at all and lay on the floor dumbfounded and empty-headed.

But the voice speaks again, forcefully, yet calm, and totally ear-filling as though echoing in space:

"I AM THE CHURCH IN YOU!

"I AM ALL PICTURES IN YOU!

"I AM THE ALTAR IN YOU!"

Now there is a deep, calm silence in me, and I feel awed and deeply affected. All thoughts, all argument, all desire to grasp with my mind have left me. I know: **This is the Truth.**

This I AM has nothing in common with my little "I" with which I am overly identified. This I AM has nothing to do with an identification. It is absolute, and I can hear IT. I partake in IT, but I am not IT in the sense I had assumed I am. And yet I know, it is true: I AM IT. Can it be more paradoxical?

I have placed gods (and I choose to use small letters) before GOD; in my religious, unconscious zealousness I have given them holy meaning. This does not mean that there cannot be any pictures or altars, but when the home altar is a substitute for the true Altar, the picture substituting for life, then something is off. And once you know the truth, why continue?

I become suddenly wide awake to the truth that it is GOD who sanctifies us. It is impossible to make ourselves worthy or to become worthy by our own efforts. HIS presence in us alone makes us worthy already. We may experience this inherent dignity to the degree we open ourselves to the divine presence and become aware of our divine relationship through CHRIST (Sonship, Oneness) and honor it.

The foundation walls that were left from that old monastery have now completely and lastingly disappeared.

In the aftermath, I reflect on my resentment toward engaging with what is given. I am shocked about my resistance and about how hard I find it to let

29

go of my own ideas, no matter how "good" they seem. I feel a deep longing for truth and clarity; I do not wish to fall for what turns out to be fantasies and illusions. The skepticism that followed me all my life has made my journey and my seeking difficult, constantly overtaking me. I always considered it necessary to question myself and others. That may be well as it is, but today I believe I also did this so I would not be confronted by life and others about my own errors and inadequacies or be seen as foolish. I did this often as a precaution to prevent experiences. I so wish to remain trusting and no longer give in to fear and preventative measures. How grateful I am that the visions and the Presence that brings them do not leave me despite my resistance.

QUESTIONS FOR CONTEMPLATION:

- What is your idea about GOD? How do you try to remember HIM? What images have you created of HIM?
- What **things** are sacred for you and replace or stand for the holy Presence in you?
- How certain is your trust in yourself, in your inner voice? Do you doubt and question yourself? With what objective, what concern?

5

The Nine-branch Menorah

I have always been moved by the Jewish menorah with its multiple branches; have been intrigued by it. That's why I was pleased a few years ago to come across a symbolism of the seven-branch menorah, new to me, in a book that has become one of the more important ones on my journey. Its title: *Talking With Angels*[4]

To better understand the vision of the nine-branch menorah, I consider it important to first discuss and describe the particular symbolism of the seven-branch menorah in greater detail. I would like to do this using an illustration that I took from the aforementioned book.

MANIFEST*ED* CREATION				MANIFEST*ING* CREATION		
I	II	III	IV	V	VI	VII
MINERAL	PLANT	ANIMAL	HUMAN	ANGEL	SERAPH	God
Truth,	flowing	rhythm,	realization,	peace,	pure joy,	
Number,	love,	motion	the Word,	stillness	power	
the law	growth	harmony	connection			

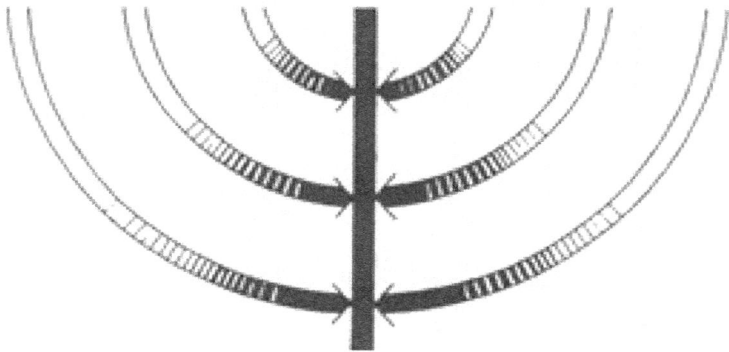

the abyss to be bridged $\Rightarrow$ $\Rightarrow$ ⇑ $\Leftarrow$ $\Leftarrow$ the human task

(Figure 7)

When I came across this illustration, it was immediately clear to me, and I felt an enormous respect for its symbolic power. Here, man is in the center between Creator and creation, between the making and the made. Man is the bridge between all created natural kingdoms on Earth and all of the creating kingdoms of Heaven. He connects both and integrates them. Even more, **man *is* the actual integration**, and it is this role that gives him his humanity. In Him and through Him it comes to pass: ". . . and the Word became flesh" (John 1:14).

32

I do not believe that this places the individual at the center of the universe (who——Heaven help us!——considers himself the center of attention around which everything and everyone revolves!). The individual is rather the midpoint and "medium," the bridge and the link, or perhaps even "the crown of creation" as he is referred to in my mother tongue, German.

In this sense, however, most people today are not yet truly human. Though I'm convinced that that is what we are all meant to be, and there is much evidence to support this. Do we not have a good and convincing example in our preceding human history? Jesus of Nazareth must be seen as the prototypical human, for he came as the only begotten Son (integrated and not divided or bipartite). He came into our midst as GOD-became-flesh, as Word realized. And with this, CHRIST was demonstrated as the midst within each of us.

Despite this revelation in *Talking with Angels*, a puzzle remained for me for a long time. Why were there a seven-branch and a nine-branch menorah? The harder I searched for an answer, the more often I came across the latter in many forms and designs. They seemed to be everywhere, and so many people seemed to be drawn to them. Although I asked numerous people, I never came across anyone who could explain to me the meaning of this difference beyond the historical explanations in Jewish tradition and the lights referring to them.

The answer began to unfold when I had the following experience. I am leading a workshop in Woodstock, New York. There is tension between a Sioux Indian shaman and me because I am menstruating, and in keeping with the Sioux tradition, I am not allowed to participate in the sweat lodge ceremony we have invited him to lead. On one hand, this particular rule is founded on the presumption that a woman is already in a cleansing period and therefore does not need the additional cleansing provided by the sweat lodge. On the other——and this seemed applicable here——on the presumption that during menstruation, a woman has markedly stronger powers.

It is explained to me by the shaman that depending on her mental and physical health, a woman in this condition could bring sickness or even death to the other participants, but especially to the shaman leading the ceremony and/or his family. The law presumes——and this conclusion is left to me to draw——that a menstruating woman *is most likely* in a "negative" mental state and is, therefore, also pre-judged for having powers of destructive intent (black magic). The risk of having an experience to the contrary is not taken. What would happen if she were to offer her total potential during this time for healing and sanctifying?

I am struck by the arrogance of the male perspective (the shaman tradition of the Sioux is reserved for the men) and by the male presumptuousness in determining what a woman is and needs. I am even more affected and concerned, though, by the fact that *fear plays such a prominent role in a healing ritual* based on the perception of two powers being at work: a power of good and a power of evil. I feel ready to break the rule and disobey this law no matter what the consequences, for I do not believe that I or anyone else loses anything unless it is meant (or even needs) to be taken from me or us.

I now try to question the apparent fear, which seems unjustified to me, for I am convinced that GOD's Laws are one (and not two), and that nothing happens that is not in HIS will. The shaman stands by his decision, but not before furiously labeling me a feminist.

The next morning during group meditation, I am given some stern instructions that I pass on to the group.

"ALL TRADITION IS LINEAR. EACH TRADITION HAS ITS OWN VALUE AND MESSAGE. THE TIME HAS COME TO LET GO OF THE LINEAR AND LIFT UP ALL TRADITIONS. IN THE LIFTING UP, THE TRADITIONS WILL JOIN IN A CIRCLE – COOPERATIVE AND MUTUALLY ENHANCING – NOT SEPARATED BY DIFFERENCES BUT RATHER UNITED BY WHAT IS THE SAME. ONLY TOGETHER DO THEY MANIFEST WHOLENESS."

I don't feel well that morning, feeling pain throughout my body. I know from experience that significant misunderstandings and illusions frequently have a psychosomatic effect on my body, but I cannot get an answer to today's problem, and also find myself in a conflict. On the one hand, I try to avoid looking too closely because I fear the intensity of the approaching "inner storm." On the other hand, I feel my responsibility to the participants to proceed with the workshop. However, I also know that I cannot run away from this situation. I am warned to attend to it without hesitation and to do this right in the middle of the house, in the living room, where all participants have access. This is not easy for me, because I prefer to retreat to a sheltered atmosphere. However, I obey and lie down on the floor.

Immediately, I feel a strong internal pressure suppressing a scream of such dimension that I am scared frozen to let it come out. I ask a woman who quietly has seated herself next to me to come to my aid by lying on top of me so that her body can put pressure on mine. I know that by doing this, I can release the pressure I myself am exerting to control my feelings——and allow the scream to come up. When it finally breaks out of me, it feels as if every cell in my body has discharged it. It is as if the Earth herself has opened inside of me, and it is her that is screaming.

While I am screaming, there are images rushing by my inner eye at great speed: These are primarily images of men, but also some women——some of whom I know, and some of whom I do not know——people from today, as well as people from human history long gone. All these beings have something in common: They have all learned to have contempt for their feelings and to suppress them. They followed their man-made laws and believed that a stoic person was pleasing to their god (whatever that meant to them). They equated bravery with the absence of feeling and tried to overcome their weaknesses (or what they perceived as their weaknesses), their feelings, the world and its temptations, by building a heavy armor around themselves. I see fakirs, monks, nuns, and everyday people, all trying to keep a stiff upper lip. And I suddenly become a Sioux Indian participating in a sun dance. I feel my chest being pierced on the left and right by small sticks of bone. Strong ribbons are attached to these bones which bind me to a ritual tree; I experience myself dancing free of the tree, my breath deep and intense. It hurts excruciatingly, and I stay with the pain.

I see all of us repeatedly in rituals, practicing stoic calm and numbed feelings so that no sound will come out of our mouths. Willing ourselves not to scream when all we want to do is scream makes a virtue out of a vice, and with that, pride arises, a fascination with the power over self.

The scream I emit seems to be the scream that everyone suppressed. It is as if they had given their screams over to the Earth (also to the body) that is being suffocated by them. Over so much foolishness, I begin to weep deeply.

After the scream and after the crying, which brought great relief, I stretch my arms to both sides. I feel as though I am bound to the cross. Momentarily, I see Jesus on a cross facing me. I am looking into a pair of indescribably gentle eyes, into which I dive without ever finding a bottom. They are like the clear water of a bottomless spring. Never in my life can I remember ever feeling such unconditional love and tenderness within myself.

Then, something becomes clear to me: This is why many people did not like or understand Him. He remained tender despite all the painful experiences. He suffered openly and truthfully for all eyes to see. He did not make himself into a hero, nor did he build a suit of armor, a shell or wall around himself, and neither did He crucify (deny) himself to escape the crucifixion, humiliation, and contempt that the world was giving Him.

Then suddenly, I see the menorah with nine branches. The middle of the menorah is raised, and the right outside branch is surrounded by very bright light, which commands my full attention. The voice says:

"THIS IS THE VOID OF HEAVEN. YOU NO LONGER CONTROL WHAT COMES OUT OF YOU. HERE INDIVIDUAL STRENGTH OR SEPARATE POWER COMES TO AN END, IS GIVEN UP."

I look to my left. The left outside branch is shrouded in fog, is hazy. However, I want to know and to become aware. I ask and listen. The voice says:

"THIS IS THE VOID OF THE EARTH – YOU NO LONGER CONTROL WHAT COMES INTO YOU."

I realize, however, that the full content of that part of the menorah appears shrouded in fog, and with it the release from this state, still lies before me.

36

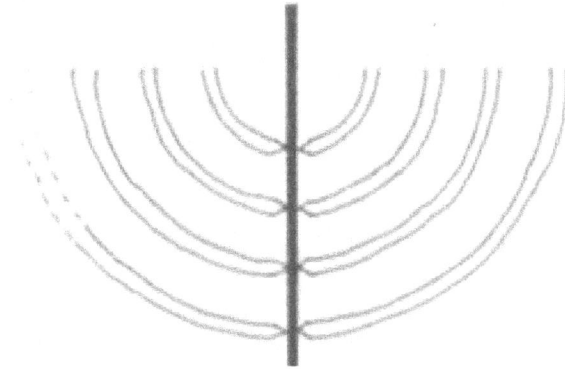

THE VOID OF EARTH	THE VOID OF HEAVEN
No more control over anything that comes your way;	no more control over what wants to come out of you
laying down all fear of the unknown from outside	laying down all fear of the unknown inside

(Figure 8)

I recognize that the specific message of this vision consists of two aspects: the perfect deed and the **perfect conception** (in the sense of devotion, surrender). Both can only be lived and experienced in their complete unintentionality, without analysis, projections, goals, plans, or wishes for myself or for others——without all that with which I previously filled my devotion and my deeds. I learn that devotion is not self-sacrifice, nor is it a generous offering to GOD to serve HIM, trying to make oneself feel capable and valuable for this service. True devotion is the end. It is allowing a self, separated from GOD, to die. It is the complete absorption of what I once believed to be my free will into HIS WILL, the immersing of my "I" into HIS "I," the merging of my heart with HIS heart. It is the awareness and certainty that there is nothing aside from GOD and that only HE IS.

In the course of the following week, I go through a liberating process, which leads me back to the very deep fears I had experienced around the time of my birth. Among these fears, I meet with my refusal to welcome and accept external life as it comes at me. I begin to understand that I have developed many defense mechanisms resulting from fear of being hurt, from fear of having to relinquish control, from fear of having my pride dismantled, and from fear of not being adequately supplied. The "seed" (provided by external expressions), which was supposed to inseminate me like a fertile field (to bring forth the fruit of its imbedded intention), I flung away from myself or ignored. I now realize that my continued attempts to control what comes into me, as well as what wants to come out of me, were and are crippling life.

It is August of 1992. I am at a Jesuit monastery in Poland. We are a German group traveling with an Indian Zen master who is teaching us together with a group of Polish Zen practitioners. The *sesshin* began the previous evening, but I already experienced difficulties with the first session. I feel the inner emotionally disturbed states of the other participants, and I see no possibility to address this openly and thus contribute to a change or their healing, for silence is on the program.

I become aware of the fact that the external monastery walls are still in us. We still follow a dogma, even if it is supposed to be one that frees us from dogma. I see the black robes of the monks and see their faces around me marked by stress, worry, bitterness, and intellectual emptiness. I notice the seeming calm of the Zen master and his students that is in direct contrast to what I feel as their internal conditions and inner unresolvedness. I hear the words of wisdom, but I decide to leave the meeting and withdraw to my room. I cannot remain any longer.

When I begin to meditate in my room, I experience intense physical pain, which opens into heartbreaking sobs. What is this or why? I feel the people who are traveling with me inside of me. I feel their disconnectedness, even though they speak of relationships and try their best to relate. I begin to pray. I feel the energy of Jesus and Mary present and very close. The menorah with nine branches comes to my mind. I also think about the walls of the monastery, the temple walls, the ashram walls, and the laws of the many different traditions. I think about the laws in us, in me.

38

Utter despair arises in me. The word "master" comes to my mind, and I burst into a flood of tears. All of the stress inside of me breaks down now. I had never considered myself a "master" and am, therefore, surprised by this experience. However, on the other hand I, too, like many others, had tried to become some kind of a master, or wanting to master something. It seemed to be such a worthwhile goal. I may have had a great misunderstanding.

I hear a voice. "NOW THE OX HAS VANISHED!"

I am perplexed. Now the ox has vanished? What ox? I ask and wait for something to come along and make some sense out of this. After sitting, waiting, and breathing——and then waiting some more——a Zen story that I once read somewhere comes to my mind about a man seeking an ox. But did the man not go home with the ox? I decide to read the story again because now I also remember that this story is in a book written by the Zen master who is accompanying us. Then I remember my condition. It feels as if I had searched for, found, and ridden the ox, and would now have to leave him and return without him. I hear:

"YOU WENT OUT TO BECOME A MASTER; NOW YOU ARE BECOMING HUMAN."

It now seems absurd that I should ever have wanted to become a master. Somewhere along the way, I seem to have made a fundamental error. Oh, how much this desire prevented me from being or becoming human! Or was this the way to become human? Up until now, I believed that I was human and had to become a master. Now it feels as if the "master" is in me, a lower rank, and has to become human. It also feels as though becoming human was the highest and absolute fulfillment of my existence.

I am struck by the loneliness of the sage who returns to the place he left, where he once felt at home. Home has become a foreign place to him.

Now I must ask myself a serious question: Is this me, or is it someone else in me? I am at a loss here; a lot of this feels foreign to me. I understand, and yet it remains foreign territory. I do not know. The nine-branch menorah appears, and inside of me I feel that the holy feminine and masculine energies——the void of Heaven and the void of Earth——are coming closer together.

Later, I come across the Zen master standing alone in the parking lot. I don't want to tell him about my experience, but I am convinced that it is directly related to him and concerns him. So ,with just a few words I tell him what I am sensing from him.

"Your back hurts!"

"Yes," he answers, and looks at me. I hesitate.

"Your second chakra is blocked!"

"Yes." Silence again between us.

"You should do something about it."

"Yes." Should I say anything else?

"It is difficult to return to the marketplace and have to feel everything! Isn't it?"

He looks me in the eye and says, "Yes." And I know that he knows.

In the weeks thereafter, many images I had made of myself and with which I had identified myself were shattered. It was very painful and frightening. I had the feeling that even the few small pegs I had used to latch onto for my security were being taken from me, the supposed security that had somehow given me a sense of belonging. But I understood; I am not a therapist or a teacher or a woman or a child or a mother——I am human, and in me is everything and nothing.

MANIFEST*ED* CREATION   MANIFEST*ING* CREATION

VOID	I	II	III	IV	V	VI	VII	VOID
Of Earth	MINERAL	PLANT	ANIMAL	HUMAN	ANGEL	SERAPH	God	of Heaven
	Truth,	flowing	rhythm,	realization,	peace.	pure joy,		
	Number,	love.	motion	the Word.	stillness	power		
	the law	growth	harmony	connection				

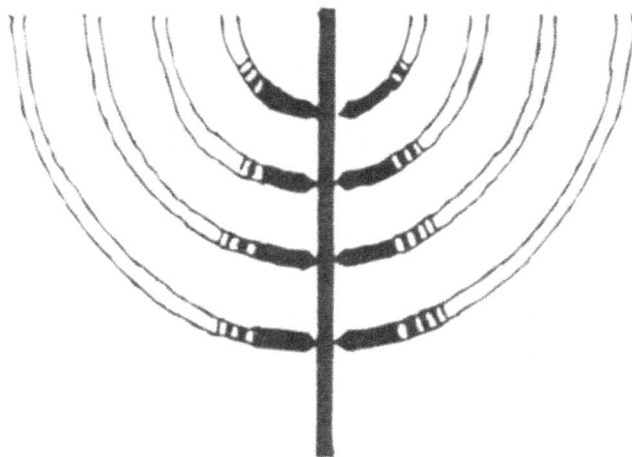

link/bridge

(Figure 9)

Then one night, I had the following dream:

I am standing at a long table covered with a white tablecloth. In the middle of the table there is some kind of table decoration, a centerpiece. When I take a closer look, I see that it is a crown of thorns. I continue to look at it with a mixture of amazement and confusion. I do not understand. Then I become aware of the presence of people that are standing around the table. I cannot see them clearly, but their personal identity seems unimportant to me.

41

Across from me, I notice someone whom I am also unable to see clearly. Then the scene in the dream changes, and I see the nine-branch menorah: It is now complete, and all of the candles are lit. But around the flame of the center candle floats a crown of thorns. The dream freezes here (I probably do also!), and I wake up.

Later that day, I told a friend about this experience. As I was explaining what happened, I am suddenly back in the middle of the dream, standing again at the table. I take a closer look at the situation and sense again the presence of several people. They have no faces. Now I recognize Jesus at the other side of the table, across from me. In his hands he is holding a piece of bread and a cup. He looks directly into my eyes. I feel reminded of a promise, but I do not know what kind of promise or when I made it. I know He stands there only to remind me to fulfill it. I am prepared to fulfill it. I feel a great sadness and cry for a long time.

QUESTIONS FOR CONTEMPLATION:

- Where and in what manner do you crucify, that is, deny yourself? Do you want to become human?
- Do you yourself wish to become a master? Or are you tempted to imitate someone whom you consider to be a master?
- What feelings and weaknesses have you successfully been able to hide and suppress?

6

God's Angels

This vision is one of a few that are closely related to other visions concerning Jesus' life and the Way of the cross. Whenever I was made aware of the personal experiences of Jesus, I have always been particularly affected by His great love in His leading me to better discernment and understanding——to the overcoming of my fallacies.

The experience I wish to share here starts with me——once again—— wondering about my severe myopia (nearsightedness) with which I have been afflicted since early childhood. Currently, a woman named Marie lives with us in our community. She has the gift of healing hands, and I ask her to help me with my eyes. I would like to know the true cause of this predicament. We go to the garden, and I take a seat in the shade of our plum tree. Marie places her hands over my eyes, and I soon notice a strong luminosity on my face and feel very grateful. I squint through my eyelids for I believe it is the sun that shines onto my face, but I am still sitting in total shade. The Light remains.

After Marie is done and removes her hands, she asks me whether I think that Jesus was present. I share with her my experience of the Light, and we both are very happy. Then she places a rock crystal into my hands and leaves me alone in the garden.

My eyes are now open, but I do not look at anything outside. I continue to sit, feel the crystal in my hands, and ponder the cause of my eye problem. Eventually my head begins to feel empty; there are no thoughts left other than my question. Jesus appears in great luminosity to the left of me in a hard-to-describe strong energy field——and says:

"LOOK!"

Right in front of me I see——my eyes still open——Him walking carrying the cross and many people that stand at the edge of the road. I hear the

43

peoples' cry: "Crucify him, crucify him!" It is devastating to continue looking and hearing, but I keep myself from averting my eyes. I feel close to tears. He speaks again:

"YOU ARE STILL ANGRY AT THOSE WHO CRUCIFIED ME!"

Wasn't that the truth! I agree but now I am also crying. Since childhood—— ever since I heard the biblical story of the persecution and crucifixion of Jesus——I feel distraught just thinking about it; that such a man had been brought to death, and all these shitheads walked away freely. I had felt enraged and helpless whenever I heard or read the story, and that was every year at least once during Holy Week. How had people been so blind? How could anyone have been so afraid of His message? What had been threatened? And what did that have to do with my own "blindness"?

I turn to Jesus. He says:

"THOSE WERE THE ANGELS OF GOD."

After some silence and my trying to digest what I just heard——it seems blasphemous——he continues:

"YOU ARE STILL ANGRY AT THOSE WHO CRUCIFY YOU!" (Present tense!)

That, too, is true.

"THEY ARE THE ANGELS OF GOD."

The light dissolves, and He is gone. He leaves me deeply affected and impressed by the truth he has spoken.

Many disagreeable memories come up in which I felt "crucified," dejected, and judged. Deep, painful anguish fills these memories with many uncried tears that I now end up crying. How often had I experienced myself as not seen, not recognized? How much had I pushed myself to please people and conforming to their image of me so that nothing would be interrupted or destroyed that "connected" us, even though that connection hardly existed?

My previous notions that injustice had befallen me began to change now. While those experiences did not seem to be less painful to me, the suffering suddenly had a different quality, made sense somehow. How confused I had been about humanity, about my "needs" and who I was! How I had strained, had worked towards, in hopes of holding onto my illusions despite all experiences of them being painfully destroyed. I had swung back and forth between self-crucifixion——that is between painful alignment and self-denial——and the crucifixion by life and others——that is the experience of my illusions being destroyed from outside.

It occurs to me how impossible it had seemed just a few minutes before to call those who had hurt or wronged me the angels of God——not to mention to actually see them that way. So far, they had been the enemies whom I had been asked to love, and that was it. I had struggled to have an understanding of their inadequacies; I had struggled to forgive. But I had NEVER, and I mean NEVER, recognized the adequacy in their being and acting. What arrogance! It dawned on me that there may not be any evil, but that in our blindness we hook into the seeming appearance of evil. I began to understand that GOD operates in HIS love and grace——even when we consider evil in others to meet **our** misunderstanding, our fallacy, our own inadequacies—— to reach us in our own illusions and liberate us from them. It dawned on me that only in being true to HIS path within me can I learn. And only thus can I let HIM direct me into loyalty to self and into that loyalty that corresponds with the freedom of divine being.

The story of my life and my experiences are changed into my story with GOD and my experiences with GOD. My perception changed——everything received new meaning.

Ah, how lost I have been! We all are. How badly we wish to continue blaming and remain in our senseless suffering. This is certainly not consciously done. But most of us do not connect the dots between our unhappiness, and even sickness, to our attitudes and misunderstandings. If we did, perhaps our minds would be quickly enlightened. Just imagine: We all suddenly stop believing that someone else is to be blamed for our dilemma, no matter what kind of dilemma we find ourselves in. We would all ask ourselves what we had to become aware of, what had to be learned——and then would end up living lovingly with this experience and the inherent, recognizable truth. I am sure this is a utopia for which we will have to wait a long time, if not forever. But you and I can start!

This vision accompanied me for quite some time and re-surfaced repeatedly. The simple words, the clear and simple message, remain lastingly.

QUESTIONS FOR CONTEMPLATION

- What does it mean to you to be "crucified"? Can you relate to this concept?
- Are you still angry with those who did not know you but wanted you to be the way they wanted you to be? What could have been the blessing in that experience?
- How is your encounter with these people today?

7

The Son of God

This morning, I am in a terrible physical condition. My blood pressure is far too low, and feebleness and tiredness in body and limbs have become a problem. The retention of fluids in my legs has filled up the tissue around my ankles, has swollen them immensely, so that I find it difficult even to walk and fulfill my daily chores. Despite this, I try to ignore my condition until I am simply no longer able to do so. Finally, my stubbornness gives way, and I decide to lie down on the carpet, enter silence, and ask to be given help for understanding the cause of all this.

Immediately, an image of a water hose appears in front of my eyes, with a valve at its end. The hose is bulging with extreme pressure, but the valve is closed to such a degree that only small drops come out slowly. I know at once that nothing could have described my condition more accurately than this image. I recognize my dilemma and know two things simultaneously: It is I who have taken control over "the valve" and am responsible for the consequences, and it is I who **suffers** from the consequences. It hurts to see what I am doing to *myself*, and I feel clueless about why I do this, repeatedly, for the problems with my legs are not new to me. I need to cry.

Then I sense Jesus as a great, bright Presence to the left of me. He makes me see by leading me to images of the path that led to His crucifixion. Today, He shows me the garden of Gethsemane (and do not ask me how I recognized it, I just did), and I am aware of His struggle for willingness, surrender, and the final acceptance of "the cup."

The image leaves and another appears. Together, we now look upon the road to Golgotha, and I see many people yelling, calling Him names, pointing disdainfully, and spitting at Him. I look, I see, I ache. Then the image changes to the crucifixion itself, His dying.

And then He speaks:

47

YOU **ARE** WILLING TO ENTER THE GARDEN: YOU ARE NOT AFRAID TO RECOGNIZE THE CUP AND TO ACCEPT IT, TO SURRENDER YOUR WILL TO THE ONE AND ONLY WILL: YOU ARE ALSO NO LONGER AFRAID OF DEATH.

BUT YOU FEAR THE PROCESS OF DYING, YOU FEAR RIDICULE, NAME-CALLING, ABUSE, THE ABANDONMENT BY FRIENDS AND FAMILY; YOU FEAR PAIN AND DESTRUCTION, TO BE MISUNDERSTOOD AND TO BE A STRANGER AMONG YOUR PEERS.

Nothing remains undisclosed, and there is nothing to question. All is true. A gut-wrenching pain takes hold of my body, leading to many tears. All the heaviness and debilitation in my body leave instantly. The swelling in my legs goes down. I see the valve on the water hose is open, and a fresh, strong, clear jet of water comes through. I decide to face up to and wrestle those of my fears that Jesus spoke about.

The vision of the Way of the cross remains. I am now where I was before. I see that Jesus breaks down under the heavy wooden cross He is carrying. I would so much like to avert my eyes! It hurts having to see this. But suddenly——and I do not believe my own eyes——I see that He detaches His glorious light presence from his suffering physical body, stands in front of His own physical suffering, and——laughs! I struggle through doubts, thoughts of blasphemy, my entire realms of skepticism. I just cannot believe He is laughing! But He is!

He waits for me to overcome my struggles. But then He asks:

"DO YOU TRULY BELIEVE THAT SPIT COULD HARM ME?"

I am speechless, and immediately also skeptical. Can I trust these images? My understanding of biblical history is thoroughly questioned by them. It is almost thrown overboard! At the same time, I carefully approach what He has said. I do not know what I would rather do, cry or laugh. I am shaken, but also register an increasing, all-encompassing exhilaration that desires to prevail and against which I no longer can defend. I start to laugh, louder and louder, and I cannot help myself: I become laughter itself. The vision disappears and so does Jesus.

Up until now, I never thought about how Jesus as the SON OF GOD experienced His "I and the Father are one" while simultaneously being confronted by such indescribably blind expectations, blind rage, and contempt. I remember other visions through which I was made aware of the kind of suffering He experienced and the physical pain that was never negated——also how much he was afflicted by not being received or understood by "His own," even though he grew up in their tradition, in their town and land, and even though he related to the same teachings and the same scripture. Totally new to me is the idea that spit and hateful words (to my ears) did not harm Him, not even physical death. What a prodigious thought! Truth! While everything was happening, I remain certain he also experienced it *but NOT in His spiritual body*, not in His identity. Perhaps he experienced it somewhere else. But where? His true integrity remained untouched. He was not the body! He dwelled in it——the temple.

What does this all mean, and what **am I** supposed to learn? I ask. I continue to ponder. I can clearly see how dependent I have been on the perception, opinions, and approval of others and why I, therefore, feared their disdain and rejection. I had also dreaded physical pain, beating, violence. I must seriously ask myself:

- Do I truly believe that I am a child of GOD and have been created in HIS image?
- Do I believe that only in HIM I have my being and life?
- Is it possible to live so utterly abiding in this holy relationship that opinion and thoughts of others, even their possible violent threats, become irrelevant and no longer worry or sadden me?
- Am I willing to pay the price that possibly has to be paid for this freedom? What may that price be and what possible loss?

Though I still experience a deep fear in my heart, I know that my unfolding and increasing love for GOD surpasses it. Also, my desire to follow unquestioningly increases——whatever that may ask of me.

When I reflect on *this* vision again, together with the one in the chapter **GOD'S Angels**, I recognize a correlation. It is the experience *between* the surrender in the garden of Gethsemane (Matt. 26:36–46) and the "dying" in which my perception and the subsequent attitude and behavior are challenged. I become aware of my previous dichotomy between my physical incarnation and my spiritual identity. It will now be impossible to continue seeing them as two different existences. Only in true consciousness of my spiritual inheritance——that is, in the divine Sonship——may I be willing and able to accept the Way of the cross and walk it. How else could that be accomplished? How else could I possibly be able to deal with the loneliness of my illusions and their disillusionment, to overcome them? How else can I possibly find willingness to consciously be disappointed, disillusioned, and struck——even by those whom Jesus called the "Angels of God"? How else will you be able to do so?

I began to understand that only the completed and, in the final analysis, accomplished dying (and I do not mean physical death) can lead to actual resurrection. I believe I understand, and yet I do not. How many little deaths will have to be died until it is accomplished?

Much later——years later——I was once more and newly prompted to face this vision. Once again, I was deeply affected by Jesus's experience of physical exhaustion and indignity. His physical nakedness and weakness, His vulnerability and soreness, and His being at the mercy of humanity still horrified me profoundly——a degree of debasement that makes a continuance of any self-created dignity impossible. Pride? Where did it go? There is no complaining, no protest; there are no proud words, no threats, no hatred, no resistance, no defense, no blame, no attempt to convince——only Truth Itself as witness and confrontation.

I know very well why I am confronted with this again. I am aware that I still try to preserve "my" dignity and try to prevent my veneer from being scratched. I cannot acquiesce to everyone or everything. And even if it is only having the last word, I must distance and protect myself. At least that!

And yet, when I see Jesus, he allows life to happen to him. I cannot take it! Just imagining what that would be like creates strong tension and resistance in me. I would like to step aside, find arguments against this. I hear myself say: "He could do this, but it is not asked of me," but I know simultaneously that that is a lie. I know I am asked to walk the path completely, not halfway, and not with only one foot. There is no safety net that I can obtain, ask for, or try to keep.

That is why I take a chance and embark on accepting all the inner experiences that are entailed. I feel a strong, almost crazy-desperate struggle; all energies are wildly upset and confused. I want to bail out and leave my body so that I will not have to feel. I am okay with looking at it, but not being with it or being it. I want to resist, want to break out with my voice, want to hit something, lash about.

Suddenly, the formerly only imagined event becomes my personal reality. I am now present in a burdened, maltreated body that is on the verge of breaking down. On my back is the cross. I feel the weight and desire furiously to shake it off and be done with it. I am aware of many people around me who loudly and insistently talk at me: "Where is this going to end? What you are doing, and where you are going? Now you can see!" They argue and offer many rational explanations for what GOD is, what HE wants, and what life is. They speak of security and common sense, and I feel **their** fear. So finally, I answer and scream: "Yes, I know where it leads! It leads to the crucifixion, the final death!" And more! I cry.

All my tension dissolves with my tears, and I feel a degree of loneliness in me like never before. Concurrently, I gain willingness, slowly (it feels stiff, like slow motion), to walk through it *and to feel everything.* I also feel a new permeability, a kind of porosity in my physical body. I know this death also means no longer having a skin that separates me from life, from others. It means accepting the suffering into the deepest cells of my being, also the pain and suffering of others, however hidden it may be beyond their fear and pride. It means being raw and visibly vulnerable. It also means no longer having a dignified "departure" available, no matter the situation. It means foregoing name and rank, greatness and approval, personal dignity, and protection. It means living the truth at all cost and without reservation or censorship——and it means infinite freedom.

Only a few days have passed. GOD certainly has a hold on me! It is pre-Christmas week, and yet it feels like Holy Week to me. Since I have been pondering Jesus's humanness, vulnerability, and His surrender to being at the mercy of whatever, nothing much seems to be happening in my inner process. My resistance to experience this death, this not-being, is immense, and, like a roly-poly, not giving up. I take small steps during these days——as long as I renew my commitment and vow not to give up and to continue to walk. I know I must do this on my own. No one can help me here; no one can take it from me. O God, how lonely this is!

The weekend is here. Sunday morning, we all sit as a small group for Sunday worship service at the Community House in Virginia Beach. During the half-hour meditative silence, I am taken right back into the passion of Jesus, into His body. Everything, but **everything**, hurts. I feel a wreath of thorns on my head, and I remember a dream I had (see the nine-armed menorah). I am now ready to fulfill my promise, still without knowing what I had actually promised at the time. Many tears run down my face for a long time. A sense of an infinite lonesomeness has taken over. There is nothing left aside from this aloneness: no resistance, no rage, no pain——only aloneness and full abandonment to the occurrence. I hear the words Jesus spoke on the cross: "My God, my God, why have you forsaken me?" (Matt/ 24:16), **but——I do not feel forsaken by God**. It is as though they were the words of the people under the cross, and as though He cried the words they were not uttering. I feel His mercy and love close and present within me. NOW I KNOW the human form of Jesus died, but CHRIST was and remained and in HIM, Jesus.

I had never wanted this crown of thorns. I may have been willing to die, but with decency, and a certain grandeur, not looking weak and being speechless, and not in such utter, inescapable loneliness. I had also not been free from expecting something from it, even if it was the resurrection.

But Jesus had warned me:

"YOU WISH TO RESURRECT," He had said, and laughingly added: "I HAVE NEWS FOR YOU: YOU WILL NOT RESURRECT. I WILL RESURRECT IN YOU."

I had not known at the time whether to laugh or cry.

Only now do I understand what Jesus meant in the vision, when He said I did not want the experience between willingness and dying. The others? At this moment, they become irrelevant. It is not about others; it is about God and me. NO, it is about God or "me." The struggle comes to an end.

During the hours that followed on that Sunday, I spoke to a number of people who, I know, were going through great loneliness themselves. I felt their condition as though it were my own, and I could voice for them what they found difficult to do. It changed something in me. But it was only in the evening that I realized that the still present crown of thorns on my head was changing into a flower wreath. I say this out loud, amazed——and I hear my own words: "It is as though in dying, I'm going to a wedding!" I was so very deeply moved! I cried tears of joy and relief.

O GOD, I thank you!

In dying I became Bride,

and Love remained—

No longer me—

Fulfill your creation

and Be.

QUESTIONS FOR CONTEMPLATION

> Are you able to apply Jesus's way of the cross to your life? What is "the cup" to you? And what is the "spit"? Do you consider yourself inviolable?
> - Everything has a price. What price are you willing to pay for your freedom and wholeness? And what is the cost to remain where you are?
> - Look closely at what you are not willing to surrender and ask yourself whether you actually have it or whether you only believe you have it.

8

Mother Earth

During meditation, I was surprised by the appearance of an image of one of my oldest friends and lovers. It has been over twenty years since we knew each other, and nothing that I am aware of has triggered this memory now. As I see him standing before me, he looks happy and satisfied with his life. This is also my memory of him from the time we shared; he was mostly in good cheer, always knew what he wanted and did it, but seemed neither to know nor understand anything about my very reduced self-worth at the time.

While I reflect on this, some other male friends, acquaintances, and clients appear, standing right next to the lover mentioned above. Then suddenly I see the energy bodies of each of their mothers behind them. They are attached to their sons, overshadowing and permeating; one could almost say possessing them. The moment I recognize this, the mothers' bodies separate and leave behind extremely malnourished beings who neither know their own feelings nor are aware of their neediness. Emotionally, they are almost unable to exist. I am deeply moved in my heart and feel an intense sorrow that dissolves with my tears.

I learn that in man's forlornness and unawareness, the mother-energies dominate the sons and the father-energies the daughters. I also learn that this domination essentially happens because many mothers and fathers find their own well-being dependent on that of their children, on their behavior, and in turn, hold them responsible for it. Many may remember a parental sentence like: "You made Mommy very unhappy with what you did," or, "I am very unhappy with you." Sons and daughters in turn are not only burdened by their concern for the well-being of their parents and by their more or less consciously engaged in it, but they also feel responsible and experience guilt. This way, the unconscious ideas parents have of living——life used for fulfilling their own heart's desire and purpose——are projected onto the children, whereby all other parental wishes and longings, denials, fears, and every unprocessed, painful experience are passed on and taken into the lives of the children as well.

I learn that the true cause for these displacements and transmissions originates somewhere else. They are created in our parents (and all generations before)——in all humanity, for that matter——by not recognizing that God is Father and Mother of us all and by not having found (remembered) their home in their own divine essence. For most of our parents, we children were not God's, but theirs. They did not understand that they were helpmates in raising us——God entrusted us (and Himself in them) to their care ——so that the children could fulfill their true purpose. All too often, parents remain set in their understanding that the child ought to be the way they envisioned and wanted the child to be. And we, as long as we considered ourselves as theirs, adopted the same misunderstanding and believed ourselves to be flesh and blood instead of GOD's children and of Spirit.

I learn that we had no clue that through the bodies of our parents only our bodies were created for the incarnation on Earth——in every way perfect for what we had to learn, to overcome, and to contribute to the evolution of consciousness not only, but also, in the family and previous generations into which we were born. Every genetic determinant as inner condition, and the social environment as outer condition, had to be considered thus. That does not mean we are the children of our parents or that our parents ought to see us as theirs. If we believe that, we forget that our body is only the dwelling, if not the temple, of the soul, and that we ourselves are not of this world, but of God

The belief alone that we are of our parents makes us dependent on them and misleads us into an *inappropriate, insincere* subordination. Our relationship is not by blood but by the Holy Spirit. **IT is and remains** the connection between them and us, just different: It creates communion, not dependency. If, however, we insist on our misunderstanding, it will be difficult to find our way into such communion.

Here it seems necessary for me to mention that I speak of energy and energetic dependency that cannot, therefore, be solved by physical separation or psychological arguments and contention. All too often we try to shed this dependency by physical separation. The solution, however, requires an ***inner process*** that eventually will lead to an external result. This must raise many questions, of their significance all those involved as therapists and counselors ought to be conscious.

During my work as a therapist, I have again and again come across the interweaving of parental energies with those of an individual——I may say, without exception——in everyone. The physical father and mother are present in energy patterns (forms) that intrinsically correspond to our perception of them. Each child of the same family has parental energy patterns differing from those of its siblings, to solve. Everyone, whether conscious or unconscious, will eventually have to face the necessity to *integrate* and thereby redeem these energy forms and patterns. Those individuals who are already aware of and feel their energies will find it easier to understand and engage in the pertinent healing process.

Our fallacy, I am told, does not only relate to man and the question of who he is, but also to our ideas of Heaven and Earth. It is a misunderstanding to believe that Heaven and Earth are separated, that Father is Heaven and Mother is the Earth that nourishes us. This concept separates the Earth from God, separates our soul from our existence on Earth in the body, and misleads us into duality, *the forever unresolved conflict*. It is this separation that instead of freeing us from the Earth binds us to it. Thus, we remain seduced, but also forced to have to return to the Earth instead of choosing to live on it freely or not. Then I hear these words:

"HOW CAN I ONLY BE FATHER? THERE IS NOTHING BUT I——I AM ALL AND PERMEATE ALL——AM HEAVEN AND EARTH—— AM FATHER AND MOTHER IN ONE; ALSO IN YOU I AM FATHER AND MOTHER. IT IS I WHO HAS CALLED YOU AND DIRECTS YOU; IT IS I IN WHOSE FOLD YOU REST AND ON WHOSE MOTHERLY BREAST YOU ARE GIVEN COMFORT. DO NOT BE DECEIVED AND SEEK NOTHING ASIDE FROM ME!"

I am reminded of some American Indian traditions, the separation in their teaching of the Great Spirit and Mother Earth, the Sun and Moon. I think of the questionable attempt by the white man to bring them Christianity's message. I recognize the fallacies on either side, and it saddens me. Will it ever be possible to convey the essence of the message of the All-One GOD so that it is acceptable and comprehensible? Will it ever be possible to overcome dual perceptions on so many levels of life in the different traditions?

QUESTIONS FOR CONTEMPLATION

- What are your ideas about life? Are they yours, or are they those of your parents? If they differ, in what way do they differ?
- How or in what way were you dependent on the *mood* of your parents? How and in what way did you feel responsible for their well-being?
- To what degree did you surrender the responsibility for your own actions and being?

9

Renunciation

One day, I decided to fast for a week. Up until then, fasting had always been rich in experiences for me, and so I began in joyful expectation. I have often fasted for much longer than a week, gaining healing through multifaceted experiences of "symptoms" that appeared during the fast. However, to my great surprise, I found myself awakening one morning towards the end of the week feeling extremely hungry. Always in earlier fasts, the feeling of hunger had left me right after I started, and it stayed away until the fast ended. This was why I was totally stunned, for not only was I very hungry, but I was craving spinach, of all things! And I mean craving! What was I to do? Anyone that ever fasted knows that you have to break the fast slowly and cannot eat everything right away.

I pondered, am I lacking something in my body? (At that time, I still believed that spinach had a lot of iron!). I generally can rely on what the body tells me, but as yet I did not want to break the fast. I stopped thinking and decided to cook spinach for the family dinner instead of eating.

When it was time for me to begin cooking the meal, I started with rinsing and brushing potatoes in the kitchen sink, to go with the spinach. I was leaning over the sink when I suddenly heard a voice directly behind me (no one was physically there! I looked!) say loudly:

"YOU DO NOT HAVE TO RENOUNCE ANYTHING!"

I straightened up, stopped brushing, let my hands rest on the edge of the sink. When I lifted my head I saw, totally bewildered and with my eyes wide open, an image of a dinner fork loaded with spinach and potatoes floating through the air towards my mouth. It seemed I had no other choice but to open my mouth and receive this food. Before I even realized what was happening, I felt my mouth filled with food and also tasted it. I chewed and swallowed the nourishment. Once done, a second loaded fork appeared and headed straight for my mouth. Again, I opened my mouth (there was no time to think of anything else to do); I ate and swallowed. With this I noticed that my craving for spinach had become totally satisfied. Then came the voice again, repeating:

"YOU DO NOT HAVE TO RENOUNCE ANYTHING!"

What just happened? Did I eat spinach, or did I eat air? The spinach actually tasted like spinach and had substance in my mouth. But I also know that there was another reality; "our" spinach was still in the freezer. It appeared as though reality levels had gotten mixed up, or as though a lighter level had permeated another, denser level. I did not hold that fork, and yet I did taste the spinach. It occurred to me: "Man does not live by bread alone" (Matt. 4:4; Deut. 8:3) Even though I am still convinced——and perhaps you are, too——that we need physical nourishment[5]. Bizarre thoughts enter my mind: What if it were not true that we "have" to eat? What if we have only always believed that? What if something totally different could sustain our physical bodies as well? What then?

I now know there is something that can replete me physically without it being physical. Would there be a similarity to the manna appearing as food in the desert during the exodus of the Israelites from Egypt? Hindus call this energy Prana, the all-creating, all-maintaining life force available to us. In the Hindu tradition saints existed, and still exist, that do not eat but continue to live. Therese Neumann (of Konnersreuth, Germany), a stigmatic, did not consume any food or drink during the last 30 years of her life and lived through the "Redeemer"——as she called the *quarter* of the wafer given during Mass——that she not only consumed daily, but had to have.

What was it again I heard? "YOU DO NOT HAVE TO RENOUNCE ANYTHING!" I was given a gift! I feel completely seen and known in my dilemma, my needs. I feel comforted, nourished, satisfied, and led into the true meaning of the psalmists words "to fresh water and onto green pastures" (Ps. 23).

But the words also move something else in me: I feel caught. What attitude did I have about renouncing or renunciation? What did it mean to renounce? I grew up during the last years and postwar years of World War II. In 1946, my father began rebuilding his business that had been destroyed, and every

59

penny went into it. For all of us that meant ongoing poverty and a continuous waiving of wants and desires. My sister Ruth, for example, had to leave high school against her wish, and only half a year before graduation, in order to take paid employment. I probably had the hardest time of all of us letting go of what I could not have. I resigned myself to this reality, but not free-willingly, and only because I had no choice. Subliminally, I fostered jealousies and constantly peered at and envied others, especially children who had more or other things.

It was my resistance towards having to feel and to express what I felt that eventually induced me to turn my vice into a virtue. This way, I practiced for years neither wanting nor needing anything. I developed a frugality and modesty that, while unconscious, was dishonest and insincere. Sometimes it turned suddenly into an irrational shopping frenzy or an eating orgy that was hard to understand. I can see now how closely related renunciation and addiction are. In fact, they are interdependent.

Renunciation covers up addiction, even while creating it. Any attempt to overcome addiction leads, if not differently directed, to renunciation——a vicious cycle! It is for this reason that an alcoholic cannot truly heal simply by not drinking. My renunciation was no real renunciation. So, what did it serve?

How **deeply** buried I had my neediness and to what degree I had romanticized my "renunciation." Today I know that renunciation harbors the perception and the associated fear that a wish will not be filled. To avoid the pain of disappointment, the wish is repressed, and thereby no longer noticeable——not available to the point of total denial. Renunciation may be a pious character trait, but in essence it is not. Neither is it spiritual. In no way does it correspond to needlessness or already having everything. The experience with the spinach guided me kindly but clearly to this truth.

After I had the experience, I shared with others what happened to me with the spinach. A frequent and, what seemed to me, odd reaction was: "How lovely! Then I can get myself everything I want every minute!" This reaction affected and disturbed me. The desire to be in control seemed so multifaceted! Our thoughts are filled with a desire to have control over everything, to either refuse to feel needs or fulfill our needs *ourselves* to *make ourselves* feel cared for! After my experience, such appeared to me to be a strange idea. Even though I can follow such thoughts (I, too, had lived by them for a long time), I had now gained a clear impression that I no longer had to concern myself with any of my needs, not even spinach. I do not have to renounce, but neither do I need to grab or hoard. Everything is given me. My experience related much more to: "Ask and it will be given you" (Matt. 7:7) or even more so to: "Your Father knows what you need before you ask Him" (Matt. 6:8).

My experience brought me close to Jesus's teaching about the lilies of the field, and I read: "Therefore I tell you, do not be anxious about your life, what you will eat or what you will drink, nor about your body, what you will put on. Is not life more than food, and the body more than clothing? Consider the lilies of the field, how they grow: they neither toil nor spin, yet I tell you, even Solomon in all his glory was not arrayed like one of these," and later, "But seek first the kingdom of God and HIS righteousness, and all these things will be added to you" (Matt. 6).

QUESTIONS FOR CONTEMPLATION

- What does it mean *to you* to waive or renounce something? Do you know this condition? Do or did you ever have to do so?
- Which of your needs do you fill yourself and with what? Where do you vacillate between renunciation and self—gratification?
- Is it possible for you to see that having it all is just as good as having nothing?

10

Chakras of the Earth

One evening, I was invited to participate in a Zen-meditation event that a friend of mine lead. After the sesshin was concluded, he suggested a guided rainbow meditation (see also the section on meditation) that he himself had recently experienced with great joy. He desired to share it with us. Even though it was already late, I was interested, excited, and stayed with several other participants.

We all lay down on the floor, relaxing our bodies and focusing on our breath. In front of my inner eye, the landscape appeared that my friend was describing. I found myself sitting on a bench observing this landscape. I experienced a light rain and noticed that in the communion of rain and sun, a gloriously colorful rainbow was created. I thought of the chakra colors and was very curious what would now happen in my body, as we would be taking the colors inside.

We started with the color RED. As I let the color in, a vision of absolutely alarming horror unfolded. I saw piles of human bodies, destroyed bodies, mass graves, slaughtered animals, sacrificial animals——dead bodies, all piled on top of one another. Wars and persecutions came to my mind, the entire tragic history of humans and their interactions with the fallacies contained therein. My thoughts raced. I thought of religious practices that contained such sacrifice, of cults, pogroms, and their mass graves. Only with great effort could I suppress a scream of horror and try to accept the extreme physical pain (in my root chakra) that entered my body simultaneously with the vision. I was relieved when my friend led us to the next color. I did not understand then what this experience had to do with my root chakra and how the vision related to it.

We moved on to the color ORANGE. As soon as the color filled me, another horrific vision appeared. I saw fire——everywhere: whole cities burning, fire falling from the sky onto houses and people, houses collapsing, devastation and destruction everywhere, horrendous noise filled with screams. I had to put a hand over my mouth to hold back my own screams and moved quickly——and before we were guided——to the next color. My consternation increased.

I breathed in YELLOW: and once more, a vision of horror. Three male judges sat on their bench. They sat there representing (in us all: in women as well as men) thoughts, intellect, rationality, the belief to know. They raised **themselves** above all and everything that was not familiar to them and that did not fit in with their logic. They represented judgment about the female, femininity, life, feelings, intuition, and the essentially unexplainable, extrasensory perception, and God. They were the "witch hunters," the scribes and crucifiers, the representatives of man-made worldly justice and religious dogma, the warmongers. I fled the ocean of physical pain that came with the vision and moved——again ahead of the group——to the next color: GREEN (heart chakra).

To prevent misunderstandings, I would like to mention explicitly to those who read this that the last vision was not about men and women in the traditional sense, but rather about the male and female attributes in each of us. We women, too, have those "judges" within. But we also experience them outside in those whom we encounter, who have cut themselves off from their feelings and their spiritual home and deny both—— or as such they appear.

As soon as GREEN came into me, I felt the color permeating my entire body, including the entire lower parts. I experienced great relief and soothing. The visions remained present, albeit they no longer got to me the way they did, and I did not really feel much——neither my terror nor any physical pain. I knew I had to deal with the truth that was stuck "down there," and I also knew I would have to enter all those feelings in order to be healed. During this evening, however, and in the group, I did not allow myself to yield to it.

I tried to go back that same night after I arrived home, but I couldn't get deep enough. I realized that these visions must have something to do with my incarnating into the physical during wartime——either before or during my birth. That is why the next day, I asked a friend trained in pre-natal therapy to help me. She agreed.

When we began our session the following evening, I was immediately drawn far back into the past. I am convinced that all three visions indicate what I saw at the time of my current incarnation (I was born in Germany in 1942). It had affected me deeply and thrown me into fear and consternation. At that time, my total resistance to encounter and feel any of the suffering on Earth was solidly formed! I was required to recommit. It took all my willpower, even in this session, to overcome my resistance and arrive at willingness to be on Earth at this time.

Then I was somewhat sidetracked by the surprising realization that I had actually participated in the preparations for this incarnation. I suddenly became aware that next to the visionary perception of the conditions on Earth, I was *co—creating* with my spiritual body the physical body in my mother's womb. I experienced myself outside of the body but simultaneously sensed physically (while I lay there) a subtle energy in my actual spine forming individual vertebral bodies and creating the spine. I was not yet incarnated in the body but already connected, and I know that this happened at the stage of eight weeks during pregnancy. After this little sidetrack, I returned to the visions I had had two days prior.

First vision

I now see the many victims of two world wars and of the persecution during the Third Reich. I see battlefields and mass graves, human bodies of every color and race and in many different places. I see human and animal victims of sacrifices that were performed for dogmatic reasons due to ignorance and unconsciousness of divine laws. An indescribably deep sorrow fills me from a seemingly bottomless lake, and my tears are hot and fierce. I am still crying when I hear a voice speaking:

"AS LONG AS YOU CONSIDER THE DEAD BODY THE VICTIM, YOU WILL NOT TRULY SEE LIFE. THE DEAD ARE DEAD; LIFE REMAINS ETERNAL! THE DEAD DO NOT REQUIRE MOURNING——THAT SUFFERING IS TO NO AVAIL. REVERT YOUR FOCUS FROM THE DEAD TO THAT WHICH IS ALIVE. THE VICTIM IS NOT VICTIM—— ONLY DOOR."

I can see how much I feared physical death and how much I detest all that leads to a violent death by external forces, be it war, murder, mass murder, famine, epidemic, or slaughterhouse. I also recognize how blind I have been about life itself——fulfilling laws to which we as part of creation are subordinate, in which we all participate, consciously or unconsciously, and that govern us in a reality we can neither evade nor truly understand. We can be conscious of such laws but can only overcome them by *fulfilling* them.

It had also always been my great temptation to look for culprits that I can hold responsible for all the suffering on Earth; the temptation to arrogate, to judge the content and course of life. Thus, I had kept my head above water when I could not take it anymore. How difficult it had been for me to understand the laws of cause and effect, or to accept what is: "Be not deceived; God is not mocked: for whatsoever a man soweth, that shall he also reap" (the law of Karma; Gal. 6:7). It had also not been easy for me to unmask cause and effect in my own life. However, now I know this is necessary to overcome the law and allow seeming injustice to transform into love.

Second vision

As soon as I move closer to the destroyed houses, the fire, the devastation——still on the road, so to speak——I scream again and again, "Stop it, stop it!" sobbing and sobbing. The more I scream the closer I can move to what I see. The burning of the fires, the noise of the collapsing structures, the screams of the people all seem too cruel and unbearably agonizing. But then comes the voice again:

"DESTRUCTION PRECEDES EVERY RENEWAL. AS LONG AS YOU DO NOT SEE DESTRUCTION AS THAT WHICH LEADS TO RENEWAL, YOU WILL NOT BE WILLING TO DESTROY OR ACCEPT DESTRUCTION. YOU WILL NOT LOVE THE SWORD THAT STRIKES YOU; YOU WILL NOT USE THE SWORD I PLACED INTO YOUR HANDS!"

65

The *power* of these words! I listen carefully after them as after an echo. Then I hear:

"BEHOLD, I WILL DESTROY WHAT IS OF OLD AND UPON THE RUINS WILL ARISE THE NEW EARTH AND THE NEW HEAVEN."

O, God! How continually and deeply had my misunderstandings and fear led me into suffering, created guilt and blame, and blocked and censored much of the truth in me. I had not only sympathized with suffering humanity who, despite all signals given, would not awaken, but had also suffered by it. We are being pushed and beaten, humiliated and pruned like trees that are expected to bear fruit——but we rebel against the Gardener and the pruning. What insanity has engulfed us that we continue to sow and harvest in rebellion and boundless unconsciousness that cannot discern between illusion and reality? I had felt solidarity with the victims in the world because I had considered myself to be one, *even while* I experienced renewal. I had been raging at the perpetrators, had judged them. I had recognized neither my fallacies nor theirs; had not recognized divine action. I believed it to be the human hand and had forgotten that through human hands, divine laws are fulfilled, so that divine order is constantly newly established.

Everything happens within the framework of His laws!

How can I come to truly own this truth without wavering?

As though scales were falling from my eyes, I suddenly realized that I had never accepted the destruction of my dreams, my fallacies, my projections, as liberation. Instead, I had considered them punishments, injustice, and as incomprehensible, unjustified hardships and lovelessness. In the final analysis, I had also not accepted myself as perpetrator, and had refused to appear or be seen as perpetrator/offender. I had felt guilty whenever my Being created difficulties for someone else. I had suppressed myself because I did not wish to be confronted if people considered themselves a victim of my words or doings, believing I could not bear having to accept their anger and blame.

All of this is difficult to understand, for it seems paradoxical! Most people consider inhuman what happens in the world, and it is. We are inhuman, and

66

that is why inhumanness occurs. We desperately need to wake up! *As long as we do not fulfill the laws, the laws will fulfill themselves on us!* We cannot change the laws or make them ineffectual. They are perfect!

I ask myself: Am I willing to live fulfilling the law? What does that mean for me? For me it implies always being sincere and genuine from love and being willing to experience that there might be——or very probably will and must be——breakage and shards not only for me, but for others as well. It also implies that I will have to learn not only to accept, but also to recognize God's love in that. HIS SPIRIT has promised to lead me and all of us out of illusions and attachments.

We all will continue to "sow" (be), but in love and consciousness, while the sprouting of seed is not our business. Being aware excludes hurting someone on purpose or out of revenge or retaliating because of wounded pride or jealousy. It does not exclude, however, being conscious of expressing and living truth——in fact, it is necessary, even while knowing it may not be easy for the one on the receiving end and might make that person feel hurt.

I am unable to prevent someone from feeling hurt. But it is also no longer my wish that someone will withhold truth from me from fear that I may feel hurt. For I know now that lies and pretenses are hurting me more. I remember a poem I wrote a few years ago:

> Not wanting to hurt someone
>
> is the pain that I avoid myself
>
> in that it pains the other
>
> and me again
>
> with a different face.

Third vision

Here, too, rests a deep personal pain. It relates not only to what happens in the world through judges, but also to personal experiences when I find such an attitude within me or in my immediate surroundings. I ask about my inner judges first and ponder their possible misunderstandings. But I cannot get anywhere. I am only given the opportunity to deal with my hurt feelings from perceiving myself to be judged. Months go by before I can get a better grasp on the issue.

I had experienced such judgments——many, as a matter of fact. But they had also provoked me into overcoming my attempts to adapt, into becoming more faithful to myself by practicing withstanding the judging remarks and the implied lack of understanding, and into letting go of my self-justifications that were nothing more than feeble attempts to defend myself with self-righteousness. What was there to defend? My life? My being? My feelings? My humanness? My experience of God? Does any of this need defense? Can anyone take this away? Who?

By facing the exterior judges, I was able to expose and overcome the inner ones. I had been afraid of them, saw their hypotheses and the claim of power based thereon. What I also saw——but only much later——was that I had to learn to discern between the judgment of the messenger and the message, as, due to my sensitivity to judgments, the message often got lost.

So often during these periods of learning, Jesus was my guiding light through His attempts to bring truth of a loving, all-creating, all-maintaining GOD to the world. He spoke of a GOD who calls us to seek HIS kingdom and at long last to return home, like the prodigal son, so that HE, as Father, can give all.

He also spoke of GOD's laws, that they were made for men. Did we understand, did we hear? Or what **did** we hear Him say? In John 8:43 we read: "Why do you not understand the language I speak? For you can't hear my word!" The words Jesus spoke to Pontius Pilate in whose hands it lay to have him crucified come to my mind: **"You would have had no power whatever over me, had it not been granted you from above"** (John 19:11). His kingdom was not of this world, He said. It still is not. Is our kingdom, mine, yours, of this world? Today I can answer: "No!" But do I dare to put this knowingness into action? Do I dare to live accordingly? How else is His kingdom to manifest on Earth? How else can it dwell here?

Your kingdom come

Your will be done.

QUESTIONS FOR CONTEMPLATION

- Do you consider yourself a victim of life or circumstances?
- Do you commiserate with the victims in the world? Do you feel solidarity?
- Who is *your* scapegoat? Who or what is to blame for your suffering?

11

Adam, Eve, and Fig Leaves

My legs were swollen, and they hurt terribly. Once again, both the kidney and liver meridians were blocked on my legs and needed opening. During meditation, I was asked to help heal someone I know, which I obligingly did. It appeared that this man's emotional body had "slipped" inside of me to become conscious. After this work, my physical condition completely changed. But the question lingered: What actually happened? What was the cause? So, I asked.

I saw the following image: Two individuals, whom I immediately know as Adam and Eve, are standing before God after they have been called by Him out of their hiding (you may remember the story in the Old Testament——if not, read it in Genesis 3). Both are covered with fig leaves, and I notice these leaves to be mainly over their pubic regions and covering their sexual organs. In the Bible I read: "But the LORD God called to the man and said to him, 'Where are you?' And he said, 'I heard the sound of you in the garden, and I was afraid, because I was naked, and I hid myself!'" (Gen. 3:9 ff). I sense that it is the nakedness (not only physical) that is especially connected to shame, the shame about humanness.

But soon it becomes a matter of responsibility for the action, namely the eating of the apple of the tree of knowledge of good and evil. Without any sense of remorse or personal responsibility, Adam blames Eve for his action, while Eve blames the snake for her action——and now we can see where our own story about guilt, blame and excuses started.

It is within seconds that I recognize this correlation, and immediately I find myself in the body of Eve. I look over to "my" Adam. I have known this man for a few years, even though we have what we call a non-relationship. While looking, I feel instantly an ancient, deep sorrow, and I hear myself say: "I am your feeling." I weep and weep for a long time. I feel separated, disconnected from him, from man. I also feel that he left all feeling to me so he would not have to feel. How willing I had been to take this role, even in our non-relationship——again and again! So often this feeling had made me call him, write to him, console him, or ask him: "What is the matter?" He always waited for me to ask. His shame and fear were too overwhelming for him to display his naked neediness, his feeling vulnerable and weak, his being human instead of a man.

The dilemma we women know, mainly from our relationships with our fathers and men, and men know from their relationships with their mothers and women, is instantly obvious to me. I recognize the way the projected masculine and feminine deeply affect men and women alike and are the cause of a lot of confusion in relationships.

This confusion arises particularly where consciousness is slowly awakening but is not awake enough to move past these misunderstandings and mechanisms of denial; where the projection is felt and recognized but cannot (yet) be pulled back to the cause. I can feel the fear that induces people to hide behind masks (fig leaves). It is fear that causes us humans to blame others for our feelings: Adam blames Eve, Eve blames the snake, or in today's terminology: the child blames mother or father, or blames the teacher, the father blames his boss, the boss blames the IRS or the terrible economics. From very early on one can say humans hide, think in terms of good and evil, blame whomever or whatever for their terror, pain, and helplessness, and cannot get rid of their own sense of guilt. It makes them prisoners of their fear.

How difficult it is for most people even today to simply admit and stand up to a mistake, a misunderstanding, an unjust action, a negligence, or a spiritual disobedience, and to simply say: "Yes, that is true, it was me. I did it, I believed this, I thought this." We find ourselves dominated by the idea that we can keep a self-image that is immutable, that we need to defend and self-justify——even while we run around with a guilty conscience. I participated in this as well, but no longer want to do so. And you?

Once I realized all of this, I decided to look carefully at my own fig leaves. I closed my eyes and looked at myself. I see the fig leaves sticking over various places on my body, and I asked what they were covering. I can only

71

advise everyone to do that same exercise and look for their own fig leaves. It is worth it and amazing! They not only cover our shame in the literal, but also the figurative sense. It is as though no time has elapsed since Adam and Eve and the Fall——whether it actually happened or whether it is just an allegory. We still cover up what we do not want to own up to, and what we feel ashamed of before ourselves, where we do not want to stand naked before others, before GOD. We long to avoid feeling and bearing the consequences from our actions and non-actions, from our straying and illusions. Unfortunately, that, concurrently, is also what hinders us from experiencing the grace of liberation and forgiveness, and from experiencing the fact that we are loved by GOD the way we are. What a dead end, what a trap, and what a fall!

While working with groups to whom I impart the principles of these teachings, the subject of vulnerability is raised. We are vulnerable when we are naked. But what does that mean? What is vulnerable in us? What are we trying to protect, to preserve, to maintain? Our integrity and our Being? They are in no need of protection. They are eternal; they live and wish to be lived no matter what the circumstances. So, what indeed, do these fig leaves cover? We know the saying: saving one's own skin. What is meant by that? Our body? Our soul? Does the soul have a skin?

In my view, fig leaves are basically created by our fear of truth and loss of control. They cover our fright, our entire suffering, our loneliness, and our remorse. **With** them we nurse our vanity and our self-image, in which we believe we recognize ourselves and which we wish to maintain. We are afraid of not being, and therefore, refuse to let go of our phantom existence (barely existing).

If we would be willing to be known in our helplessness, our inadequacy and limitation, our fallacy, and our total nakedness, we could immediately let go of all fig leaves——our masks——and never, ever look back for them. The vulnerability that we fear so much is exactly what makes us able to **feel** when our illusions are cracked and taken, when we are being unbound and delivered from attachment and addiction, bondage, and captivity. And we wish to cover this vulnerability? How shall we see, how shall we learn to discern truth from illusion? Do you know one human being who "awakened" without experiencing pain, whether physical, emotional, or mental——even one?

This vision and its teachings made me realize something exceedingly valuable to me which fundamentally changed my attitude and approach to life and people: Had Adam and Eve admitted to what they had done in their unconsciousness against divine order, forgiveness would have been instant, and **paradise would not have been lost**.

QUESTIONS FOR CONTEMPLATION

- How difficult is it for you to be naked and seen (I do not mean physically)?
- In case GOD called you (and He does call you like He calls every one of us), how would you answer? And how would you stand before Him? What are your fig leaves?
- Where do you take upon yourself the feelings of others (for example of your partner)?

12

"AND" is Cooperation

During my studies at Atlantic University, where I got a good look at myself taking trans-personal courses, I concentrated intensively on the teachings of Gurdjieff. George Ivanovitch Gurdjieff (1877–1949) had become famous in many countries as a spiritual teacher and mentor. During the 1930s and '40s, he headed a center and school outside of Paris. I was very taken with his multi-layered and multi-faceted self-awareness models and was especially intrigued by his perception and extensive knowledge of the laws of creation.

In the midst of my studies of this man's life, his teachings, and his models of the laws of creation, I had the following nightly dream:

I am shown a horizontal line connecting two points. Under the line the words "not only . . . but also" appear. I look at this more closely and recognize the equality of the points. It is as if I am at school, and someone is waiting for me to understand what I am looking at. Then I am instructed:

"ON THE SPIRITUAL PLANE THERE IS NO 'EITHER-OR', AND THE 'NOT ONLY-BUT ALSO' EVOLVES HERE INTO 'AND'."

After these words are spoken, two lines slowly begin to move up from either point of the line to form a triangle above it. The sides forming the triangle unfold and burn like fuses towards the top. When they meet there is an explosion of light, and the point of their union remains as a star, brightly burning at the top of the triangle.

Then I am further instructed:

"THE THIRD POINT, FUSING THE OTHER TWO POINTS, IS LOVE— —IT IS LOVE, THE BRIDGE, THE 'AND'."

I know that this explains the law, which Gurdjieff describes as the Law of Three Forces. This law corresponds to all the creative processes and the unfolding of creation; one could even say to all births. Two forces come together chafing against each other (in the sense of irritation and provocation). They desire and are supposed to complete, complement, renew, strengthen each other, and stimulate each other's potential, which leads to the creation of something totally new (something third and other than the two but including the two). This is the nature of their being. I understand this law much better now, which makes me very happy.

I awaken. As I am waking up, I feel a triangle attached to my face, which has positioned itself over my forehead and physical eyes (and stays there for three weeks!). It is as though my physical eyes as well as my third eye are looking jointly through this triangle upon all there is. Everything appears in a totally new light: things, people, and my relationships with them. I am moved by the simplicity of the message, and I feel the deep truth that has been communicated to me. I think about the bridge and the "And," and also about how much we are in need of them——how important it is for all of us to change our attitude so that this "And" becomes part of it, is in accordance with it and realized.

Are we not practicing delimitation and separation, either/or, winning and losing, the deductive model? How little practice we have in true cooperation suggested by this "And." The "And," which can only come into being through love/acceptance, means more than a simple adding or accumulation. It means potentiating and multiplying everything that is found therein. It means cooperation.

This experience, however, seemed like a prelude to another one, which I was later led into, and that gave me the requisite understanding. Sitting in a meditation group one day, I heard the following words:

"PRACTICE COOPERATION. COOPERATION IS NOT COMPROMISE. IN COMPROMISE, EACH PERSON MUST MOVE AWAY FROM HIS OR HER ORIGINAL IDEA——IN COOPERATION, BOTH IDEAS ARE JOINED AND MAINTAINED. EACH COOPERATING INDIVIDUAL FEELS ACCEPTED AND ENHANCED RATHER THAN REDUCED. IN TRUE COOPERATION, *ALL* PARTICIPANTS FEEL GIVEN TO AND EXPERIENCE THEMSELVES AS ENRICHED. A FEELING OF LOSS IS

THE SIGN OF AN UNSUCCESSFUL ATTEMPT AT COOPERATION. THE PRICE IS HIGH.

"FEAR CHARACTERIZES COMPROMISE, AND IMPATIENCE INCITES THE DESIRE TO INFLUENCE ONESELF AND OTHERS TO COMPROMISE. COMPROMISE IS ONLY HALF A LIFE. BUT IS THERE SUCH A THING AS HALF A LIFE? HALF A LIFE IS NO LIFE AT ALL. COMPROMISE IS, THEREFORE, DEATH, AND TREASON TO LIFE. OUTCOME AND INNER EXPERIENCE SUFFER ACCORDINGLY.

"THEREFORE, PRACTICE COOPERATION WHERE IT IS NEEDED AND DESIRED. LEAVE COMPROMISE BEHIND. NO ONE CAN SERVE TWO MASTERS."

It became clear to me that true cooperation can only be achieved and experienced within spiritual intent. It requires an open and flexible mind, which is not attached to a fixed concept of how anyone's idea should be realized but inspired by the question of how this idea can be joined with that of someone else's. This requires an open and loving heart, which can receive and accept *without fearing new experiences*. Cooperation absolutely requires that both parties be prepared to allow their *shared idea* to mature out of their individual ideas *until* there is satisfaction on all sides.

As I am sure you will soon realize, cooperation employs all the gifts of the spirit: love, patience, trust, commitment, perseverance, and, above all, creative power. Any compromise can only be foul. Either one party pushes his agenda through and the other gives in, or agreements are reached that display a minimum of consensus and a denominator of fear rather than courage.

We have certainly seen evidence of this in many political decisions. We as citizens are often left feeling greatly frustrated with a growing sense of resignation and a lasting loss of trust. Any type of creativity is suffocated, and problems are never really solved. Can this lead to growth and satisfaction?

Our internal tendency to compromise and the lack of willingness to cooperate resulting from this are both very tenacious forces. Both tendencies correspond to our willfulness and denial. They show our refusal to accept what is right in front of our eyes and noses as reality. We hang on and *still* want to prove something to those who have little or no willingness at all to welcome us as who we are and with what we bring. We also do not want to give up the hope that perhaps someday things will be the way we want them to be.

I believed for a very long time that the psychiatric clinic where I worked years ago needed me but that my colleagues were (still) simply unable to recognize that fact. Due to this, I prolonged my painful path of compromise because I just did not want to accept the fact that my understanding of healing——and my corresponding experiences——were hardly of interest to anyone there. Also, I did not **at all** share the belief that a person can be helped with psychiatric drugs, to say nothing of being healed! I simply could not keep myself from trying to sway people to my point of view. Why did I do this?

Could there be any good reason why I voluntarily extended my own, in the final analysis, self-generated suffering? Yes, there was a reason. In truth, there were three. First, I did not wish to acknowledge the level of fear and rejection surrounding me; I insisted on believing that people really wanted to be healed, not just be free of symptoms. Secondly, I preferred to accept *some* suffering (self-pity) so I would not have to feel a different suffering, namely, the pain of loneliness due to not belonging or being welcome. And thirdly, this clinic represented for me a secure job, complete with an extra month's salary, long paid vacations, health insurance, and retirement pension. I wanted to hold onto this "nest" of security.

I also did not wish to be compelled to feel my *own* fear, even though I had constantly witnessed it in clients, colleagues, and doctors. However, the fear appeared anyway, and I *had* to feel it when, after a long period of discord, I finally came to my senses and was willing to move on. I had not wanted to feel so alone, feel who I am, and therefore did not want to start out on this obviously solitary journey filled with uncertainties. Like many others surrounding me, I had preferred to stay put, becoming tired and resigned, nursing the lowest common denominator as a minimal consensus, and feeling more and more truncated, tired, and angry with others. That I remained so long was also due to my ability to make virtues out of vices to avoid having to act. I foolishly made, what you may all, the *best* of things. There are so many people I know today who act and think the way I did at the time! Are you one of them? How long will you continue to do this?

You may ask: "Yes, but how is cooperation possible there?" *It is never, ever possible* where fear and narrow-mindedness reign, where concepts and self-maintaining structures water down the solutions to the problems and make people run around in circles, where the spirit is not permitted to soar freely, and where, due to fears and illusions, each person is eager to feather his own nest, save his own skin, and take no risks.

The clinic and I were unable to cooperate by my remaining there. My leaving was an act of cooperation, because, with that, I accepted the clinic for what it was and myself for who I was and wanted there. It is through my committed and decisive action outside of the clinic that an "And" came to pass. Possibly this will result in friction, which may lead to something third/new (remember the law of three forces). Possibly.

I hope that you ask yourself where your "And" is and what it means to you. That is why I would now like to provoke you a bit.

Imagine there is a married woman in Nebraska who has thought about what she would like to do for her vacation this year. For a long time, she has wanted to go to a nice, warm place with rich vegetation where the sun is guaranteed to shine——maybe Hawaii or Florida——and where no one wants anything from her.

Her husband has also been thinking about vacation. He desires to fulfill a long-cherished dream from his youth and go fishing in Alaska. However, neither of them wishes to be alone while fulfilling their dreams. After all, they are married and want to be together. So, she would like to lay on the beach in the sun *with him*, go out to eat *with him*, cuddle from time to time when she feels like it, and maybe share the book she will be reading.

He thinks it would be great if *she* were sitting behind him in the boat and he could show *her* the fabulous land- and seascapes, and his catch. And then, when they were both tired at the end of the day, they would head for shore to set up their simple but adventurous shelter. They would then prepare dinner——the fish he caught——and together experience the approaching nightfall.

What is this couple going to do? They may travel under these circumstances to the Merritt Reservoir in Nebraska——great for fishing and camping. Maybe she will lay in the sun (if it shines) while he fishes. Maybe they book a hotel somewhere in California, which——because they could not make up their minds and did not want the entire vacation to go down the tubes—— they found as a last-minute deal. "Oh, that was also quite nice . . . better than we expected!" Well, one always makes the best of it.

What would cooperation be like in this situation? One year they will go here, the next they will go there? One spouse is open to the idea of the other and tries to see through his/her eyes at least for one summer? Each spouse fulfills his/her dreams completely and then back home joins up again with the other and shares his/her experiences? Other solutions are also possible! Only the fruits (results) of this endeavor will disclose if this was an example of cooperation or compromise. Cooperation has very much to do with each person knowing himself, accepting and representing himself, and refusing to incorporate or plan the other person into the pictures of his own dreams and ideas.

QUESTIONS FOR CONTEMPLATION

- Where do you try to win instead of inviting another to a mutually new and common awareness or to contribute to a solution?
- What do you do when the other person does not wish to be included or when there is no space that you both can enter together with your full being?
- Do you know situations in which you thought that someone was cooperating with you, but, in fact, it was just a compromise – with all its consequences?

13

The Bodhisattva

I had become tired of standing in that indirect way by the man I felt closest to in my life, the way I had practiced so far. For someone like me, who feels the suffering of others on and in her own body, her personal well-being strongly depends on the willingness of the sufferer to become **aware** of his suffering and its cause and also be willing to process it. As this man——in my perception and experience——did not develop such willingness, but constantly split off from his feelings that I then felt instead, I, for whatever reason, became angry, impatient, and asked in meditation to be relieved of this responsibility. I also asked for someone else to take over. My plea was heard; I saw a light being come and take his ethereal emotional body with It, which until then had been constantly around me. I felt understood and immensely relieved.

However, the morning following this experience, I was filled——already upon awakening——with the deepest sorrow ever. I was in the midst of preparing for a trip from Germany to Los Angeles with a group of nine others that I had organized. In two days, we were leaving for the celebration of the Kalachakra Initiation with the Dalai Lama. I had felt drawn there, even though at this point I had no clue about any Tibetan initiation rites——or so I thought. A friend who came visiting to say goodbye said, coming directly to the point, that she perceived a deep sadness in me. What was it about?

To respond honestly, I finally felt into the condition, I could only define it as that of a widow and express what that meant to me. It was like having been abandoned by someone, leaving me utterly inconsolable. I was permeated by this despair but could not find a cause for it. Whenever I asked in meditation in the hope to better understand this, I received the same picture: I stand in front of an altar in mourning attire. Around me is a sea of white Easter Lilies known to me also as flowers of transformation.

The image depicted my condition perfectly, like a mirror. Despite all sorrow, I had the sense of a promise of change and transformation. Something was to die to become new, but nothing was revealed of what and why. I felt urged to be patient and accept this, though it was not easy to do in the face of not feeling any relief from my condition.

The trip to Los Angeles turned out to be much more strenuous than any of my many other flights to the US. We missed the connecting flight in New York and thus arrived in LA past midnight, only to find the dormitory where we were to stay closed with no one there. My condition was unchanged. Even though I kept asking, nothing was given.

We finally found a room. Totally exhausted and hoping for any hint to help me better endure, I drew a tarot card from the Rider deck. And what did I draw? The *five of cups*, or "Sorrow after Upheaval"! The book interpretation of the card reads: "It has been lost, it is over, go through your pain"! It seemed true, but I did not understand anything. What was over? What was lost?

The daily events with the Dalai Lama started. Around two thousand people participated. I learned that the Kalachakra Initiation pertains to **the orientation and vows** for the various stages a person passes through on the Bodhisattva Path. I am familiar with the Gestalt of the Bodhisattva. I had already recognized earlier that IT is the lover who renounces his own enlightenment for the sake of love and compassion for unredeemed humanity. To serve human deliverance is his only motivation, his sole intent, to be on Earth. Therefore, much of what I heard during these events I was acquainted with; it was not new. Yet——I had never had a direct link to it.

Some days went by without anything changing in my condition. When we were led through the fifth stage, I felt a longing to remove myself from the auditorium and all the people, including our group. Everything seemed to be too much. I returned to my room at the UCLA dormitory and remained in meditation for several hours.

After staying in silence and breathing for a long time, I asked once more for help. I waited. Then came the voice:

"YOU ASKED TO BE RELIEVED OF THE RESPONSIBILITY FOR THE WELLBEING OF YOUR FRIEND?"

What friend? Oh, I dropped my own question right away. I knew what was meant by the question I just heard. I had lost patience and asked that someone else take care of the emotional body that constantly circled around me. I still felt justified. But in the same breath, I also realized that I had betrayed the core of my being, I had betrayed CHRIST, and thereby my most fundamental task and sincerest concern. Once I realized that truth, all sorrow disappeared, as if someone had turned a switch. A deep regret replaced it. The voice spoke:

"TAKE BACK THE REQUEST!"

It was not difficult to obey immediately, as my willingness had already been forming while I recognized what I had done. I knew that my inner peace depended on this. But other truths came along and became clear to me. For I had totally misunderstood this responsibility. Up until this point, I had believed I had to do it "for" my friend due to his unconsciously wishing for this and his refusing to take responsibility. I had not seen that I did not do this for anyone, but because I AM THAT.

This responsibility was the fulfillment of my core Being, and I can give and do what I am prompted to give or do. I had the feeling of having to carry him: I, Christa, and woman. I knew now that it is not true this way——instead, it is quite different from what I believed. How can I explain this? IT carried him in me. It just dawned on me that this kind of responsibility belongs to impersonal love and may require actions that appear to be unpredictable and will not allow being in line with what is commonly considered help. I renewed my full-hearted willingness to serve the Highest and to leave the entire space in my heart to this impersonal love——to serve in all conscience however I am able. I now felt so happy and calm. Everything inside of me and outside looked new and good, put right.

During the next morning session at the auditorium, the Dalai Lama spoke of the sixth stage of the Bodhisattva. How great was my surprise when I heard him say: "At this stage, the Bodhisattva vows to **accept** responsibility for the healing of others." I felt very well-prepared and lighthearted. What did I know? With what presumptuousness had I believed I could carry my friend, and at the same time, petty-mindedly refuse to help him? My shame had left me, though. What remained was a tremendous veneration for the omniscience of God, and I was deeply impressed, as I always am, by what tools HE uses to lead me to wherever HE will and to where the soul is drawn and needs to be.

An impression may form that this experience is contradicting the experience I described under the heading "The Human Dilemma." There it is explicitly explained that I can only help and raise him who has lifted his head and has accepted my help. I was asked about these seeming inconsistencies. For this reason, but also because the same question came up in me, I would like to try to contribute to a better understanding of the seeming paradox.

First, I need to say that these two experiences are separated by years, and to me the first vision (Human Dilemma) was an essential step in correcting my exaggerated opinion of myself and my pity. The experience described above has nothing to do with "my" help. I am a channel, and the Essence is much more and variedly capable and has different and greater insight than I do. After this experience in Los Angeles, other experiences accrued that made me more aware of what can and sometimes has to be taken off someone and to what extent this was my purpose. There is only one rule: When, who, what, and to what degree is not mine to decide, because here I am very seducible, I know. But I also know that for me, only willingness and obedience remain, not time and content.

QUESTIONS FOR CONTEMPLATION

- Do you sometimes feel you are carrying someone and no longer want to do that? No longer wanting to help?
- What could it mean for you to take up the responsibility for someone else's healing – do you recognize that feeling? Do you understand what kind of responsibility I speak of here?
- Would you be willing?

14

You are Spirit

For some time, I had been engaged with a question: What may it mean to contain the various created kingdoms of nature on Earth within us? I wanted to know how it was possible to experience the macrocosm within the microcosm, to experience the energy within rather than as an engagement with the exterior, namely the physical existence that can be observed and touched. That is why I had studied the energies of plants, trees, and animals, had integrated them into my healing work, and had had very interesting experiences in using them in different initiation rites.

Into the middle of these experiences entered some very painful realizations that led to many revealing observations, and eventually to being essentially freed. For while I was pondering the above question, I was also confronted by having to deal with a relationship, painfully unresolved, which weighed on me and affected me in everyday life. That is why I found it surprising on one hand but appropriate on the other when I suddenly experienced myself as an eagle——sitting on my meditation pillow, stuck with questions, seeking answers.

Here I go——As an eagle, I sit on the ground and find myself waiting for another eagle by my side to come with me up into the air. In case you are interested in analogies and symbols, you will immediately grasp what is being shown and why this is happening.

Somehow, I must have believed that it would help my partner if I stayed on the ground and from there encouraged him to fly, instead of showing him by my own flying, exemplifying. In Germany we call this a **helper syndrome.** That is it! I recognized it immediately. I also recognized the nonsense (no sense) of this situation and decide to fly and go up in freedom and soar. On my way, however, I notice with consternation that this was not as easy as I thought, for an elastic rope is tied around my foot that first stretched and then pulled me back toward the ground despite my trying to find my own flight.

This rubber band seems to me the perfect symbol for the bonds I feel with this man and his condition. Nothing could depict more clearly what I am doing, thinking, and their cause and effect in this relationship.

I arrive at a decision to change this attachment. I have to "fly" back to the ground and rip off the rubber band, which is not possible without intense crying. I see the necessity to dissociate from my partner and his problems; I also see the necessity to stop experiencing my life as dependent on his life and his fear of life. I will have to be willing to walk (or fly) without him.

Back as the eagle, I fly again. Tears wash over my face; I feel the pain of this separation. I hear, gently spoken:

"FIRST YOU CRY YOURSELF TO EARTH; THEN YOU CRY YOURSELF BACK TO ME."

I cry and cry and cry. When I have calmed down, I find myself, still the eagle, cruising above the spot where I left my partner behind——until I hear:

"WHY DO YOU CURTAIL THE SPACE YOU ARE GIVEN?"

That is a good question. Why do I restrict my space? Why do we restrict our space? How dependent am I on not wanting to walk alone, dragging someone with me at all costs? How does this dependency affect my relationships? What illusions am I pursuing that I will not let go? I am deeply affected by the truth to which the above question directs me. Again, in pain and again feeling liberating tears, I decide to leave behind the point of attraction, extending my "air space". My newly gained freedom is exhilarating, indescribable. How could I possibly have willingly disclaimed this?

The next morning, I woke up in a new, energetically charged state. Everything inside of me vibrated——it felt as though I was burning up. I hoped to gain insight during meditation. And indeed, I experienced something interesting and liberating. As soon as I closed my eyes, I saw myself standing there, and simultaneously I **felt** I was a brightly glowing figure. In my hands I held the complete plumage of an eagle. I heard the voice:

86

"YOU ARE SPIRIT AND FREE! YOU MAY DWELL AT ANY TIME IN THE FORM OF YOUR CHOICE. YOU ARE SPIRIT OF THE SPIRIT THAT PERMEATES ALL AND DWELLS IN ALL. WITH IT, YOU ARE ONE."

After this, I played around like a child that has discovered a new toy. I dwelled in a tree; I dwelled in many other trees. Each one differed in energy from the other, each one corresponding to its kind. I could feel them all and their differences in vibrancy. I dwelled in various animals, and there, too, I could just move in and leave again, just as I wished. Each one had its own specific character, and I could feel its particular nature by which it was discernible from other kinds. I experienced the same with stones and minerals. Ahhh——such wonders!

It is so vital that we can personally experience being one with all. This is not simply a question of a philosophical disquisition. It is Being, BEINGNESS of which we partake, in which we share. Once we are conscious of this BEINGNESS, we cannot continue to live the way we have so far. Our relationship with humans, animals, and plants will change, and we change, too. We will see that there is only ONE LIFE and not many little, private, single lives, separated. So much that pains us is relativized and appears as a different face, a different truth. Our seeking and addictions on Earth—— which drive us to look in the world for love, fulfillment, and gratification of needs——also come to an end. We will see that we are one and, therefore, there is no lack. We can stop taking medications and wanting to brighten, influence, or change our energies with Bach flowers or healing with stones. Everything is energetically available, directly and without detour or diversion. **All is already in us** and, if not yet experienced, wants and needs to be integrated. We separate ourselves from the essence of all life and then consider and feel ourselves separated.

Where separation must be made——from our illusions, our ideas of separation, our fears, and our self-restriction, needs, and expectations, which no human being can fulfill——we only reluctantly let go. But we will not be able to experience true ONE-NESS——we will not know that in truth we are not separated from that which alone is reality as long as we are not willing to be disappointed and disillusioned, as long as we are not willing to be

87

liberated from self-created dependencies and fallacies. And, more than anything, we will not find the peace and love, the inner home that we are seeking.

QUESTIONS FOR CONTEMPLATION

- Do you also have such a rubber band on your foot? If so, where does it pull and to whom or what does it attach you?
- How dependent are you on not wanting to be alone on your journey? How does that affect your relationships?
- Do you still wait on having your illusions fulfilled? Or something changing at your workplace and then finding the perfect conditions there? Or possibly meeting a human being that fulfills your hunger for love and life, eternally and without any conflict?

15

The Servant

I had been invited to a sweat lodge ceremony in Richmond, Virginia. It is a traditional Native American ritual for cleansing, healing, and other intensive prayer concerns. This ceremony is a **women's sweat,** and the invited guests arrived steadily until noon. It is the first time ever that I will participate in such a ritual——at least in this life——and I am excitedly looking forward to it.

In the early afternoon, we women go and collect wood for the fire. The stones that will be heated in the fire during the ceremony are already stacked, and the wood is distributed over them and lit. The leader of the ceremony, a female Cherokee tribal member, explains the stages of the ritual and discusses with us who will be laying the stones in the various directions and saying the prayers. The ritual starts: We place the stones, and once the prayers have been spoken, we wait until the stones in the pile are hot enough to be carried into the sweat lodge by the fire keeper to start the sweat.

We are sitting outside around the fire. Next to me sits a woman whom I will call Jean, who——in her own words——is walking the Indian path and knows it well. We have a full moon tonight, and Jean tells me enthusiastically about the significance of the moon in the Indian tradition and how blessed we ought to feel that we experience the sweat lodge ceremony at the time the moon is full.

I know some bits and pieces about the influence the moon has on the Earth and the oceans, have read Rudolf Steiner, who studied the cycles of the moon and its effects on life——beyond that, I always considered the moon to have assumed the role of a mirror of the sun, as it does not have its own light but shows light by reflection only. I am not very open to what Jean shares and feel rather harried by her.

Finally, we are ready. The stones are hot and red. We move into the lodge, the hot stones are brought in and the ritualized sweating begins. I had decided that I will accept everything that comes and not avoid any experience. After the first round, it is already getting so hot in the airtight tent that I try to lay down on the cool ground——to the degree this is possible——despite the close sitting arrangement. The moment I do, I leave my body and move forward without delay. That is, it is rather that I am being *pulled* out of the body to find myself before a group of five Light Beings that are standing there in a half-circle. One of them steps forward and asks:

"YOU TEACH THE LAW OF REFLECTION?"

I feel caught and think immediately of the conversation with Jean by the fire. Simultaneously, I feel that this is only a rhetorical question, for all of them already know the answer. I say, "Yes!" and wait. I hear:

"THERE IS SOMETHING YOU HAVE NOT UNDERSTOOD! HE WHO DOES NOT HONOR THE SERVANT DOES NOT HONOR THE LORD."

It is true. I did not understand. I know the Law of Reflection (Hermetic law)——or so I believed——quite well and have learned to deal with it and to view, use, and teach it as a useful instrument. The law opens up to us: *Above is as below, below is as above*——and, in addition, outside is as inside, inside is as outside——a cross forming relating and encounter. I have known for quite a long time that there is nothing I encounter in the outside world that I will not find in me as well, no matter how deep I have buried it and how much I want to be in denial of it.

I also know that "mirror polishing," i.e. arguing with others, does not help. Instead, it separates me from what I need to integrate or engage with. But here is exactly where I suddenly see my problem. I never really related to the "mirror." My experience was more an analytical observation of projection without my gratefully realizing that this mirror is a mirror for me and truly serves me becoming conscious. Yes, the mirror serves! Once I see this, I feel ashamed and grateful at the same time and find myself back in my body.

I consider the sun and moon. It dawns on me that the moon not only reflects the sun, but also the shade that the Earth throws. It suddenly occurs to me that the Earth is right between "lord" and "servant" and throws shade. So many questions arise! Questions about light and shade, about my perception,

90

about my not recognizing the light inside where the Earth throws its shade in me and upon my fellow beings.

This entire questioning is suddenly interrupted; I feel myself being lifted up, carried, and experience a memorable weightlessness. It is as though I am a very small child, a baby, who is lifted in cradling arms to which I have totally surrendered. Very gently I am brought to the moon and am embedded into its energy. I experience absolute bliss. Were I a cat, I would now purr. The energy around me is feminine and motherly, and I remember that in many languages, the moon is considered to be of feminine gender (oddly, not in German, though). I now know how appropriate this is.

How to become a *conscious* mirror I learned some years later during a retreat I led in New York. A friend had invited me and organized the week. She asked me at the beginning if it were okay with me that her old, beloved Indian Hindu teacher come visit and spend some hours with us. She would love to have me meet him. I was happy about this, and she drove one morning to fetch "Guruji", as she so lovingly calls him.

Guruji is quite old, over eighty, but he is physically agile and very lively when speaking. When we all sit together and he talks to us, I notice he does not look at anyone. He seems to be in an entirely different world and is not present in his eyes. They look empty. I am severely shaken by this, but I see that the others are surrounding him lovingly, seeking to be near him and enjoy his presence. Many of them have known him personally for a long time. He suggests that we all go to the meditation room in the basement. My friend asks me to take a seat to the left of Guruji, facing the group, while she sits at his right.

Guruji speaks of enlightenment and illusion. He points to various things in the room and says, waving his hand as though wishing to chase everything away, "Everything is illusion." He tells us we only need to meditate——he himself had meditated three years without interruption, and then he was free. The more he speaks, the more uncomfortable my body becomes until I feel completely split. My left side is entirely missing; I exist only as a right side——masculine/mental. I know what that means, but I do not know what I can do to change it. I ask GOD and I hear:

91

"COMPLETELY UNDRESS, STAND NAKED IN FRONT OF HIM AND SAY: 'YOU ARE A STRONG MAN!'"

A storm breaks loose in me within a split second. I see myself run away as fast as I can. Like a child I run and hide under a table behind a tablecloth to protect myself from the adults. My fear is immense, and my heartbeat is all the way up in my throat. I think: "GOD cannot want this of me! If GOD becomes so unpredictable through me, I will stop right here. I no longer want to have anything to do with this!" Due to all this thinking, I have already missed the moment and can no longer implement anything. Now I feel even worse, but I can only blame myself for having succumbed to my fear.

I sit there, frozen. I no longer can hear anything that is being said and withdraw completely inside, away from the room and the event. I refuse to participate in the love circle that my friend forms next with everyone standing up. I stand but stay away, confused, and thunderstruck, until I finally leave the room. My friend follows me after a while and asks what happened. When I tell her, she laughs her head off. "I only know one person who would have the courage to do this: You!" she says. But I did not have the courage, and I am still totally confused. The group returns from the meditation room, and I sit down with everyone. We draw pictures. I draw what lies on my soul.

My friend leaves with Guruji to take a walk. She immediately returns again with a little songbook in her hand that Guruji had asked her to give to me. It is a beautiful song adoring the invisible, unnamable, formless DEITY. Now I feel even more ashamed, as two days ago I had heard clearly to sing two verses of the song "I am the stars and the rainbow" to him, the song that one day out of the blue fell into me during a shower. It is a song about **all form** being permeated by GOD, about HIS creation, about every cell in which HE IS. I am distressed. How obedient Guruji is, and how disobedient I am! I want to make up for it and know I have a new chance to "undress", but on a much less threatening level. So, I follow my friend outside.

I thank Guruji for his love of GOD and for his exemplary obedience. I tell him I have been disobedient and that I will now sing one verse of a song. He taps repeatedly on my arm and exclaims, "No! No! No!" and points to his song booklet, which on the back cover shows——like an odd contradiction——his photo and copyright.

A great strength comes over me. I stand there like a tree, rooted, and begin to sing "my song" (that neither carries my name nor my copyright):

> I am the stars and the rainbow
>
> I am the Earth, Sun and Moon
>
> I am the trees, eagle, and dove
>
> I am the heavens above.

I have barely begun when Guruji gapes at me, shocked, throws both arms high into the air, turns and runs away from me as fast as his feet can carry him down the footpath while wildly gesturing with his arms. My friend stares after him, her mouth open.

I am happy and return to the house. I know now exactly why I was asked to undress. I would have been the Earth, the woman, form, naked corporeality——perhaps also temptation. I would have been all and everything that no longer had any place in his life. I came to him, not undressed but with the song, in a somewhat moderated appearance. Guruji, as my friend related to me later, had asked her over and over again: "Who is she? Where does she come from? What does she teach?" I asked myself what would have happened if I had actually taken my clothes off . . . that question remains unanswered.

Months after this event——I have long since returned to Virginia Beach——I received a letter from my always sincere and understanding friend. She has been a respected companion on my path, though at times also admiring me inappropriately and to my discomfort. The experience with Guruji had an aftermath and has destroyed the pedestal she had placed under my feet. But she resents me for it, berates me, dishing out various allegations and her conclusions drawn belatedly from the experience. In her eyes, I did not honor the old Guruji, " you had only "your" (the word "your" underlined five times) workshop in mind." She adds that everyone felt that way (whoever everyone was!). I felt I had been judged in absentia, and that really hurt. I

93

was especially hurt that she, with whom I shared my fear at the time, was the one writing this.

After crying and releasing the immediate pain, I wrote a return letter and by doing so hoped to clarify a few things. But something was nagging at me. I decided to leave the letter for the time being. Days later, in meditation, I heard the voice:

"*I* PUT THE WORDS INTO HER MOUTH!"

The word "I" is strongly emphasized. Something awakens me. I suddenly can hear the words of my friend completely differently, and, incontestably, they are true! Again, I had missed hearing and seeing! My ears had been stuck on how "she" had worded it, on her judgments. That way, I could neither hear nor receive the true message. I had not recognized God in it, nor had I honored the servant.

I now saw the truth in the words, but they had nothing to do with the interpretations of my friend. These interpretations were of no concern to me; they are hers. **It is all true.** I had not respected Guruji. If I had, I would have gotten undressed. It is true I was thinking of "my" workshop; I feared the participants' reactions to my action because they were devotees of Guruji. And that had significantly hindered me.

I am so grateful to my friend for expressing what she did. I committed to receive the words of others differently and to untie them from the judgments attached to them. I also committed not to interpret "my" truth or to embed it in judgments, only to express it. I recognized that our uncomfortable mirror becomes visible and noticeable where we interpret and are interpreted, where we judge and are judged, and where our illusions are being crushed and we are crushing the illusions of others. But I will also remember that other part to the mirror analogy: The Sun and its reflected light, the Sun that recognizes itself and meets itself.

QUESTIONS FOR CONTEMPLATION

- What attitude do you have towards your "mirror" outside?
- What does it mean to you to be a mirror for others? What makes you a mirror?
- Can you imagine taking more seriously the words that others say or tell you? As seriously as though GOD or HIS SPIRIT had placed them in others' mouths? Would you stop judging or stop assuming the judgments of others to be about you?

16

The Thief on the Cross

My body feels totally distorted. Another body that pushes my body out of whack and out of trusted familiarity has entered mine. I am taller, my head further away from the floor, slender, and male. My face seems changed by his, my head is not mine——and I know whose body this is. This annoys me. Not that this is a new experience, but it bothers me, and I resent the man for leaving me with this (I had not had the Bodhisattva experience by then or I would have been more willing). I still have not gotten used to allowing certain human or interpersonal conditions to mature, evolve, or heal within me. I harbor an enormous resistance, and still try very hard to get rid of any of these conditions. But often enough it does not work, and it also does not today. Like a stranger to myself I sit in the subway (S—Bahn) to Munich to meet an old acquaintance, whom I will call R, for tea. I do not know what to do about my condition: meditating, praying, asking, none of these have helped so far.

That evening——nothing has changed——a friend picks me up at R's place to take me to her meditation group in midtown Munich. While driving she asks, somewhat irritated, about the condition I am in that she senses. I cannot tell her much, but I continue to feel my own annoyance. She says she does not want to participate in carrying this condition with me and urges me to do something, anything. That makes me even angrier. I now develop strong pains in my liver; the organ swells so that I cannot stand the waistband of the pants I am wearing and have to move it off. My friend starts feeling pains in her chest, the heart.

The only thing that we can think of is a Bach flower essence, *Sweet Chestnut*. According to Dr. Bach, it is "the remedy for that terrible, that appalling mental despair when it seems the very soul itself is suffering destruction. It is the hopeless despair of those who feel they have reached the limit of their endurance."

I hear the sentence: "My God, my God, why have you forsaken me?" (John 27:46). After all this time——driving in the car, ending up in a cul-de-sac (not only with the car) and having to turn around——we finally make it to the meditation center.

When we enter the room, we find two women there sitting quietly and listening to chants from Taizé.[6] We join them, when suddenly I hear from the CD player: "Vater, in deine Hände lege ich meinen Geist (Father, into your hands I commend my spirit)." Deep sorrow suddenly fills me. My liver is still swollen, and once more my friend urges me to do something. I do not know what, but anything may do. I surrender, lay down on the floor, and try to go deeper into the condition I feel. But the door seems blocked, and the energy is arduous. I need someone to hold my feet, but my friend puts her hand on my forehead instead and says: "I hear the words: 'old, old.'"

Now I am pulled backward, deeper, very quickly, and before my mind can figure anything out, I find myself hanging on a cross with two others crucified to the left of me. In me is such a rage that it smothers any sense of pain from actually hanging on the cross. I cannot feel the cross, only the rage and the words that begin to form in me wanting to be expressed. Foul-mouthed curses and vulgarities from a vocabulary I am totally unfamiliar with come screaming out of my mouth. They are directed at those who are standing around, at people who have judged and condemned "me" for my actions, who now witness my subjection and perishing. I feel an all-consuming hatred. I hear myself scream: "I will show you! You will not break me, you shitheads! You assholes! I do not need you or anybody!" and many more curses. I am livid.

I know I have been caught red-handed, stealing, but I still feel as though I only took what I deserved and had coming to me. I am also angry that I allowed myself to get caught. I do not feel any guilt or remorse, just rage and justification. I notice that I do not dare look to my left, where I can sense Jesus. I avoid his glance. When I finally do look, I see him hanging there and scream at him: "And you I don't need either!" At that very moment all my rage collapses, and I cry many tears.

The body that had been in me all day pulls out the moment the rage collapses. I see this man now standing before me. Currently, there is only despair in him and a deep pain about life, the injustices and irreconcilability of human experience. He looks exhausted, tired. I have my own body again and feel okay and well. My liver is no longer swollen. The job is done.

During the rest of the evening, the topic remains with the group who witnessed the process. We ponder some more the three crucified men—— Jesus and the two thieves that were crucified with him. We remember the stories from the New Testament. When we enter their conditions (we do not look at them, but become them), we realize how different these crucifixions are, let alone the difference between the two thieves. The one is conscious of his actions and finds his punishment comprehensible in view of his actions. He also discovers that the "man in the middle", Jesus, has something he is lacking, and he longs to have it. Jesus has somehow accepted his fate, and in accepting his cross, he becomes the cross itself.

The other thief hangs in front of the cross. He rages to such an extent that he feels neither the cross nor the pain, and definitely no contrition. He mocks Jesus and despises everyone and everything around him. Surrendering to his suffering and helplessness is extremely difficult for him. "The feeling" to the left (the thief on the left) is much more capable of accepting the suffering than "the thinking" to the right is. But then, who wants to change his thinking, losing control? Who does not want to be right?

During the evening, we also remember our own experiences of "hanging on a cross", being caught. We are aware that sometimes we can accept the cross with more willingness than other times. We also remind ourselves how we have raged against those that judged, condemned, and held us responsible for our actions, but we are aware that while "being crucified", we have a longing for something we cannot quite grasp. How often are we the thief in our left side and hope that we can find what we lack!

We then direct our attention to Jesus. Oddly, we all find Him rather behind the cross, as though He had transcended that which the other two are still struggling with. The pain with which He looks upon those who surround him has nothing to do with feeling guilty or being disappointed. There are no self-justifications, no accusations, no lack. It is rather that He is the Center between guilt and self-justification. Love and Truth remain. Here it seems that "Adam" has returned. That Adam once felt guilty and hid himself, that he tried to justify himself directing blame somewhere else——all has been brought into the present and is redeemed. In Him the circle closes, the cycle ends——beginning becomes completion, is reconciled. We are deeply moved by these experiences and for what we recognize.

The man, whose troubles had been with us at the beginning of that evening and who, as it turned out, had promised my friend to come and join us for meditation, tells me three days later of his total breakdown on that particular evening and the resulting exhaustion. He had not been able to drive anywhere. He had carried a horrendous rage within him that exploded the following day when he had to hand over his house, which he had lost through speculation using not only his own money. Even though he had known that he himself was responsible for having to sell the house, he had felt humiliated, punished, and powerless. When I share with him what words had come out of my mouth that evening, he tells me that those had been his thoughts, which he had partially expressed during the handover, and the degree of his rage had greatly shocked him.

During later encounters with people and their miseries, the image of the right-hand thief appears again and again. He is forever crucified, forever angry, forever jealous, and ferociously straining within most of humanity. It is he who hinders all surrender and dying, and thus also all transformation and renewal. His resistance is enormous against whatever life provides or does not provide. What we humans need, and how long it will take, expresses Rabindranath Tagore:

> My desires are many and my cry is
>
> pitiful, but ever didst thou save me by
>
> hard refusals; and this strong mercy
>
> has been wrought into my life through
>
> and through.[7]

99

QUESTIONS FOR CONTEMPLATION

- Are you aware that the unredeemed secrets you carry around are palpable to others?
- Are you aware that you can contribute to easing the human dilemma at any time when you fathom your own shadow and become more open and honest with your feelings?
- Are you of the same opinion as the thief on the cross that life owes you something? Or that if life does not deliver what you expect, then you will have to take it?

17

The Rosary

How it began

This experience opened a number of personal encounters with Mary, the mother of Jesus, whom up to that point I only had known and respected as a female character in biblical history. All the encounters equally describe the loving aid to me and others that comes to Earth through this Being. They resemble all other interventions by the Holy Spirit that are spoken of in this book. Some of these encounters I will share here. It began like this:

My sister Ruth had joined a group of pilgrims to go to Medjugorje, the town in Yugoslavia (now Bosnia Herzegovina) known for its apparitions of Mother Mary. Ruth had just returned. Her adventure and experiences were fresh, and her heart ran over. She recounted many healings and encounters and spoke of her decision and commitment during the trip to participate in a prayer circle, praying the rosary every three hours, corresponding to the message of Mother Mary to a lost and anchorless humanity, which, to Ruth, is very badly needed.

I agreed with her that humanity is lost and in great need of prayer and intercession, but I am surprised that Ruth is so vehemently concerned with the formal Catholic prayer of the rosary. We were not raised Catholic but come from the Pietism side of the German Alliance of Protestant Churches. I had never believed the Protestant derogatory judgments about Catholic beliefs that I had often heard in childhood and youth. But when Ruth suggested that all members of our joined households get involved with this ritual, everything resisted in me. That is why I said to her, "I can well understand that you are so moved by your experiences that you wish to pray the rosary, but I have nothing to do with Mary, nor with the rosary. I will support you in prayer, but not with the rosary."

She considered and having calmed down after some time, said, "I probably ask a bit much. Praying with me is okay, and that is what counts." So, we agreed to that and ended the conversation, as I was expecting a client for a healing session.

The client arrived, and I led her downstairs to my room. She lay down on the daybed, and I sat next to her in a chair. We both closed our eyes and entered a meditative silence from which I always start my work and in which I like to remain during a session. I had barely closed my eyes when, in a matter of seconds, I had the distinct impression of being pulled out of my body. Before I realized what just happened, I "landed" right in front of a very bright Being whom I recognized immediately as Mary. I myself was also in a light body. In my hands I held a wreath of fresh roses that I offered to her. I was totally shocked and started to cry, for I still had my own words in my ears: "I have nothing to do with Mary." I felt so, so sorry.

Gently, without words, and devoid of any judgment, Mary accepted the wreath of roses from my hands and now held it herself. I returned to my body and my work. She remained present during the entire session with my client. When the client cried and her body found relief and healing, Mary broke a rose from the wreath and handed it to me and my client into our session.

For three months, Mary remained a continuous presence during "my" work. If the session was successful; that is, if the client risked entering his/her feelings, Mary validated it with a rose. If it did not go well, she'd just stood there with a Easter Lily in her hands, consoling me, but also urging me to be patient in the work of transformation that I am involved in and of which urgency and failure often quite pain me physically. I felt so blessed by her help and touched by her continuous, gentle, motherly love. I slowly got used to bringing the people and their condition straight to her on the spiritual plane and asking for **her** help, which she often and directly granted. One amazing thing I observed: *The wreath of roses never depleted!*

After three months, something changed unexpectedly. An acquaintance was visiting to speak to an English friend of ours, a medium and healer. I was present during this conversation, and since our friend closed her eyes to ask for help from "above", I, too, closed mine and went "up" with her. When I was "up", I again stood in front of Mary, who now had crossed her arms in front of her chest. I was shocked about this closed gesture and returned swiftly back "down". When I realized that I had just fled, I went back, as I did not even ask or understand why. When I again stood in front of Mary, she said:

"DO NOT ALWAYS BRING EVERYONE HERE; JUST DO YOUR WORK!"

I felt shame, for I knew I had begun to make it easy for myself, becoming lazy and leaving all the work to Mary. The message was clear yet loving. I was sad about myself, and I was waiting for my friend to return. How surprised was I that when she finally opened her eyes again, she looked at me and said, "You will have to work with this woman."

I told her, "I know. I was there."

She came back with, "I know!" and we both laughed.

Do not ever worship me

Months after all of the above——I continued to do my work——an elderly lady came to visit me who is Catholic and greatly adores Mary. She sat with me at the table, held her rosary, and let the pearls slowly glide through her fingers. I now also owned a rosary that my sister Ruth brought me from one of her pilgrimages. I liked it, but I did not really connect to the traditional rosary prayer. Sometimes I just held it in my hands during my work, just like my guest did now——and there it is present like a tangible mantra.

We speak about what the rosary means to us. The lady tells me that she often uses the rosary to speak other mantras she prays, for example, "You Queen; You Beautiful." I enjoyed her love for Mary, this beautiful greeting, and said to her that I would like to say this prayer with her. Meanwhile, Ruth has joined us, and all three of us close our eyes and enter silence. I repeat the beautiful greeting to Mary that I have just heard. But after a few seconds, I feel an immense pressure on top of my head. I ask and. listen. I see Mary again, and she says in a very strict voice:

"DO NOT WORSHIP ME—WORSHIP ONLY THE MOST HIGH!"

The pressure is off, and Mary leaves. I realize how much I love her for her clear, simple, and single-minded service. Her words have corrected something in me, and I renew my commitment to only ever serve the Highest while honoring all HIS servants. I am deeply grateful for her intervention, but I am also ashamed, for I see how quickly I played along without any discernment and without asking.

Later, I feel prompted to read Mary's song in Luke 1:46 *ff*, which I have seldom read and rather know only from pre-Christmas readings in worship services or from the *Magnificat* by Bach. I was touched by her words of adoration and awe: "My soul magnifies the Lord, and my spirit rejoices in God my Savior, for he has looked on the humble estate of his servant."

The nun

I sit on an Intercity train to Munich. It has just entered the Würzburg train station and come to a halt. Many seats have emptied during the long trip from Northern Germany to here. The seat next to me is also available.

Some travelers enter, among them, a nun in habit. All pass the seat next to me. The nun, too, has gone through the entire car seeking the "right" place, but turns around again and walks out of the car to the one behind. I observe her, wondering. Soon she is back and asks whether she may take the seat next to me. The moment I nod my head, Mary appears. Without her saying one word, I know: There is something for me to do. But I do not like it. *Here on the train?* I think with trepidation. *A stranger and a nun at that, an official representative of the Catholic church? No! She may believe me an occultist or think that I am crazy——this is too much for me. Find a Catholic!*

Mary stays calm and waits until I have struggled through my resistance. When I have finally managed to arrive at my willingness to serve, I think of how to start a conversation. Turning to the nun I ask whereto she is traveling. We begin a normal conversation like any other two people may do who meet

104

on a train. I am watching Mary still standing there waiting for me to create the bridge for her to meet the nun. The nun relates to me that she is in a leading position and on her way to a national Head Sisters Conference somewhere in the south of Germany. After we exchange a few more words, Mary says: "NOW!"

I do not know what to say, but here I go! "I don't know how to convey this, but Mother Mary is present!" The nun looks at me baffled and questioning. She, too, does not know what to say. I explain——and I can feel how I am still trying to get out of this——that it is so, that I cannot change it, etc. In the meantime, Mary has told me why she is here. She says, and I pass the words on, that the nun has a great concern and that she, Mary, came to help.

The nun blushes deeply, but after a very brief hesitation she says, "Yes, that is true!" and then relates to me about a house that she leads in a major German city where women of the street can find beds, food, help, and guidance. The Church has decided to close the house despite its successful work, claiming lack of funds. She talks about the work they do, and I can see this conflict tears on her nerves and on her heart. Mary says:

"BUT YOU ALREADY HAVE AN IDEA, HAVE FOUND A SOLUTION!"

The nun blushes again and looks at me as though I had just caught her doing something illegal. Yes, also true, she admits. She had thought and thought about how this work could be saved, and then she had the idea to form a nonprofit organization that would support the house and the work—— without the Church. *But*, she emphasizes, that would bring her into a conflict of loyalty with her order and with the Church, and she did not know how to solve this. Mary says:

"FOLLOW YOUR HEART, NOT THE CHURCH, FOR THE CHURCH HAS LOST ITS HEART! ALWAYS FOLLOW ONLY YOUR OWN HEART!"

We speak about the heart (CHRIST within us) and about heart-following. Mary turns to me and says:

"SPEAK TO HER OF MY SON!"

The nun laments how hard it has become to speak her heart, even among her sisters, and how much lovelessness, intrigue, and fear is among them, especially among those in leadership positions. I share some of my own experiences, speak of the feelings of loneliness that unavoidably arise once you commit to that path, and I encourage her to keep her eyes on Jesus, who never betrayed His heart, which brought him constantly into conflict with institutionalized religion.

Her heart is warming and filled with joy now, and I feel her great love for GOD, for Jesus, and for Mary. Our encounter comes to a well-rounded end just when the train enters the station where she must get off.

Her eyes shine when she says goodbye, and her cheeks are lightly flushed. What a wonderful experience we just shared! Sometime during our conversation, Mary left. The nun leaves the car, but she knocks on the window standing on the platform, waving a last goodbye. Her face beaming, she waits until the train leaves with me on it. We have become allies, without exchanging names or addresses.

About receiving

I am in the midst of packing. In a few minutes, someone will pick me up to drive to Weyarn (near Munich) where I will lead a one-week intensive retreat with a group that has often worked with me before. At the very last minute, when everything is ready and loaded in the car for departure, I ask whether I have forgotten something. I am told to take with me a small wooden statue of Mary that currently stands on my bedside table. Though a bit surprised, I go to get it, wrap it in a cloth, and stick it in my bag.

After we all met, shared some coffee and cake, and "found" ourselves a little, I begin with the retreat. Intuitively, I take the statue of Mary with me into the meeting room and place it on a silken scarf, together with a lighted candle, in the center of the circle in which we usually sit on meditation pillows. I ask everyone to join me in closing our eyes and entering silence. Mary is present. She seems sad and says:

"MANY HAVE COME, BUT NO ONE CAN RECEIVE. ALL WANT TO DO AND GET. BUT NO ONE CAN ACCEPT. BEFORE YOU GIVE, YOU WILL HAVE TO HELP THEM TO OPEN THEIR HANDS!"

For three days we do exercises exclusively to learn to let go, to have space into which something can be received. Three days we practice "yes" and accepting. Three days Mary stays with us during the healing process. The fourth morning, she has left. Instead of her, Jesus is present and with Him some other male Beings and teachers, who all stay through the remaining days of the retreat. The energies change, and that which is to be taught has now a different quality.

I was deeply grateful for this immediate supporting presence and the love therein that I felt. Sometimes I just did not know how to express this in words, and yet I wanted to call out to the entire human race: "Wake up! When do you finally wake up? Everything for which you long is there! Open your eyes and ears!" But I also know all of that can only be seen and heard if one is ready.

In many ways, Mary became The Gift. Not only because of her great love for humanity, but especially because of her total commitment and dedication to GOD. During and after these experiences, I often pondered the question about the feminine aspect of GOD——ITS motherly safe-keeping and nursing expression. The vision related in the chapter Mother Earth specifically mentions this. However, what Mary showed me was something different: It was the devotion of man as it is explained in the chapter The Menorah as "void" of the Earth. Mary was so completely permeable, transparent. Because of her being so, I had to newly ask myself how well I was doing with my devotion to GOD. I still experienced resistance as my first reaction, a fearful alertness.

My experiences showed me how stuck I still was in my prejudices (the nun). However, they also opened my eyes to how much I love doing this work. And how gladly I will contribute to the healing of humanity and the Earth once I have overcome my inhibition threshold (fear).

QUESTIONS FOR CONTEMPLATION

- Do you have prejudices toward others? How firmly are you set on the beliefs of your own faith?
- Have you encountered any divine intervention in your life? The intervening surprise? Are your eyes and ears open for such an experience?
- Do you believe that GOD can move anything if HE so desires, to give and bring anything to you or others that is needed or even wished for?

18

The Shack and the Palace

Today is a beautiful day! After breakfast, everyone living in the house left to do their jobs. I am ironing, which I love to do, and the task is easy. Out of the blue I have horrible pains in the area of liver and gall bladder, and from one minute to the next I feel extremely nauseated. Placing a hand over the painful organs, I seek a chair to sit down. The entire area under my hand feels like solid stone.

"Show me, GOD! What is this?" I see a black stone on which is written "Hunger." I go deeper into myself. I sense two different male forms in my body. One of them I know right away; the other, I do not.

A young woman who currently lives with us joins me. She can see auras and says: "You have two men in your aura."

"Yes," I answer, "I know. One of them is F, but I do not know the other." With her help, I find out. Both men have been important to me at one time, and I have always been aware of *their hunger for life, love, and their own self.* I cry, for I remember that they had neither shown willingness to feel at the time and accept that hunger **themselves,** nor wanted to hear or accept what could have satisfied it. I am quite aware of my own incessant reactions to that hunger, repeatedly experiencing rejection, especially from F.

After crying, my organs are free again, the nausea is gone, and so is the stone. I realize how overwhelmed I always have been by this unacknowledged and unresolved hunger. I continue to sit for a while and ponder when I am given this vision:

To my left there is a small shack. It is dilapidated, extremely sparse, and bare. Living in it is a small boy, perhaps five or six years old. He appears malnourished, joyless, hopeless, and hungry for food, touch, and acknowledgment. He looks at me forlornly. Attached to the right of the shack is a palace. Inside the palace is bright light, and it is filled with gold and silver. The walls are covered with tapestries and pictures, collected treasures, documents, certificates. The man who lives there is well fed, complacent, and very busy with the treasures and things with which he has surrounded himself.

I stand exactly across from the double wall that separates both dwellings. I have been attracted and called by the hunger of the child. I stand there, a jug of water in my left hand, a slice of bread in my right hand. I offer the bread, but the man comes hurriedly out of the house and looks at the bread to see whether he wants it (make use of it, but not to eat). He will either take it or throw it away——all of that is shown to me in quick succession. The child gets neither bread nor water. Now I hear these words:

"STOP THIS AT ONCE!"

I immediately understand the urgency, as well as the necessity to stop. I remember now that I had been told a long time ago: "You will have to learn to show the door to a hungry child." I understand that better now. Back then, it did not even occur to me that a palace dweller may come to me with his hungry child and bring it to me to feed it——not feeling responsible himself for the hunger inside. I somehow never recognized the palace dweller, only the hungry child.

It definitely hurts to be confronted thus. How often did I feel this arrogance (and of course, the fear behind it) with which "my" bread was considered and assessed. And still I continued to offer bread and water, having no doubts. I threw pearls before swine without discernment and assisted the palace dweller in embellishing his palace with gifts that ought to have been the bread of life——no comprehension whatsoever of what I was doing. The many words that were flung at me, the ridicule, derision, lies, denial, disdain, and the judgments I had ignored . . . I could not and would not see that the palace dweller has to **feel** his own hunger (not just "know" something about it) and walk towards the source before he can even receive the bread. I must have considered myself innocent rather than naive and unconscious.

Some weeks after I had been given this vision, I wrote to F. I wanted to share with him its content and what I recognized. I know that he is not only the hungry child and the palace dweller, but also she who stands in front of the wall with bread and water. While I was writing, I confused the two hands: I said the bread was to the left and the water to the right. That starts an inner turmoil that will not let up until I finally ask, "Why can that possibly be of importance?"

I feel myself standing there, with the bread in my left hand. It has shrunk, and no longer has substance. The water jug to the right is over-dimensionally large——both are totally out of balance. When I change them around again, the balance is immediately restored. What does that mean? I hear:

"IT IS OUT OF BALANCE BECAUSE YOU SPEAK OF YOUR FEELINGS INSTEAD OF BEING THEM!"

That is true. I cry. A lot of tears want to be cried when I think of the way I stand in front of the hut and the palace, not being received, and without being able to do anything for the hungry one, even though bread and water are available. But when I have cried enough, bread and water disappear from my hands, and I become filled with a deep love and joy. I hear:

"YOU ARE BREAD AND WATER."

Now I know; bread and water are life and are realized in every honest encounter. However, true encounter can happen only with openness and honesty on both sides, by lived feelings and deeply felt living. To that, I desire to pay attention.

QUESTIONS FOR CONTEMPLATION

- Do you try to give to people without their asking because you feel their need? Is it difficult for you to separate yourself from their need or what you think their need is?
- Do you recognize the palace dweller inside of you? What do you do with that which is offered or given to you?
- Do you feel responsible for the hungry part in you, or do you prefer to leave it to others – to your partner, your parents, the doctor, a teacher, a God of your own making?

111

19

The Crucifier

Once again, I am fighting a guilty conscience. Since I separated from my husband, this bite of my conscience haunts me. It has a voice and says: "You should have remained with your husband and nursed him because you knew for certain at the time of your separation that he would need care. And you did not want to have anything to do with it." That is true! I knew it, and I did not want to have anything to do with it. Now I have difficulty owning up to this. But this time, I will take the bite and not calm my conscience with explaining arguments or by suppressing it.

Instead of giving myself answers, I turn to GOD. It is so painful to think of the suffering man from whom I separated: old (much older than I ever knew before his passing), sick, alone, speechless——but also an alcoholic, a notorious liar——and as it turned out also a bigamist. I hear the voice:

"YOU DID NOT SIN BY PUSHING HIM AWAY NOW. YOU SINNED BY NOT PUSHING HIM AWAY **RIGHT AWAY!**"

I am oddly affected by the word "sin," for never before had it been used by the voice. I realize, though, that this word perfectly fits the pricks of my conscience. It is, so to speak, its language. So, I see the love coming my way by using what is contained in my conscience. Love uses the language that the "conscience voice" in me understands best, and thereby aids that particular identity to become conscious, which it must. Instantly, I remember the primal and more exact meanings of the word *sin*: failure, being in error, missing the mark. At the time of which the voice speaks, I had had so many warnings———warnings that even then I recognized as appropriate. But I did not listen to any of them. Arriving at this thought, I hear:

"YOU HAVE GREAT DIFFICULTIES DEALING A BLOW TO AN ALREADY SUFFERING BEING!"

That is true. I cry. I remember the first encounters with the man whom I had married after a very brief courtship. My heart had been filled with love, and I had been convinced that I could save him from his loneliness and unhappiness. His constant drinking I had ignored, hoping that he would stop once he had a good home, and that was what I wanted to provide. It had taken thirteen years of marriage for me to finally give up wanting to save him. I knew I could not. Again and again, I had given way to the temptation of trying to ease his life. But also again and again, a guilty voice had plagued me, as though it wanted to say: "Cling together, swing together!" (The literal translation of the German phrase is: "Caught together, hung together".) I still believed I had to lay in the bed I had made: At first, I thought I had to save him, and once I recognized I could not, I believed I had to stay on. Somehow, I still wanted a result that was acceptable to me. There was no limit to my arrogance! What disguise!

Back to the voice, I cry again. I know what the voice meant with "not pushing him right away", but I am also certain that I do not have to continue in my fallacy. Somehow, I am caught by the expectation that I sense in the words: "You have great difficulties dealing a blow to an already suffering being." Pictures appear and memories of experiences with people, in the years after my separation and up until now, in which I had desperately tried to avoid dealing out this extra blow, even though it had been the truth in me. I can feel my resistance and desire for control, and that affects me. I hear Jesus:

"LOOK!"

and I see Him hanging on the cross. He says:

"YOU ARE NOT WILLING TO CRUCIFY ME!"

I freeze and recoil. That is no praise! That is a challenge. It is as though I ought to do this, or, at least, it is a request to be willing. My God, this cannot be true! What is true, however: I am not willing! I do not wish to count myself among the crucifiers, and, more than anything, I do not want anyone else seeing me as such. How can I possibly share this with anyone? Imagine me speaking of this to Christian church members! I do not want to know what I just heard from Him. I want to put my hands over my ears! I cry, I resist, and I wish to terminate the experience——but it will not go away. He does not budge. He waits until I can surrender my resistance after crying and ranting some more. Then He says:

"HOW LITTLE DO YOU TAKE INTO CONSIDERATION THAT **GOD** IS LIBERATED!"

That hits home! I am rescued from an enormous and serious fallacy. As much as I longed for liberation, as much as I wished it for others, I had totally *missed* considering the liberation of GOD in man, in me, and in others. What had I believed liberation was? What had I been longing for? My eyes had never been directed there. Now I know my own liberation rests in the liberation of GOD within. I can stop longing for freedom and stop wanting to bring it to others. I am stopped! I totally comprehend that suffering is nothing but resistance to the shattering of illusion.

Still somewhat shy and skeptical, I walk on and consider the possibility of free-willingly becoming a "crucifier". A book by Irina Tweedy falls into my hands: *Daughter of Fire.*[8] Reading it, I feel relieved, supported, and I somehow totally get what her teacher is doing, as painful as it is to her. Now my resistance feels even more inappropriate. How arrogant (another disguise!) had been all my judgments about "suffering" in the world and within me. Will I ever **be able** to be a crucifier, willingly and consciously? Will I ever be ready to accept, even attract, the hatred of others without hitting back? I realize that my own crucifixion will be accomplished by this.

I remember an earlier experience where Jesus spoke to me about the crucifiers, calling them "the angels of God." I still have not recognized their innocence. Now I believe He had been wanting to tell me already then what he does now. Deeply and anew, I experience the words, "Father forgive them for they know not what they do" (Luke 23:34). Do I know what I am doing? No. I believed I knew, and I believed I had to. I believed in good and evil, and I believed in guilt. I know this all needs to sink in to where there is no more muddy thinking or doubt.

Suddenly, I have a radical question: Did Jesus provoke His own crucifixion? Did He know how the priests and scribes would react? I ask Him, but he does not answer with words. He laughs.

114

I wake into a place of truth where I have never been before: Jesus never attacked the Romans for their brutal reign. He never demonstrated against political suppression, wrongful ruling powers, or wars. He solely attacked the hypocrisy of the high priests, Pharisees and scribes, and their repugnant dealings with the Roman dictatorship for the sole purpose of maintaining their status——the compromise with the world and its thinking! He questioned their "knowing," their power, their blindness with which they led the blind, and He questioned their self-justifications and self-deification. With it, He provoked their hatred and broke through their duplicity. He laid them bare, and with it He "crucified" them. Everyone was and is given the choice to meet such a challenge either with hatred and resistance or with admission and realization. I, too, have this choice when my own hypocrisy and duplicity are being attacked. I experience a complete switch in direction – 180 degrees – a kind of twisted world. What I did not want, I am to accept; what I did not wish to do, I am to do. Or, in the words that Jesus once left with me:

"LEARN TO KNEEL WHERE YOU DON'T WANT TO KNEEL—— LEARN TO STAND UP WHERE YOU DON'T WANT TO STAND"

I want to learn this. I have to learn this and remember!

My prayer is filled with entirely new content. I commit to allowing my willingness to increase to accept the hatred of those who hypocritically try to hide it. I pray for the strength and courage not to defend myself. In amazement, I realize that wars could stop this way——and **only** this way!— —when the beaten give up their illusion of being perishable and separate from GOD, and no longer defend themselves I cannot expect this from anyone but can adhere to it myself.

I have hardly started with these new prayers when I receive four letters from a German woman who had been one of my students for some years. The letters increase in accusation: she calls me loveless, contemptuous, a judge, and finally, the "biggest judge I ever met". The first letter has me stunned. I write back and wish to find out: what created these accusations? What had I done? My questions and remarks only intensified the name-calling in the letters that followed.

115

Then suddenly, I got it: Of course, none of what she called me had I wanted to be, ever; nor did I ever want to be seen as such. I cry and reconcile myself with being seen or appearing as a judge in the eyes of others. I have no control over what others think of me, no matter what I do or believe I do——it is okay **to be seen as disdaining and judging** while being neither disdainful nor prejudiced. Entirely new to me is the thought that even Jesus must have been seen as such by some of those around Him. After all, He did insult them, calling them names such as hypocrites, brood of vipers, blind fools, serpents, and many more (Matthew 17 and 23). I begin to reconcile myself with the high priests and also with the truth that I may be stuck in my own hypocrisy.

The idea that from now on I can say anything that wants or needs to be expressed makes me cheery. The very idea that perhaps someday there may be nothing ever again against which I want to defend myself, or nothing as what I do not want to be seen as, creates an almost unbearable joy in me. I also look forward to all that people may say to me that may remove and destroy any leftover "paint" or the false masks I unknowingly still try to keep. What freedom!

Just one day later, after I have journaled all of the above, I sense during morning meditation that I am not done with the subject. It is as though I had overlooked something essential. I ask for revelation. It feels as though the entire text I have written runs through my body, filters out anything that is not understood or is off. What is left discloses this truth: *With everything, and that means everything, that I had not wanted to be – and BECAUSE I had not wanted to be it – I had created circumstances, conditions, and encounters for being exactly that.* It is my own confusion that forced me. How incredibly ingenious you are, GOD! I am so happy. When I am "allowed" to be everything, then everything outside is "allowed" too. Of what should I ever be afraid again?

I am still stuck on the question I had asked Jesus: Did He provoke the high priests on purpose? It is eating me, leaves me dissatisfied. (How stubborn can one be?) Therefore, I ask Him again. Silence. He is watching me. I wait one more day and ask again. Now He laughs and says: "WHAT HIGH

PRIESTS?" I get it and laugh, too. Pure joy remains about not remaining dependent on the limitations of the human mind.

QUESTIONS FOR CONTEMPLATION

- Can you empathize with my consternation about Jesus's teaching?
- Are you approachable by the thought of being a crucifier yourself, to be allowed to be a crucifier?
- Are you willing to impose yourself on someone when you know quite well that it will hurt his/her feelings, pride, and expectations?

20

The Cleansing of the Temple

We are having a group session at Community House. Residents and outside guests are present. As members of the circle begin to talk about how they feel and what is going on in their lives, I feel an unexpected surge of rage towards one of the women the moment she speaks. I am aware that for the past year, this woman has come here with the very same problem week after week. Each time I encouraged her to search in her heart for what she would like to do in the coming week to solve it, and she would commit. But each time she did not do what she had set out and needed to do. This time the problem is not the same, but I asked her if she accomplished what she had decided to do about the other. "No," she said, adding many explanations.

I am furious and scream at her, "Who is supposed to take care of your heart? Am I? When are you finally going to trust your heart and obey it? For months I have taken it upon myself to get you to pay attention to the voice of your heart. Am I crazy?" I go on for a while. Then I leave her sitting there, crying. I have nothing more to say.

We continue on around the circle. At some point, I experience the same anger towards a man in the circle. Similar words came out of my mouth. "How long are you going to sleep hoping that someone else is going to live for you? Man, open your eyes! Otherwise, life is just going to pass you by——just hanging around, waiting! For what? For whom?" I feel as though I am a blazing, all-consuming fire. After this outburst, there is absolute silence in the room, and I begin to calm down. Then I hear the voice:

"THAT IS ENOUGH. BECOME QUIET AND ASK YOURSELVES WHAT WAS NEW TODAY!"

I hear the question and pass it also on to the group.

When I close my eyes with all the others, I find myself not in our house, but instead I am standing in an enormous old and spacious stone building. There is a great mess before my eyes: Wooden tables lay overturned on the floor, merchandise is all over the place, people are lying or sitting on the floor, and they are looking at me in total shock; money is scattered all about. Like a blazing flame I stand there holding a thick, looping rope in my hand. It looks as though I, like a maniac, have just destroyed everything in the room. But oddly enough, and despite my own shock, it feels actually very good. Then I see Jesus standing to my left. He looks at me, laughing, and says:

"YOU TOOK IT LITERALLY."

I immediately am reminded of a time when I lived in constant fear. At that time, I did not dare to attend a regular church service because I deeply feared that GOD would make me stand up, open my mouth, and shout, "What have you done to my Father's house?" This thought alone was so terrifying that I did not step into *any* church for a long time. I admit now that I had taken the message of the temple cleansing literally and am relieved that I was mistaken. But I also confess, more to myself than to Jesus, that I am in general simply terrified of the unpredictability of GOD's power and have always connected certain ideas with it. I recognize that what just happened was totally in accordance with this powerful unpredictability, which I had always feared.

Now it does not appear to me to be so bad or threatening anymore. Not only that, but it also seems to be quite in keeping with what was needed and——I could feel this clearly——it was filled with love! It had been rushing past me before I had a chance to control it.

Jesus remained standing there while all of this is going through my mind. He then says,

"I AM GLAD THAT YOU ARE WILLING AND HAVE BEGUN TO ACT!"

Now I realize that the temple cleansing relates to internal cleansing, and immediately I ask myself, "Who, then, are these moneychangers whose tables I have overturned?"

But I do not have the chance to delve into this question much further because Jesus has become serious. He is still looking at me. Then I hear:

"BEWARE! FOR THOSE WHO CALL THEMSELVES THE LORDS OF THE TEMPLE WILL CRUCIFY YOU!"

I do not feel threatened by that, even though I hear the seriousness that lies in His words. I sense He is not speaking these words as a warning so that I will take steps to prevent it. It is rather so that I am prepared because it will happen. Before Jesus leaves, He encourages me to look at all the stories that speak of Him and to see them as current in my own life, in our lives:

"THEY CONCERN YOU AND ALL PEOPLE. IT IS THE SAME, AND IT IS NOW. I AM NOT HISTORY. I AM NOW AND IN YOU (PLURAL). BRING THIS TO THE PEOPLE!"

The following day, a woman comes to visit. She is looking for a room in Virginia Beach. Even though I tell her that we are not renting, she insists on speaking to me. She says she has heard of us, is searching, and is interested in becoming a healer. Sometime during our conversation, I mention how happy I am that more and more men are willing to open to this deep emotional work. I am very touched by this and very grateful. The woman looks at me, and her facial expression hardens. She says, "Don't you know that 98 percent of the world's money is in the hands of men?"

"No, I don't know," I reply. "But no one owns anything on this Earth—— neither women nor men! Everything is given to us so we can love, and it is unimportant what it is or in whose hands it rests."

She turns rigid in her seat and says, without looking at me, "Yes, well, we all have our private lives and can do and think what we wish."

"No," I said (or perhaps I should rather say, it came out of my mouth?), "There is no private life. There is only *one* life, and we are all part of it. The sooner we realize this, the better. No one can do or not do without affecting everyone else." Barely have I uttered the last word when the woman straightens up and places the water glass she is holding very slowly and softly on the table. Standing up, she says with an icy and extremely tense voice, "Thank you very much. It was very nice to meet you. Goodbye!" and runs out of the house.

Later I hear that she told people that I am the new and dangerous "Charles Manson" (the sect leader who convinced his followers to murder the pregnant actress Sharon Tate and her friends) and am leading the young astray. She felt committed to do everything possible to encroach upon my business and disturb my work.

I am getting an ever-clearer picture of the significance of the lords of the temple. Interestingly enough, I find it to be exactly as described in the biblical story where the high priests and lords of the temple are only affected indirectly by Jesus's cleansing of the temple. It more affects the moneychangers who stand between the world (Rome) and the sacred (or what should be sacred) and re-coin the secular into the sacred while making a profit in the process.

In the following weeks, in various retreats, I invite all retreat participants to focus on the moneychangers, their viewpoint (a very confused heart chakra), their fears, and their respective loyalties. It often seems that internally they have a rather neutral and accepting position. However, upon closer observation, it becomes clearer that they are trying to belong to both sides, as though they wanted to dance at two weddings and cannot be a guest at either. It feels tepid, neither cold nor hot. All of us recognize that the moneychanger in each of us has a very personal face and that we all actually do know him.

I have decided to maintain a keen awareness of these moneychangers. In the various lessons I am given, they turn up again and again, each time with a different face, and because I know them very well within myself, I can also recognize them in others. I am ready to overturn these tables and accept the consequences. In the two years since this experience, I have had to shed a lot of skin, but I still cannot say that I no longer have any.

QUESTIONS FOR CONTEMPLATION

- What does the story of the Cleansing of the Temple mean to you? If you do not know the story, read it (Mark 11:15–19).
- Do you know such a condition of a fire in yourself? To whom or what is this righteous anger directed? Do you dare to show it?
- Are you familiar with your moneychanger? What are the "coins" with which *you* try to buy Heaven?

21

The Ghetto

When the movie *Schindler's List* came to our theater in Virginia Beach, I dared for the first time to see any film footage about the Holocaust. Up until then, I had managed successfully to dodge it, and even now it was not easy. But since I knew I could not get away forever, I decided to face it.

In the theater, I sat among mostly Americans. The moment the film started, I suddenly no longer felt like a person watching a movie, but like a participant in the story. I feel German and as though I am now in the center of the screen, visible by all and everyone, identified and judged. I realized I cannot avoid carrying the burden laying on Germany——even when I had been only three years old when the war ended——whether I lived in America or somewhere else. In this burden, I currently felt less the guilt than the judgments and accusations, the impotent rage and desire for revenge, unexpressed in the silence here in the cinema. I started to cry and was unable to stop. I cried and cried, and no longer saw anything of the movie. Therefore, I left.

A few days later, I went back for a second visit; also, to overcome this seemingly bottomless pit of pain that had opened. This day, it was a bit easier. I no longer felt German, and I also identified less with the victims. I went back two more times. The fourth time, I was finally able to look with compassion at everyone: Schindler, the individual men and women, the child in the red coat, even the Nazi camp commander. The unfathomable humiliation experienced all around was still very present on my mind and in my heart, yet I knew: Life will eventually reveal all to me.

Some months later, a friend from Vienna came to Virginia. She told me of her strong desire to cut off her hair and shave her head. I had shared this desire, secretively, for many years, and I could already taste the opportunity to do it now with thoughts of "jointly we will have the courage." I was very aware of my willingness and ability to flee forward and jump into something new whenever I am afraid of the new. But what may look like courage it is not. That is why I decided that this time, I would walk slowly through every stage of fear and feel every bit of it up to the actual act. I soon learned I mostly feared the visible nakedness and what the people who see me may associate with a shaved head, like cancer, sect involvement, etc., and also that I wouldn't be able to reverse this. Once the hair was off, it was off.

It took me four days. We cut each other's hair with the shortest level on the hair clipper. My eyes were closed and while my hair was falling to the ground, memories of past lives flashed by (as a nun in France, as a Tibetan monk) in which my head had been shaved for religious reasons. How surprised was I to recognize that this ritual had had absolutely no meaning whatsoever. The hair had no meaning other than what I gave to it! The truth I came across in *A Course in Miracles*[9] suddenly sank deeply into me in that there is nothing that I see outside of me that has any meaning other than the one I give it. It moved so fully into me and filled me that I felt fat like a Buddha: filled with pure joy, cheerfulness, and bliss.

About a week later, probably triggered by this experience with the shaved head, I felt a strong urge to go to one of the concentration camps, which would be possible during my upcoming trip to Germany. Since I will be in Munich, it seemed natural and easy to drive to Dachau for this. While I spoke to a friend about it, I felt great anxiety about actually going there **with my shaved head**. I did not know what I feared more: the German or the Jewish visitors. Yet despite my fear, I was willing to go.

Two days later, during morning meditation, I found myself suddenly out of my body, in Dachau. I am wearing the long, coarse linen gown that I wear often for worship and am walking slowly, barefooted, past one of the barracks. Then I heard the voice:

"THIS IS HOLY GROUND! NEVER HAVE I BEEN CLOSER TO MAN THAN HERE!"

I am torn up, ripped open. Love had just touched me in a way that no judgment remains. I cried, deeply affected by this love and this truth that transcends everything that ever happened, here and also within me. The peace that filled me simultaneously with the love was beyond words. I would not have to travel there (although I did during my trip, just to face my fear regarding my shaved head). I thought of all those beings that experienced and recognized this truth during the Holocaust and felt at one with them.

Months later, I had a nightly dream that enhanced these experiences significantly——

I am standing in an open exterior doorway, leaning against the left door frame and looking outside. There, to the right of the little front steps, stands an old man. His body is so deeply bent that he cannot lift his head anymore and his face is turned toward the ground. While I watch him, a long, seemingly unending trail of people comes from the right that all look like the rounded-up Jews in *Schindler's List* on their way to the ghetto: men, women, children, young and old, in clothes that speak of poverty and wealth. Some are carrying bundles. One of the men, while passing, gives the old man at the steps a pat on the back and says in Yiddish: "Ir hobn tsu geyn, Alterchen!" (You have to go, old man!) The man laboriously begins to move.

Now my heart fills with compassion. I start to move as well and follow the old man. When I reach him and am walking next to him, I ask: "Can I help you?" He does not answer. He hands me a little package with a wrapped sandwich and hooks his arm into my right arm, which I offered him. We walk a bit together. I realize I have no idea where we are heading, but I actually do not care. My heart is filled with love, but I am rather unconscious and indifferent towards what is happening around me. Then I notice that the man at my side has straightened up a bit. I am happily surprised and bend forward to look into his face. There I see——to my utter dismay——disdain, bitterness, and pride. I am shocked and let go of his arm. I wake up.

While I began pondering the possible message of the dream, I heard the voice:

"STOP THIS IMMEDIATELY! YOU CANNOT HELP ANYONE ON HIS WAY **INTO** THE GHETTO! ONLY ON HIS WAY **OUT**!"

I recognized my misunderstanding not only in life generally, but also in tangible relationships. I was deeply affected and very sad that I had continuously intervened in people's lives trying to make their lives easier (or so I believed!) while life itself had asked something of them. What had I done? What did I prevent? What was I hindering? I had a hard time admitting this because I preferred to keep that self-image of the loving and helpful. And, of course, I also wished to believe I was conscious. I did not like having to recognize how unconscious I had been in whatever I called "my" compassion, how arrogant. I felt totally rattled in the foundation on which my understanding of the meaning of life and "divine destiny" had manifested.

Now I remembered many situations in which others gave *me* such misunderstood assistance. I realized how the delay in my awakening related to that, as my illusions were preserved. With a soothing vigilance and gratitude, I remembered the few times when someone had been clear, honest, and disallowing with me, thus giving me what I acutely needed. I wanted to shout, "The love of God, the presence of God, is limitless!" because I could see IT right there where I was thrown back onto myself. And again, I heard the voice:

"TRUE HUMILITY IS NOT GAINED BY BENDING, BUT BY BREAKING!"

I understood that only **after** such breaking, or rather, after letting oneself be broken, could true upright standing be born, from inside out, and not by clutching the arm of someone else. Pride bends, resigns itself, and waits for the opportunity to continue with one's actions, one's thoughts, and one's beliefs, in bitterness and with the wish to retaliate.

I remembered a message that came to us in meditation a long time ago:

"IN TRUE HUMILITY, HUMILIATION IS NOT EXPERIENCED!"

. . . Not any longer! I wanted to add. No longer any humiliation! However, I still experienced it.

May true humility one day overtake and fill me and us all.

I find it difficult to form questions for this chapter. The still raw and unprocessed agony and the accompanying fury about the events during Hitler's reign seem to be too present and are still being nursed. I hesitated a long time to take this chapter into my book, but I did not wish to spare you the imposition. I wish you willingness, courage, and strength to reconcile with your pain and anger.

Many of the thousands of people that perished during the Holocaust or died after, returned (reincarnated) quickly back to Earth. Not all of them who returned were victims of the times, but some were also perpetrators. I have met a few of them. On either side, the pain is equally excruciating, and the lessons to be learned in **this** life are difficult. How could it be different?

However, in the grace of GOD we are all in the safest possible hands, each of us, unconditionally, as much in the suffering as in the actions. In this grace and unconditional love, we can afford to open our eyes.

22

Exodus

(Brace yourself, this is a very long chapter.)

"When Israel was in Egypt's land . . . let my people go!" Who does not know this well-known gospel song? I have always particularly loved it. Its music as much as its words affected me deeply. They speak of GOD's calling Moses to go to Egypt and lead the people (also me and all the various parts in me) out of captivity. They speak of the suffering of the black slaves in America and of their deep longing for freedom and salvation. For a long time, I did not understand why it affected me so much; I thought it was empathy with the historic fate of all people in dependency and bondage. But I did not relate their experiences to myself. I did not consider myself "enslaved," as the time of slavery had gone.

In the last few years, I increasingly noticed how much this subject directly impinged upon me——well, upon all of us. I began to understand that the external appearance of slavery can only be an effigy of our inner human condition in which we share. More of this came from a completely different angle. For this I have to put some puzzle pieces together. So please bear with me.

Over New Years of 1993, during a retreat I led in a monastery in Germany. I had the following nightly dram:

I am traveling by air with my son Oliver. In the dream he is young, about seven or eight years old, sitting cheerily next to me in his anorak, wearing his little yellow rain boots, and having his headphones on.

We land and depart the plane near a big, beautiful, crystal-clear lake——a vast body of water. My attention is drawn to a big white mansion on the opposite shore. I bend down to Oliver's height until I can see from where he is looking and point to the mansion and say, "That's where we will go!" I see that he is still wearing his headphones, but I do not pay it any mind.

He turns towards me, points, and asks as though to confirm, "That's where we are going?" I nod and am totally shocked when he runs straight toward the house, directly into the water. His totally blind trust in my words stuns me, but I also recognize his complete lack of discernment about the external reality.

At first, I cannot even move, but then I run and pull him out of the water. His body is lifeless, and he seems to have drowned. I put him over my knees and struggle to get the water out of him, to get him to breathe. I make it but wake up exhausted and crying.

Upon waking, I remembered that Oliver at that age had gone through a deep crisis, had even expressed thoughts of suicide. He had kept talking about not knowing where he belonged blaming his two brothers who got on well with each other but to whom he did not feel any connection. At the time, I had not recognized the extent of his lostness on Earth. It made me weep as it dawned on me. His lostness did not differ from my own when I had been his age. During the silence that followed my pondering, I heard that I had projected one of my problems onto this child and would have to take back my projection so that Oliver could live his own free life (here I remembered also the vision about the energy of mothers and sons in the chapter Mother Earth).

The "problem" that I saw in him was his credulity and carelessness, which was also apparent in the dream——perhaps the somewhat creditable characteristics that are disproportionate in relationship to the external reality. In his case, especially in relationship to money. I asked myself why he acted like this in the dream. For in the dream *I am* of the firm conviction we will have to walk the very long path around half of the lake in order to reach the house——the exact opposite of Oliver's intent.

I discovered a conflict within me: on the one hand, I carry a blind trust in the words I hear, whether they come from outside or inside, but on the other hand, there is also a longstanding belief that I have to work really hard for everything. I believed I belonged neither to Heaven nor to Earth. I had always efforted to face the earthly realities, to see as the world saw, and to try to fit as well as possible into it. My own sense of not belonging to anything or anyone was——once again——deep and very painful. I had not realized that there was still so much pain left about it, unresolved.

My attention went back to the headphones. What did they symbolize? I barely asked the question when truth came to me about the entire dream: My trust in man, in life, and in GOD had continuously (as it had Oliver) filled me with a basic cheery, positive attitude. Most of the time, I knew what direction I had to take and what I had to do. But I had GOD mixed up with the world. Time and again in my life I had overlooked——especially in my younger years——listening more carefully in order to experience what it was *supposed to mean, how and when* I might had to go, *how and when* it was to be done, and what it was that the voice had actually said. Instead, I drew conclusions, and, believing it had been my idea and, therefore, I knew what it meant, I followed my own interpretations and concepts as soon as I heard the words, became aware of the idea, and believed to know the direction. Without asking for the necessary steps that were required for implementation, I worked hard trying to figure it all out or ran into the "water", as my son did in the dream. It often seemed rather coincidental that things in life went gently, fast, and perfectly——as it ought to be or could be, if I were more conscious.

Countless tears followed. It was very painful to realize how hard I had made life for myself in that I did not inquire and listen more closely. A strong desire arose in me to take off my own "headphones" and learn to listen. I knew I wanted to hear GOD clearly inside and in people; I did not wish to give more importance to interpretations, opinions, and judgments than to the word itself. I wanted to listen and get it.

After my tears dried, I went once more back into the dream: To my surprise, the lake had now parted, and I thought of the parting of the sea during the exodus from Egypt in the story of the Old Testament. For now, in my changing dream memory, a small white, sandy path led between two walls of water directly to the house and I experienced deep peace and bliss.

I turned to the Bible to read once again the story of the exodus (Exod. 12:1–18,27). I read that GOD had heard the lamenting of the people and had asked Moses to lead HIS people out of Egypt. I read how the people themselves, out of fear and feeling trapped in their suffering, initially considered this a joyful opportunity, but soon it also became a threat. I read that the people, when experiencing difficulties during the exodus, would have preferred to return to Egypt, back into bondage, instead of weathering through. I am again deeply affected by this story, and it stays with me.

A few days after the above dream, I called my dad, to whom I had not spoken in months. When he realized that it was I who was calling, he remembered my birthday that had passed a few weeks before. He said cheerily: "Happy belated birthday, child! **Had you come to me, you would have gotten something**!" For a moment I was absolutely stunned, but then I laughed and laughed, for suddenly those words become a double message. I had heard my father and pretty much knew what he meant, but now I also heard GOD and knew what HE meant. For in front of me on my desk was a list of numbers amounting to 13,000 DM (German Marks = about $ 6,500) that I had borrowed from various people for the Community House in Virginia Beach and that had to be paid back in a few days. I had no idea how to get this money. It had concerned me, and I had gone back and forth thinking about what I could do or whom I could ask. Now, through the words of my dad, I knew what to do and was very happy that I was not wearing my "headphones". Our conversation ended on that note of gratitude. There was not much else to say. He lived in his world, and I rarely had felt he understood where I am. He did not understand now why I was laughing, but he also was not interested to hear. We said goodbye and I placed the receiver back. I was very grateful to him that he expressed what he probably considered his own thought. I felt so abundantly given to and was reminded that GOD supplies and knows of all our concerns, that HE constantly leaves me with signs to strengthen my trust in HIM. Remembering this, with renewed trust and still cheerful, **I shoved my list of debts to the back of the desk and went to bed.**

The retreat that I had come to lead began the next morning. Before we started, I was given an envelope by one of the participants, who extended greetings from friends whom she had visited the evening before and who had given her the envelope. In it I found a card with loving words of gratitude and a check for 5,000 DM. I burst into tears of joy and could not believe that only yesterday I still had had doubts. Why did I still believe I was on my own, that

I would have to make it happen, and I would have to see to whatever was needed myself? That on my shoulders rested everything?

It took only a few more days and the entire amount came together. Among other things, an anonymous giver left a 1,000 DM note on my desk during a gathering we had in my room, and others, however motivated, decided to support my work financially.

By now you may ask: how does all of this relate to the exodus from Egypt? To make the bridge, I will have to relate yet one more incident that happened after returning back to the States about two weeks later.

A friend had invited me to meet a group of people at her house. Those present had questions, to which I attempted to respond, but I noticed that the attendees' avoidance to address their suffering, or anything else that was essential, was starting to irritate me. That is why I decided to change the direction of that afternoon and after a few minutes addressed a man who appeared to be quite calm but whose terrible suffering was palpable to me. At first, he defended himself with strongly expressed emotions and gave explanations for his condition. I asked inside how I could help him and was given an image for his dilemma that——upon asking—— I then described to him.

I see two adults. In one of them I recognize his mental body that has filled himself up with studied (read and heard) spiritual knowledge and is able to recite it. In the other I recognize a counterpart that is able to emotionally react but fails to comply with the emotional body. The latter is a thought form, emotionally charged, created for defense and resistance against the outside world so that true feelings cannot emerge. A cloche shape below the two adults covers up his being and true feelings in the form of a child of around seven years old, who sits there cowering and resigned.

After I had described the image, I asked the man to allow me to speak to the child. He consented. I spoke words of compassion and what I was seeing of his truth, upon which the man began to cry.

132

But that was only the tip of the iceberg. I knew that and was not surprised to find the man's emotional body in my own on my way home. I accepted it and was not concerned. I would be shown what to do.

The following day, Sunday, we, the group at Community House, met for worship at 10:00 a.m. As we sat down for prayer and meditation, again I felt the body of this man within me, but now I was a child (or the child). I needed a moment to determine his truth and try to pray for him and accept him in his lostness, which, however, did not change my condition. So, I spoke to the others of his presence and described the state I was in. They agreed to be with me. I felt it imperative that *his* words and *his* truth be expressed, no matter where that would lead. I began to do this and listened to the words that came out of my mouth:

"Stop preaching to me. Stop telling me endlessly about God, how He is, what He says, and of his love. I can't hear it anymore!" my voice screamed. "The love you don't feel yourself, the love you yourself do not believe in and do not live by. You don't see me, you don't know me, you don't feel yourself, nor the others, no one!"

My voice became louder and louder, and a deep sorrow overwhelmed me about all that pious talk around me. I saw "my" father in a pulpit, and was simultaneously aware that he did not relate at all to me or anyone else. After this, the man/child left my body. (Later, I called my friend at whose house we had been and learned that the man's father was indeed a pastor).

The spiritual movement of the New Age came to my mind, and so did people who represented churches and educational institutions that sat in this trap of constantly carrying untested spiritual or psychological truths in their mouths while resisting to feel and accept their feelings (especially the painful and "ugly" ones) lovingly into their own responsibility. "It's difficult to own your own shit," I had had to utter often as teacher in my work.

But I also shed tears because I still carried memories of my parental home filled with such experiences. I, too, heard again and again such pious patter, sermons, and admonitions (not only but also). Partially, I took them to heart. Today I was glad to have been exposed so early to the contents of Christian faith, but that did not help my feeling of being unseen and unheard. Rarely was there someone who asked me something or had an interest in my thoughts or my answers, or even in my inner being; there was no one to whom the words from my mouth meant anything or who could have used them. Rarely was anyone interested in my faith or spiritual experience.

I quieted down and into this quiet I heard the voice speak:

"LOOK! THAT IS *THE PEOPLE OF ISRAEL* AND THE CONDITION IN EGYPT UNDER PHARAOH. TAKE A LOOK AT ISRAEL, TAKE A LOOK AT EGYPT, AND TAKE A LOOK AT PHARAOH. TAKE A LOOK AT THE EVENTS. IT IS IN YOU; IT IS IN ALL HUMANITY."

I repeated these words aloud——all of them. One participant in our service cried and called out, "Let my people go" (Exodus 5:1). Another woman said: "I see my dad sitting alone in the basement in front of the TV, drinking," and she started to scream and moan. I suddenly realized the role of Moses, something, or someone within me, within us, that will have to fulfill the task to lead us out and away, to never lose sight of the goal. "My God," I asked once again, "Where have we all been? What is this Egypt within me, in all of us? What is this bondage within me, in all of us?" I knew I had to ponder this more and deeper, and I wanted to speak with others about it.

That is also why I wish to take a closer look together with you, the reader, at the various aspects of this story and the mystery. I start with Pharaoh.

Pharaoh

I look at Pharaoh, his self-importance, and his misunderstanding of the deified human. He thinks himself God, *appointed himself* as God, and the people around him believe him to be God. I recognize in Pharaoh the misunderstanding created by mental and spiritual arrogance and presumptuousness, as it still can be seen today (or maybe again?) everywhere, even among those who claim to be "conscious." I can see how it manifests in individuals and in humanity as a whole. This "Pharaoh" in me believes himself in the know. He knows his way around and considers himself competent to tell me where it is good for me to be and walk——and

134

where it is not. He considers himself cognizant to tell me what I may feel and what I should not, what I can say and what I cannot. Do you recognize something/someone inside of you that has such an enslaving power over you?

What do we imagine when we for whatsoever reason, gain power in and over this world? Are we aware that everything, absolutely everything, is by the Grace of GOD——having a position, having money, having an academic title, having the inherited status within a social framework, being a spiritual teacher, or being a "good" therapist? Have we been granted, or do we use with an arrogant assumption such positions and endowment for our own gratification, self-adulation, and personal gain, as though we had it coming? Is it by our own merit that we are *able to learn, to see, to hear, and to use our mental faculties*? Or are we not especially called to always and everywhere be conscious of the task and commission that lay in the words of Jesus: "You shall love the Lord your God with all your heart and with all your soul and with all your mind and all your strength" and "love your neighbor as yourself" (Mark 12:30,31).

The Pharaoh in me I recognize in those inner voices that early on kept saying to me that the Earth was a place of suffering and I had to acquiesce. I had to carry that cross of mine, had to appear kind, which was equivalent to keeping my mouth shut, to pretend as though conditions were not very different inside me. That was my fate, the voices implied, for otherwise I would lose the love, regard, and approval of those who meant a lot to me. These voices were the protectors of "law" and the rational rulers within me, the judges and preachers of morals who placed themselves above feelings and truth. Can you recognize such a pharaoh in you? How he fears to lose his position or face before others? Do you also recognize the pharaoh who purports to the outside world that he represents you, stands up for you, in that he *speaks about* your feelings (often with rage or pity), instead of allowing you to be and show your feelings?

In the biblical story, a pharaoh comes to power who knows nothing of the formerly blessed coexistence of the tribe of Jacob in Egypt. He fears the predominance of the people of Israel in his country. As he sees them as potential enemies, who one day may oppose him, he decides to "dampen" and suppress them. It is said about the Egyptians: ". . . and they were in dread of the people of Israel" (Exod. 1:12 f). Upon his orders, the Egyptians make their lives bitter with hard service. He also orders his overseers to kill all the sons of the Israelites and let only the daughters live.

When Moses and Aaron come to Pharaoh to affect the release of the people, Pharaoh says: "Who is the Lord that I should obey his voice. I do not know the Lord and, moreover, I shall not let Israel go" (Exod. 5:2). And he orders that the drudgery be even harder and more severe.

I am especially interested in Pharaoh's fear of the potential enemies. What is he afraid of? What am I afraid of? Who are those potential enemies inside of me, and what can they do to me or take from me? The rule and control of the upper chakras (head/Pharaoh) over the lower chakras (feeling/Israel), accompanied by the excessive overestimation of self, lead to the suppression of all that which someday will scream for liberation and entitlement. Only for so long can we, too, bury and suppress our unfree and unhealed condition before it asks to be noticed——be it by disease, exhaustion, or a deep mental or emotional crisis in which collapses our "throne". But would we free-willingly surrender that "throne"? Sacrifice it? Would you?

The pharaoh of the biblical story does not allow anyone to tell him what to do about his power; he asserts it and insists on demonstrating it. Again and again, and despite plagues and pestilences, he does not give in. It does concern him that perhaps the GOD of Israel may be bigger than himself and his magicians, but as soon as the disaster has been averted and the threatening events have come to a halt, all his concerns vanish again.

I ask myself (and you) how often in life have we been afflicted and confronted by fate with sickness, problems, burdens, and difficulties? How often did we then think of GOD and HIS power that could possibly, please, relieve and heal us of our afflictions? How often did we promise things we would do, once we felt better, once we were healed, once we had financial stability?

And how quickly did we forget HIM once we no longer felt our misery and had come out of our hole? Just like Pharaoh: "But when Pharaoh heard that there was respite, he hardened his heart and would not listen to them" (Exod. 2:15) He is like that part in us, or we are like him: capricious and akin to a chameleon that, upon danger, changes its color opportunistically. Pharaoh prefers to use his experiences to strengthen his power and position in order not to be dethroned. So many of us become bitter over the repetitious, painful experiences caused by the battle for control.

We are truly stiff-necked! A blocked fifth chakra (see also the page on chakras), the seat of the will, gives us cramped shoulders and painfully stiff neck muscles. We like to have them softened with massage, learn relaxing techniques . . . but soon, everything is tight again and hurts. Do we learn, what we need to learn???

Pharaoh promises again and again to let the people go if Moses could influence GOD to end the scourge. Again and again, his heart turns to stone as soon as the problem is averted, and everything is calm in the land: Then he no longer sees any cause to be afraid. But even here, so we are told, GOD's hand is involved. He says to Moses: "And I will harden Pharaoh's heart and multiply my signs and my wonders in the land of Egypt" (Exod. 7:3). Is it possible that GOD may harden our heart and that of others? That He not only designs it but even wishes it? We often ask how can GOD allow this? But do we also ask, is HE doing this, and if so, why?

This is an especially difficult subject and yet part of the journey, and I can think of many people who will pounce on this question (or on me) with all the impotent anger they carry inside that is directly linked to this question. In this story, we are advised that HE designs and uses it——simultaneously, HE would like it changed. A true paradox! I will come to this again a bit later.
After long negotiations and many painful experiences, Pharaoh finally allows the people of Israel to leave. We are told that within *one* day, they finally do. This one day is for the "liberation movement" just one moment in time considering that Israel's bondage had lasted 430 years. In us, too, "Israel" can be given permission to be liberated in an instant. But who gives permission or decides? Who takes the lead?

This moment is not the end of the struggle for Israel but the beginning of a different struggle. Soon, the Bible tells us, Pharaoh regrets that he has let his servants go, and he chases after them. The people are frustrated and afraid and turn on Moses.

"Have you taken us away to die in the wilderness because there were no graves in Egypt? Why have you dealt thus with us, to carry us forth out of Egypt? Is not this the word that we did tell you in Egypt, saying, let us alone, that we may serve the Egyptians? For it had been better for us to serve the Egyptians, than that we should die in the wilderness."
And Moses answers: "Fear you not, stand still, and see the salvation of the LORD, which he will show to you today" (Exod. 8:11–14).

GOD tells Moses what to do and promises further signs and the salvation of Israel. In front of their eyes, the Red Sea parts so they can walk across with dry feet. As the Egyptians attempt to follow through the Red Sea, GOD allows the waters to flow in again and destroy them. That is how the pharaoh's rule over Israel is finished, even though neither Israel's nor Egypt's problems have ended.

I recognize in Pharaoh and in the Pharaonic part in me an essential aspect of a continuous inner antagonism between head and feelings, between arrogance and fake humility, between life and pseudo life, between truth and illusion, between reality and unreality, between seeming power and seeming impotence. I also recognize in this aspect my rage, my being stirred up by any act of humiliation, by tenaciously refusing to surrender to humility and to acknowledge the omnipotence of GOD.

How difficult it has been for me to comprehend that I have no control over life, no matter what I try or what magic helpers or "servants" I use, no matter what power or approval I am granted by myself or by others. I had to experience that that part in me that is so tenaciously fighting for its dominance, the survival of its power, had to back off and die. How long had this part in me suppressed, ridiculed, and humiliated my feelings instead of gaining humility? How long had this part manipulated them into serving him? But even for him, all the painful experiences had become too much one day and, with letting go of the control and letting the feelings be, he gave in. **This had not been easy!** Just like Pharaoh in the story, the pharaoh in me

138

regretted this relenting again and again and tried to get back his power and rule.

For many people, the Old Testament is a history book of many brutalities and senseless killings. I understand this view, but do not share it undifferentiated. I have asked myself for example, why did all these Egyptians have to drown? Was that necessary? Why is GOD so cruel? But we could just as well ask: Why does the seed have to die in the ground——why can it not remain a seed? Of course, I can never grasp this if I focus on form, material manifestation, and external perishable reality, if I do not recognize life as a continuum that is subject to many laws that completely surpass my limited and mostly physical perception of things. I know this: Pharaoh, his power and self-aggrandizement, and any additional expression of this deified fallacy, must die in me if I want to find life and true liberation.

The People of Israel (in this analogy)

Who is (are) the people of Israel in me? How often have I asked myself that question. Even as a child, whenever I heard biblical messages directed to Israel, I believed that with Israel not only a specific political or ethnic group was addressed——even though its people manifested as such in history and humanity——but that we were all addressed and we, who felt called by GOD, chosen (that is seen), and spoken to, were meant to hear this as well.

In view of the biblical story and as possible analogy to myself, I recognize the people (also called children) of Israel as a quality, a part in me that, even though aware of and close to the All-One GOD from the beginning, has to be constantly reminded because it always forgets and gets lost in the forgetting. But perhaps this part is also so lost, so deeply stuck in matter, that it cannot find its way out by itself since it cannot even remember what it needs to remember, namely where it came from. GOD commands Moses to say to Pharaoh: "This says the Lord: Israel is My son, My firstborn, and I command you to let My son go so that he may serve [worship] Me" (Exod. 4:22,23) It seems evident that we ought to consider this liberation from Egypt as a "leading back" to GOD, namely, leading back to what was "first", before all else was.

What could "firstborn son" mean here? Let us consider this question in relationship to our (suppressed) feelings——or perhaps to all else that is suppressed within us: suppressed truth, thoughts, ideas, actions, and sounds. The suppressed in us is mostly the "firstborn"——that which arose and evolved in an instant and could have been "born" had it not fallen victim to our fear, censorship, and control (Pharaoh)——become enslaved and maltreated, because it was not expressed and thereby not freed.

However, this is not about jurisprudence or equal rights, guilt or atonement, or a condition to be moaned over in self-pity. It is about understanding and letting "my son go, so that he may serve Me." In this lies the entire message of liberation. The firstborn is HIS, is created in HIS image, is HIS expression, and is to serve HIM. A great challenge——this idea, this call.

If we compare the history of Israel with the philosophy, teachings, and history of other world religions, we may recognize that Israel forever tries to find a home on Earth, to deal with the realities of the world (even though they were lamented), to engage in the world, to settle, instead of shunning, despising, or even denying it as a deceptive place of illusion——as can be observed, for example, in many respects within the Hinduistic tradition. The constant persecutions, the repeated expulsions from nations that had become "home," and the strong inner sense and external reality of homelessness have exacerbated the painful longing for shelter on this Earth.

That's why Israel for me has much to do with our longing for but also willingness to *inherit* the Earth and inhabit it, not as a temporary place, but as a contribution to fulfilling HIS kingdom and being "as in Heaven so on Earth"——Matth.6,10 (and **in** the Earth/root chakra). It was the pain of homelessness that caused the people of Israel's longing for permanent shelter (also in us). But does this longing for permanent shelter not also bring the temptation to put ourselves into captivity? Does not our fierce longing to belong somewhere create our various imprisonments? Perhaps it is our dilemma to desire a "home" at all costs instead *of being conscious of our true home,* whether in Heaven or on Earth and, therefore, feeling home wherever, indigenous, *because we are aware* of our true home, the kingdom of GOD.

With that, the *captivity* in Egypt is of importance. It is written: "Israel sighed because of the bondage, and they cried out; and their cry for help because of their bondage rose up to God. So God heard their groaning; and God remembered His covenant with Abraham, Isaac, and Jacob" (Exod. 2:23,24). When Moses comes before the people in Egypt and speaks of the move, the people at first are very elated. But their own elders react with anger to the consequences when his first talk with Pharaoh leads to the worsening of their living conditions. The longer the realization of their release takes, the more difficult it becomes for them to hear and accept GOD's promise that they will be delivered from the burdens of Egypt. "On account of their despondency and cruel bondage," (Exod. 2:6,9) they cannot develop trust.

Perhaps we, too, could do such a step only in the first exuberance, while——quite astonished——we perceive the possibility of freedom. Yet, the longer we think about it, the more difficult it gets. We do not like to leave our captivity free-willingly. Free-willingly, we do not like to leave the warm barn, even when it stinks, even when it becomes increasingly uncomfortable for us, and even when someone speaks of Heaven and Earth. After all, it could get worse than it already is. That is what we fear, and——being creatively talented——we color the things that we fear enough so that they seem reasonable. Due to this, many people do not wish to truly reflect on their own "imprisonment" or situation.

When we yearn to gain consciousness and clarity, we have to ask, "How did we get into this mess? How is it that, on one hand, we do not recognize our dilemma, and, on the other hand, we also do not recognize divine intervention?" This inner entanglement of Pharaoh and Israel is probably not accessible to us, or we would have to follow the call of our inner Moses expeditiously, get up, and move out! Perhaps we do not recognize Moses, don't hear his voice, do not trust it——or he has not arrived! The inner quality of Moses is, of course, the key; he is the obedient emissary who gathers us and teaches. Perhaps Gurdjieff would have said, "Moses was the auxiliary steward who evolves into the main steward and eventually becomes the master." But before we spend more time with Moses, I would like to take a closer look at the relationship between Israel and Pharaoh.

I am saddened by discovering how little most people know and how little they care to experience who they are and which inner voices they follow. They do not have a clue who or what is currently calling the shots inside, let alone who is actually in charge of the inner house or who is responsible for the inner condition. They are mostly so over-identified with, that is, dominated by, emotional states and thought patterns that they can neither discern nor dislodge from them. They are mostly convinced that the true ruling powers are outside of themselves.

There is some truth to this, but we must recognize that the external can only have power over what has power internally. For just as the people of the biblical story worshiped Pharaoh as god, we, too, worship pharaoh within ourselves and make him our god. Likewise, we also give to those with political or religious authority, our parents, our employers, our partners, and our teachers godly power over us, without seeing in them GOD and HIS PRESENCE IN ACTION and without being able to receive HIM in HIS love and wisdom. And without asking ourselves why we are experiencing certain things and what we are supposed to learn. Such confusion!

We seem to have difficulty discerning between gods and GOD, and do not know how to confront the former. Even if it is against our heart, against our better knowing and conscience, we allow them to determine our actions, thinking, and feelings. We become corruptible and justify our regulated action or non-action by explaining that we cannot do anything else, or that we must howl with the wolves. We tend to nurse a questionable "spiritual view" and see our behavior as wise and loving since we do not wish to offend or hurt anyone. In secret, however, we hope that circumstances will turn miraculously better, or at least not change or get worse. We hang on and follow for we believe that our hands are tied and that there are no other possibilities, while inside we are furious and frustrated by our situation and are constantly busy with scapegoats and boogeymen whom we hold responsible for what we feel.

I remember a man (I hesitate to call him a friend because he is disgruntled with me and unforgiving toward what I have to say) who for years has bemoaned his situation at the university where he teaches. He loves his work but hates the university operations. This can be recognized in all his

142

comments. For years I suggested he leave, as he probably could do his work in a more satisfying way outside of the university. I suggested also that it might be good or sensible to create an alternative teaching institution. Once too often he liked the idea but answered: "Yes, that is true, but one needs a lot of money for that, and competent personnel." I suggested he be willing to lower his standards in the beginning for the sake of his work and purpose and to refrain from immediately wanting to create an equally big and "efficient" machine, only now under his own reign. I never knew whether he truly understood me.

This is how we, like the people of Israel, deplore our trap year after year, do not listen to our Moses, even defend our prisons. We do this on one hand by finagling through, stealing away in cowardice and fear, fearing the consequences of our truth, and on the other hand by not standing with ourselves, acting accordingly, and (unfortunately!) *not fearing* the consequences of that. At the same time, we judge ourselves, our situation and the alleged causers.

Torn between the suppresser on one hand and the suppressed on the other, we jump back and forth. We feel our bondage, but also have answers and explanations for why we have to accept our fate. Pharaoh, mind you, has twisted the truth. He believes himself god and knows where things are heading, what is good and what is right. But of GOD he knows little, and I question that he wishes to know unless he can make use of it in his own game of power (i.e., to speak of feelings, of what is spiritual and what is not, what is worthwhile and what is not, what is God-intended and what is not). Otherwise, all would have consequences for him and his reign, which he values greatly.

As long as we find ourselves in what I may call the pharaoh-state, we will refuse to allow what is deep down in us to come up, get out, and be known. As long as we are in the Israel state, we believe ourselves to be impotent to change anything. Who mediates between us? Who connects and bridges this dichotomy? Where is *our* Moses? Eventually, we all have to consider this question——and better sooner than later.

I would like to come back to the above-mentioned paradox in the biblical story: Moses tries again and again, at the behest of GOD, to soften the heart of Pharaoh. Again and again, Moses speaks to the people, encouraging them to trust GOD and to leave. But the people cannot hear due to too much lamenting and too much fear. And, by GOD, Pharaoh's heart becomes obdurate (imagine!!) while GOD is still sending Moses repeatedly to move Pharaoh to agree.

Moses is like a voice between fronts, and it may look as though he is fighting a losing battle. The situation becomes critical. GOD sets signs. HE demonstrates HIS power one time after another over Egypt. And nothing seems to change. Signs of the OMNIPOTENCE become more severe, for the people cannot be convinced that they will be led and saved——they hesitate, lament, and fear. Finally, the hardened heart of Pharaoh, as difficult as this may sound, becomes rather a blessing to the people. Because of the renewed appearance of plagues, pestilences, epidemics, and devastations that not only hit the Egyptians but also the Israelites, both sides experience a condition of "enough is enough". And slowly, both sides develop willingness for change; in Israel to leave and take upon themselves the risk, in Pharaoh the **necessity** to let the people go. I am amazed seeing this process!

At this time, I would like to call to mind the two triangles in **Divine Manifestation**. We may easily assign them to this relationship as well. For better illustration, they are once more depicted here, somewhat supplemented:

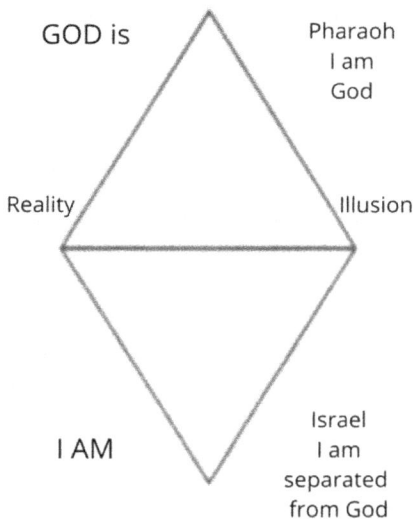

(Figure 10)

As long as we do not feel one with all, we are within the polar perception of being——we experience ourselves as having a spiritual *as well as* an earthly identity. However, on this plane of consciousness, we also encounter reality and truth and are motivated on one hand by love to evolve/grow, and on the other by fallacy and illusion and the suffering caused by them (because we cannot help it). Even though the movement of becoming is still on the polarity plane, this becoming is already full of being, as long as we understand the becoming as an unfolding-into-being.

According to the triangle image above, GOD IS and I AM are reality——the illusion: Pharaoh and Israel. On both sides there is a personal relationship needing a mediator and bridge to reach ONENESS and unity. **In illusion,**

there is an antagonism; in reality, same is attracted to same (light to light). In order to benefit from the story of the exodus from Egypt, we must understand that healing and deliverance from the antagonism is the key to leaving illusion behind. Let us look at that.

In the illusion, I recognize the upper triangle——the "spiritual" identity of man——as Pharaoh (the three upper chakras) and the lower triangle: the earthly identity——as the people of Israel (three lower chakras). As long as they are separated as such and see themselves as separate poles (master and slave), either must remain trapped in their illusionary condition. The upper part (pharaoh) considers itself to be god and is lost in its ego-created "spiritual" identity (better, different, holy). The lower part (Israel) thinks of itself as flesh/blood and separated from God. Pharaoh despises and suppresses the lower part as evil in origin and potentially destructive (for him!), while Israel looks for a home on Earth, feels lonely, suppressed, homeless, abandoned by GOD, and does not know how to overcome its pain.

The lower part also represents the multifaceted divine form-expression on Earth, HIS creative thought manifested. But these multi-faceted expressions are not recognized as such. They are separated and adherent to form; animals are animals, trees are trees, a man is a man, a woman is a woman——form and appearance are more important than the oneness of all BEINGNESS in GOD. A true relationship does not exist. The All-One GOD is not all-one. Our perception obstructs such BEINGNESS. It is not a surprise, then, that divine intervention is required to cause the dissolving of this illusion and belief in separation, *AND* effecting transformation and integration. We, as humans, have needed this divine intervention since the beginning of time during our evolution and were also given it so we would not get lost even deeper——in illusions and fallacies——but would grow in consciousness and better understanding. Prophets, saints and mystics are forerunners witnessing to these interventions.

When Moses asks God what he should call Him, God gives Himself the name I AM THAT I AM (Exod. 3:14). Jesus accomplished in Himself (in my eyes) this transformation and integration process that started a long time ago and became Christ: God became Man——He BECAME and IS. By walking the path and fulfilling all law, Jesus prepared for all of us the path *but did not*

146

take it from us. The Star of David symbolizes the integration and permeation of the One in All and All in One——He is in me, and I am in Him.

Heaven and Earth are one——Jesus came and is to fulfill the law. In Him IT becomes reality. Will we ever fully understand this mystery? Are we willing to walk this path of following Him to which He invites us? Will we respond to the invitation?

I can hardly express how grateful I am that life has familiarized me with the life and history of Jesus so that I am able to look up to Him and have Him as an example of living evidence. How grateful I am to Him that He was willing to walk where no one else I know of had walked before, without any model, which He then became for me by His path, His BEING. However, in the case of our exploration here and for the point in time of our inner conditions of consciousness that I mentioned and that correspond to the story, the divine intervention is Moses.

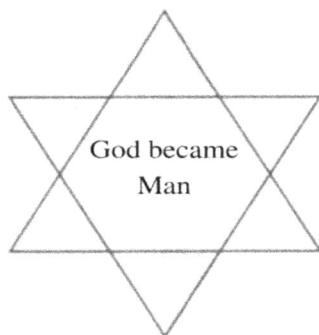

(Figure 11)

Moses

At the beginning of the biblical story, we learn that Moses should have been killed. His death had been a decided matter on the part of Pharaoh, just like the death of all the Israelite sons. But he was miraculously rescued and raised in his own Jewish family as a son and foundling of the *pharaonic family*.

147

The name Moses, given him by the daughter of Pharaoh, means, *I pulled him out of the water*. It is true: he was recovered from the river where his mother had set him out in a basket to save his life. But we can also say: Here is a human being——or a part of us——who was seized from the water, the element of unconsciousness and feelings. That may also mean on one hand to be free of the trials and tribulations of a people that feel homeless and in bondage, and on the other free of the illusions of a self-deified Pharaoh—— someone who is no longer stuck in, has perhaps at least partially overcome those illusions, is more awake, has heard the voice of God, has opened himself to IT, and struggles with obedience.[10] Only such an entity, such inner authority, with quite a chunk of integrity, is adequate to the task of leading us out of captivity and away from the attachments to *our* illusions.

Moses appears to be standing between cultures and is dismayed by the interpersonal lovelessness that he recognizes among his Hebrew brothers as much as between the Egyptians and Israelites. This dismay tempts him to fall into the same lovelessness that he judges, and he murders someone. But when the deed comes to light and he is chased by Pharaoh, he flees to another country.

On a particular day, years later when GOD calls him, Moses is herding sheep. GOD makes Himself known and speaks to him about the fear and suffering of the people of Israel. HE commands Moses to go to Pharaoh and to lead the people out of Egypt, but Moses is not that easily won. He argues back, "Who am I, that I should go to Pharaoh . . ." (Exod. 3:11). He has doubts. What shall he say to the people in Egypt? To Pharaoh? To Israel? "Suppose I go to the Israelites and say to them, 'The God of your fathers has sent me to you,' and they ask me, 'What is his name?' Then what shall I tell them?" (Exod. 3:13). He is not satisfied with GOD's answer. The whole thing seems to scare him, and he comes up with every objection he can think of. Then GOD gives Moses two signs——today we would call them miracles——so that he believes it is GOD he hears.

But even that is not enough. To his objection that he may not find the right words, GOD answers with an especially important promise: *"Now go! I will be with you as you speak, and I will instruct you in what to say"* (Exod. 4:12). But again, this promise does not calm Moses. Finally, the story says,

148

GOD becomes angry and points to Moses' brother to accompany him. "He shall speak for you to the people; and he will be as a mouth for you and you will be as God to him" (Exod. 4:16).

In this duo——with one that hears and receives, another that speaks and expresses——a needed quality of relationship within us is fulfilled. It is an analogy to the feminine and masculine sides of our heart chakra, which as a unity becomes the mediator between Israel and Pharaoh right at a very particular time of our awakening.

Gurdjieff described the "normal" condition of man as that of a drunken loudmouthed coachman who sits in a pub and insists on being the owner and lord of the carriage. Gurdjieff taught his students how important it was in order for gaining consciousness that the coachman recovers his senses, gets up and leaves the pub (no matter how drunk), that he assumes responsibility for the carriage and the horses and learns to listen to what the master, the owner of the carriage, has to say. This picture of the coachman I find particularly suitable for the quality that corresponds to a Moses in us, who also does not know where things will lead and how he can possibly fulfill his task, but who still decides to take the risk and follow obediently.

So, Moses returns to Egypt. As soon as the first difficulties arise, he quarrels with GOD because it is not working the way he thought. I am deeply affected by this struggle with GOD, his questioning, and yet his growing obedience. I am so like him! I asked myself whether I would have been willing to go to Pharaoh repeatedly, to speak and do as I was told, while knowing ahead of time that he would close his heart and not listen. Would I have wanted to lead a people from captivity that do not want to leave despite the great suffering and obvious hardships and that later would reproach me as soon as there were difficulties to overcome? (Now, years later after I wrote this, I have to admit I tried and believe I failed).

To some degree I can find such obedience in me, but only rudimentary, since I throw in the towel in much less critical situations, get angry, resist, and look for emergency exits. I have learned much, though, by applying obedience. Moses slowly matured in me to increasingly new phases, new awareness levels. I, too, kept going to the hungry child and the palace dweller (see

149

Shack and Palace——how all this interrelates becomes clear to me only now). But I had misunderstood so much, had my "earphones" on, had mixed things up. The Moses of our story keeps going and going again: he is the perfect tool for demonstrating to Israel, as well as to Pharaoh, the Omnipotence of God. He eventually feels committed to God and the task. I, too, am longing to struggle through my own patterns and mistaken perceptions——to let my passion and Love be fulfilled in and to God's glory.

Moses speaks to God about his dilemma, and God says: "I am the LORD; and I appeared to Abraham, Isaac, and Jacob, as God Almighty, but by my name, LORD, I did not make myself known to them (JAHWE)" (Exod. 6:3). Had not God said to Moses at the time he called him: "I AM THAT I AM. Thus shalt thou say I AM has sent me" (Exod. 3:14)? What an assertion! What a tremendous message to Israel! Actually, to anyone! In that message there is so much to ponder for us as well!

Which task does Moses have in the human evolution? The external Moses as much as the inner Moses. And which task is his to fulfill within us? What is his message?

There seem to be parts existing in us to whom GOD is unknown, to whom His name has not been revealed. In the chapter *The Human Dilemma,* I speak of the forlornness that is stuck in our root chakras, the earthliest and most deeply "fallen" manifestation in us.

Is it possible that the exodus from Egypt may be just as current now as it was then——that today this exodus may be about our own inner bondage, especially being *earthbound* in our lower chakras? Is it possible this is about the chakras being opened, involved, and integrated, instead of being "overcome" in the sense of being disowned? It is certainly about our misunderstandings and our question, whether we are at home: on Earth or in Heaven. Is it possible that we, too, have first to become aware of an UNFOLDING GOD in us? May perhaps the unfolding life and our unfolding consciousness be the UNFOLDING GOD?——the unfolding presence of HIM who then IS? What is CHRIST in us? Is it GOD-BECAME-MAN, the accomplished journey, the end of any and every path? A place? Thus, many questions arise.

How is it possible not to fall into Pharaoh's old trap and consider ourselves as god and in charge of our lives? From the esoteric traditions, we learn that this was not only a problem in Egypt, but already in Atlantis——man repeatedly forgot that GOD IS and there is no other God. We are just as in danger today, as ever, to misunderstand. We still believe we have to "make it", to fix it ourselves and believe *we can* make ourselves spiritual and conscious. We still believe that by collecting knowledge we know something. We believe ourselves righteous while only desiring to create our own self-righteousness.

We also suffer from a paradox: We are called to let GOD express HIMSELF through us in word and action and to become the living word, while at the same time not to believe that *we* are doing everything ourselves. Who is "we" in this case? We are so tempted to act when we ought to stand still——or to procrastinate in censorship and judgment when we *ought to go or do*. We do not trust that GOD leads us out of our fallacies. We do not trust that if we ask Him and listen to Him, He will respond. We do not believe that we can relentlessly depend and rest on HIS promises given through the ages. But we can, *we must, rely* on His eternal pledge to never forsake us! Do you have any idea what this may mean?

The history of the people of Israel during the exodus from Egypt and the time thereafter extends over many pages in the Old Testament. When I continued reading, I was affected by how unwilling, how unconscious, and how closed-minded the people were towards their helpers——how tenaciously they held onto their thinking, their fears, and their need for security. The challenges to be met did not end, nor did the people's vacillation in their relationship to the ALL-ONE GOD. They bemoaned their situation, scuttled about, and continued to defy and ignore the messages and signs given by GOD.

The first commandments were not enough; more and more rules and laws were issued, and everything seemed to have to be dictated, even the details. Repeated hardships and distress continued, and so did pestilences and endangerment of life. Again and again, GOD speaks through Moses and others to HIS people, and the people remember the GOD that brought them out of Egypt, only to forget quickly again looking for something else, for something material and more physically visible and tangible, more promptly

151

convincing, and seemingly giving more security. Fears were many, the confusion was big, and the journey was long.

Our human dilemma is well-depicted in this biblical history. Just as with Israel in Egypt, I recognize our own bondage in thought patterns (solar plexus chakra), in feelings (second chakra), and in our longing, seeking, and homesickness (root chakra). It is necessary for us to open the doors by which we keep life captive and let it come out. Is there something in you that will assist you to do that? One "I" that is willing to assume this task, which prays and listens for GOD's words? If not, look for it, find it!

Our fear is as immense as that of the Israelites, and our "journey", too, seems long. But does any one of us have a true alternative? We may need to consider how it might be possible to stop continuing the circuit of repeating history. When will we as humanity be willing to solely worship the ALL-ONE, to let Him fulfill His Plan for Earth, also on and in us? When will we stop our judgments and begin to live in love, abundance and cooperation instead of lovelessness, sadness, addiction, lack, captivity, narrow-mindedness, self-aggrandizement, hypocrisy, and delusional grandeur? When?

In the book of Deuteronomy, GOD speaks again to Israel, and it would be good for us to hear as well.

When all these blessings and curses

I have set before you come on you

and you take them to heart

wherever the LORD your God

disperses you among the nations,

and when you and your children

return to the LORD your God

and obey him with all your heart

152

and with all your soul

according to everything

I command you today,

then the LORD your God

will restore your fortunes

and have compassion on you

and gather you again

from all the nations

where he scattered you.

. . .

The LORD your God will circumcise your hearts

and the hearts of your descendants,

so that you may love him with all your heart

and with all your soul, and live.

…

Now what I am commanding you today

is not too difficult for you

or beyond your reach.

It is not up in Heaven,

so that you have to ask,

Who will ascend into Heaven to get it

and proclaim it to us so we may obey it?"

Nor is it beyond the sea, so that you have to ask,

"Who will cross the sea to get it

and proclaim it to us so we may obey it?"

No, the word is very near you;

it is in your mouth and in your heart

so you may obey it (Deut. 30:1,ff)

These words move me deeply. I hear them as an offer, as a promise. It is, however, not a promise of a life depicted in some romantic Hollywood films in which all our whims and fancies are fulfilled. No, our heart being "circumcised," our illusions destroyed, is a very painful experience which hardly any of us is willing to take on without resistance.

That is *why* I share my own struggles, my own overcoming. Today I rejoice over the pledge that my captivity will be reversed, that I am gathered from all my distractions and forlornness. I feel relief that "Egypt" will end. I am willing to go, to love GOD with all my heart, my soul, and mind, and love my neighbor as myself. *I will guard the Word in my mouth and in my heart like the apple of my eye, and act IT!*
Do you hear and understand? Do you know what it means that the Word is intimately with you? That it dwells in your mouth and heart, so that you do it? How much would I love to hear your answer!

In the beginning was the Word,

and the Word was with GOD,

and the Word was GOD.

154

He was with GOD in the beginning.

Through Him all things were made;

without Him nothing was made

that has been made.

In Him was life, and that life

was the light of all mankind.

The light shines in the darkness,

and the darkness has not comprehended it (John 1:1–5).

"When Israel was in Egypt Land . . . let my people go! Go down Moses, go down to Egypt Land!" I had heard myself called long ago and still had not gotten it. I went to the enslaved, the imprisoned, and the sick, to "Israel." I recognized their dilemma and listened to the lamentations. Their suffering induced me to want to help them, to lead them out of their captivity - without realizing their unwillingness to feel the fear that kept them there, without considering their need for security, however false that security was——and last, but not least, *without having any awareness of my own condition*.

Not seeing their own fear or feeling it——the same as I——they neither wished to have their attention drawn to it nor to be forced to feel it. Instead, they defended their condition by blaming God and the world (and people, and circumstances), and held them responsible for their fate, their sickness, their crises, and their dead ends.

Like Israel, people even today continue their laments while hoping that something or someone will free them, heal them. This constant lamenting and the concurrent refusal to get up and walk, to take up the cross of the journey, keep them in "Egypt," in institutions, in hospitals, in the waiting rooms of doctors and therapists, in work places, and in marriages and relationships that all speak of the same: of constriction and dependency, of betrayal, of the prostitution of heart and essence, of the crucifixion of the living GOD, of the self-justification of fear, weakness, constraints, needs, and of the coziness gained by surviving in rigidity and comfortable numbness.

I suffered and, concurrently, it made me very angry. I felt impotent and helpless vis-à-vis all these misunderstandings and what I considered follies——angry also towards many individuals' insistence to stay where they were, to keep their "jails" even *after* they had taken small, initial steps toward freedom and had gotten a whiff of its fragrance. *I kept returning to the same stubborn belief that I had to become a better therapist.* I looked for ways and means for an exodus for "Israel," because I believed I heard in their complaints, cries, and laments the wish for healing and liberation.

This is how I betrayed myself and them: I began to sit in front of their jail doors and offered consolations. I began to adorn their jails and make them bearable (I had done the same to my own jail so I could remain there). Their burden became lighter; they did not feel it as much or as deeply as before, and they felt loved. They even healed to a degree and loved me for what I brought into their jails, longed for **my presence** and to be near me. But when I was not there, the jails returned to what they had been before: the languor a comfortable blanket, self-justifications nursed——and decisions were retracted.

Only a few recognized me as external to their jail and realized that they would only understand and internalize once they **left** their own jails. Fewer yet took the trouble to actually leave their jails and walk into life. Only one or two risked overcoming their fear by continuing to walk out of "Egypt" and to "follow," whatever that meant to them. And I, finally, began to see my own jail, namely their jails.

What had made me stay there, and what had hurt so deeply when someone chose not to be free? I had not recognized Pharaoh, had totally ignored him, who profited from my own meandering, who whispered that I was "needed." It was he who retained his power by the prisoners remaining prisoners, sacrificing their freedom for their perception of security; he who used people's longing for contentedness, mislead them into misunderstanding their numbness as comfort; he who appeared to me as the people's longing for knowledge, as someone who could describe people's hunger and the feelings of being bound; he who disliked me when I began to reject what made the prison comfortable.

I begin to understand and to regret that I played into Pharaoh's hands by easing the intolerableness of the prisons. I become aware that only someone who already stands outside his prison door and whose fear of being stuck in jail with its lifeless numbness has grown greater than the fear of journeying into the unknown and into freedom. After all, this freedom is not any utopia, but truth and reality of which a prisoner may dream or imagine. But it will not be experienceable.

Lucifer comes to mind, the fallen angel and lord of the world who declared to fight GOD, who called himself God and whose pride separated him from GOD. I see a connection between him and the pharaonic quality that we study here. But I had not recognized, and had definitely underestimated, the total extent of Pharaoh's strategies and striving for power.

I feel embarrassed that I fell for it. I am embarrassed by my arrogance and that I did not turn and walk away sooner. I am embarrassed that for such a long time I considered my family's "love" and the comfort of some worldly lap more important than my salvation in GOD and HIS LIBERATION within me. I am embarrassed that I kept landing at the prisons I saw in others, worried about "Israel"——and the lovelessness I eventually recognized in not confronting Pharaoh in me. I know the time has come to stand up to him, presenting the living Word, to refuse tenaciously and convincingly any adoration Pharaoh may desire——to worship solely and without constraint GOD and CHRIST within me and within every being. I feel freshly called: "Come!"

I hear and go to the prisons and call out: "Come!"

Let the one who is thirsty come

and let the one who wishes

157

take the gift of water of life

for free (Rev. 22:17).

With daily renewed commitment I will follow this call and tend HIS sheep:

The one who conquers

will have this heritage,

and I will be his God

and he will be my son (Rev. 21:7).

"For the law was given through Moses; grace and truth became through Jesus Christ" (John 1:17).

QUESTIONS FOR CONTEMPLATION

- Do you recognize that inner conflict between the one who knows everything better (or believes so) and the one whose views, perceptions, and intuitions are constantly undermined and controlled?
- Are you willing to leave behind the seeming security of "Egypt" and enter the desert? Are you aware that life itself is at your side should you so decide?
- What is your personal "Egypt"?
- Which task does Moses have in the human evolution? And which task is his to fulfill in us? What is his message?

The story

After signing all the papers, she leaned back. For a brief moment she withdrew from her surroundings, the business-like conference room of the realtor's office, the professional advice that she felt she needed, and the friends around her who were sharing in this "historic" event. Had she really signed? She could hardly believe it. A memory of something that had happened eight years ago, when it all began, flashed into her mind.

She had left her apartment to do some errands and met a friend in the street whom she had not seen for a long time. He asked her how she was because he had heard that she had quit her job and had been unemployed for several months. Then, just like she herself and many others before him had done, he asked her what she was going to do. She had been feeling increasingly lost each time this question was asked and now had no more words. This not knowing left her feeling empty.

Suddenly, with a feeling of standing beside herself she heard these words coming from her mouth: "I want to build a healing temple. It will be a holy place where people live together and contribute to the healing of others, where people can come in order to heal and from where people will go out into the world." She was not able to give him any details for she was as surprised as he; the words had been clear and convincing and have stayed with her ever since.

The years that followed have been marked by intense changes within herself and in her life. She began to see and hear things that most people could not, and which frightened many of them. However, she knew she was treading a path from which there was no return. Her heart was filled with a deep longing for GOD and a desire to heal and become whole. In the years since there have been many encounters with interesting people and experiences that have reminded her of that special moment in the past and supported the realization of what she called "the Idea". She met people who seemed to be one with "the Idea" and also felt called to participate in its realization. But when it came to

159

taking action, they all withdrew. Fears appeared and conflicts seemed insurmountable. The major problem was the required commitment to walk the path fully and completely, to surrender totally and relentlessly to the high intent, which "the Idea" implied. It appeared to her as though she was the only one fully committed. At least this is what she came to believe. She asked herself over and over if she had done anything wrong or had misunderstood something; she felt the longing in everyone's heart, yet none had been willing to act or pay the price. She felt "the Idea" taking up so much space in her that she could hardly bear the forcefulness of its desire for realization. There was also a feeling of urgency, necessity, a lack of time. But whenever she pushed the issue or wanted to accelerate its coming into being, she failed and remained frustrated.

Finally, she had to admit to herself that, although she had access to cosmic will and desire, her greatest dilemma was her inability to bring this knowledge into the time and space of earthly life. She had forgotten and overlooked that this, too, had to be left to the Source, that Divine Will also governed space and time. It began to dawn on her that her concept of having to take "the Idea" and its realization into her own hands was a misunderstanding and had created a tremendous fear in her. She, therefore, felt the need to continually look for someone who – hopefully – would be willing to walk with her. She understood, even though it was not in her hands, that she would still have to walk and act alone. And while the idea rested in her heart, nurturing and nourishing itself in Love like a growing child, she slowly continued to walk awkwardly between great fear and increasing faith and trust.

Then she bought the house. She had felt this to be a clear and unquestionable calling and followed it with diligent obedience. It had seemed the smaller step, yet it already contained the seed of "the Idea". Here, too, her fear was still great. But when she witnessed how Divine Will manifested and guided the heart of man in his love for HIM, she experienced happily and with awe that her faith and trust increased. A joyfulness unfamiliar to her entered her heart.

People came to the house and left again. They learned and healed, experienced their resistances and their fears, raged against God (or what they thought IT was), man, and her; and many felt their prison walls tumble down. According to the Voice, which began to accompany her, the house was but the eye of a needle, a narrow doorway through which she and many would pass. The community of healers for the healing temple was being gathered and the people would be led to her.

All of this brought her ever closer to her deepest fears and the precipices of her being. Her trust and her love were tested and challenged on many levels. Increasingly, she felt the judgments and underlying anxieties of people who had once been close to her. She felt the many expectations projected onto her as the one who is walking ahead on the path, and she felt more alone than ever before. Through her growing willingness to accept this aloneness she learned to depend more and more on divine guidance and providence, practicing surrendering all control over her life, income, security. Despite her anxieties and her aloneness, she felt more alive than ever.

Then, in the first days of 1994 she heard the Voice: LOOK FOR LAND!

So, she consulted with friends and that old feeling of urgency returned to her heart. Again, it was shared by those who listened to her; it corresponded with their own longing. But how to proceed? Whenever she asked the question of where to look, she heard: MONTANA:

This was astonishing to both herself and others; her American friends nourished her doubts and discouraged her from looking for land in this northern state. "Montana is cold", they said, "and uncharitable; no one in his right mind would go there". But the Voice was firm and supportive: HOW DO YOU KNOW IT WILL STAY THAT WAY?

While she was submerged in inner turmoil her 85-year-old father telephoned from Germany, only his second phone call since she had moved to the "foreign" world. Excitedly, among other things, he cried out: "Look for land, child!" Those few words gave new nourishment to her calling. Now, however, she felt pushed and became still more aware of her lingering fear: the fear of having to go there by herself, to carry

161

the decision alone, to take the financial risk, and to bear all the consequences. In her distress she turned inward and entered her place of silence. There the Voice met her and spoke the following words:

THE NEW PLACE IS TO MY GLORY AND TO MY GLORY ALONE. IT IS NOT A PLACE TO HIDE FROM FEAR; NOR IS IT A PLACE TO CHASE AFTER ONE'S OWN DREAMS. IT IS NO PLACE TO FEATHER ONE'S NEST. IT IS A PLACE TO – OUT OF LOVE FOR ME – OFFER BACK TO ME ALL THAT WAS GIVEN YOU.

She wrote down these words, feeling both her strong love for GOD and being loved in return. Her fear continued to struggle with her love, and doubts came and went. She began to find out about Montana, checking out material from the library, reading books, and procrastinating as long as she could. Finally, after months of fiddling and hesitation, she planned her trip. Four friends went with her; they came from all directions——Austria, Ohio, and Georgia——and with different motivations and intents.

BILLINGS, the Voice had said when she asked where to fly. So, they all met in Billings, Montana. The first three days they drove many miles looking at different lots of land offered by several realtors. She did not really know what she was looking for, and she was not even able to say how large or small the land should be. Should there be fields near the mountains? Irrigated land? Land with a stream? She had no notion of the size of an acre, nor did she know what to concern herself with when buying land. However, during the hours that they spent together things became clearer for both her and the others.

Finally, she arranged for a meeting with a realtor who offered to show three larger properties. Prior to getting into the car the realtor asked her what exactly she was looking for. She told her of her experiences, shared the message of the Voice and said she did not really know herself. She was surprised to find the realtor very receptive to this lack of clarity. Then they drove off, her friends following them in another car. On their way to the first property the realtor said:

162

"I will not show you the first two properties that I had in mind. I have a feeling I should take you straight to the valley."

They drove through the beautiful countryside and were deeply impressed by the vastness of heaven and earth that unfolded before their eyes. They had heard that Montana is the fourth largest state in America with only nine hundred thousand inhabitants! With this in mind it was not surprising to see herds of deer in peaceful coexistence with cows grazing on pastures or herds of antelopes running across the road and leaping over fences.

After the small town of Roundup, about one hour's drive from Billings, they left the main road and turned into a gravel road that eventually became a dirt track (field road). After driving through the first valley, she thought maybe that was it. No. Another valley unfolded before her eyes and then still another one. "Here", the realtor finally said. Not only did this land include a valley with large pastures, but there were also hills topped with broad fields, forested slopes, and woodland paths leading through narrow ravines to hidden corners. There was no house.

By now they had all squeezed into the realtor's four-wheel drive SUV. At one of the two springs they came across they left the car. Honoring her desire to be alone for a few minutes she followed a hidden path that led around a hill. Then she heard the Voice again: THIS IS IT!

Her eyes filled with tears. Great relief came over her, as though she had arrived after a long and tiring journey. No more searching and worrying about it, she thought. But new worries appeared: "Should I test the soil and water?" she asked and saw and felt the loving laughter of the universe. What for? Passing before her eyes like a soft breeze she saw a picture of Findhorn (Scotland) and remembered all the guidance that had been bestowed on its founders. Now her own laughter drove away her worries. She went back to the others and told the realtor: "This is the land. I will buy it." Everybody had looked at her as though she had lost her mind, and all she had been able to say was: "It's not me!"

While driving around they had looked for the boundaries of this wonderful land, and for the fences marking them, but in vain. She finally

163

asked the realtor: "Do you know where this land ends?" The realtor looked at her with a twinkle in her eyes: "Do you want to know the truth?"

"Yes"

"No, I don't know where it ends!" They looked at each other and burst out laughing. Everyone was filled with a deep and joyful excitement. Only H. spoke of her fears facing the big decision she felt approaching. She lives in Austria and for quite some time she had had a deep knowing that she would "have" to move to Montana, long before the search for land had started.

Then questions came up regarding the details of the sale. "The current owner", the realtor informed her, "is a difficult man. He has never wavered on the price even though the land value has increased. However, he insists on receiving the two hundred sixty thousand dollars up front——no financing. None of the potential buyers have been able to come up with the money." "I don't have the money either", she told her, "But I still have to buy it".

That evening in the hotel her fears returned. She prayed and renewed her commitment but asked for yet another sign to strengthen her faith. Still, she hardly knew how to respond when the realtor called her the following morning to tell her that a miracle had happened. The owner had changed the terms: only half the money up front at a date to be determined and the balance over five years. "What did you do?" the realtor asked her, and she told her about her shaky courage and her prayer.

After they ended their conversation, a great joyfulness entered her heart. She remembered when she had bought the house: she had only had the courage to buy it because the owner had, as it turned out prematurely, agreed to let her pay half of the requested amount, but a few weeks later had changed her mind and asked for the full amount. With great humor the universe had presented her with this kind of déjà vu experience. She felt GOD had left her naked in her lack of trust, but at the same time she also felt recognized, understood, and loved. She now felt the courage to

164

sign the papers. She had only to wait for the check to be mailed to her since she had gone on this trip with neither money nor her checkbook.

The check for the down payment of two thousand dollars came special delivery. It had been mailed with a greeting card made by W., showing a photograph of Mother Mary with roses around her head, taken in the garden of the house. Under the photo, W. had written: FAITH and TRUST. 'My courage is also not my courage', she thought while reading these encouraging words. She began to hear, over and over again, the melody of a song whose lyrics she did not remember. She decided she would look up the song when she returned home.

Then she came back from her reverie, leaned forward, handed over the check and shook hands with the realtor who congratulated her on buying the land and called her a "land baron". Everything seemed like a dream, whose outcome unknown to anyone and whose design is in the hands of the ONE Almighty.

The others started talking about the land. Ideas, wishes, suggestions, possibilities, and visions were exchanged and pondered. But Truth stayed: THE NEW PLACE IS ONLY TO MY GLORY AND TO MY GLORY ALONE, with the addition: IT IS MY LAND AND MY PLAN. She herself felt called back from an all too independent leap ahead. A new understanding formed in her: GOD was in the process of reclaiming the land that once was HIS, free land being freed again. She felt a deep sacred appreciation and love.

Two of her friends left the next day. She and the two others went to the bank to open an account. The bank assistant asked whether she wanted to give the account a name. She asked and heard: LIVING SPRING, and so it was called.

Here my story ends for the moment. It is the story of only a few days in my life, but it is also the story of my life. When I came back from Montana, I looked up the words for the song whose lyrics had escaped me. I found them in the song sheets from Taizé[7]

Ubi caritas	Where Love
Et amor	and Mercy dwell
Ubi caritas	there is God
Deus ibi est	

The story and the conceptual ideas were written in 1994. Of course, the story continued: I was not able to buy the land that year and lost the earnest money deposit. I myself got lost in my own agendas and had to be called back on track more than once. I had to learn patience and a deep grasp of it not being *my* plan. Every year, however, I came to Montana to walk the land and ask whether I was still to buy it. This was confirmed. I asked the owner that he please wait until the finances came together. But in 1997 the land was sold to someone else. Still, I was told to be patient as this was the land for the purpose. In 1999 the land came back on the market and since the new owner had a big business in mind, it took some months to negotiate an acceptable price: In August of 2000 I bought the land for LIVING SPRING at the 1994 price. Everything, all I had and all I am, was asked of me. There are no words to describe the joy I experienced. The universe itself danced and sang, beautiful wordless choral music together with the sound of drumming filled my ears. A celebration!

Some friends built me a one-room cabin in fall of 2000, which made it possible for me to live on the land. Much of the first year I spent in seclusion; a simple life without running water (there is a good well), without electricity and an entire year without a phone.

Slowly, and as I was told it would happen, people are coming (are led) to the land. Some seeking help for healing, others are interested in joining. The area of service for the community was given by the Voice: MY CHILDREN. At first, I was uncertain what „my children „meant. Were they physical children in small bodies, or God's children in adult bodies? Today I know: It is about HIS children in small *and* adult bodies. Those in adult bodies need to assist

166

the small-bodied ones and in doing so facilitate their own healing, the bringing forth of the GOD CHILD in all.

The community has still not formed, as commitment stagnated. But it will have to be self-sufficient and as far as possible independent of commercial energy and supply. A place of sanity and health. We will, however, not lead a secluded life; what is gained here will have to overflow into the world: attitude, expertise, and service.

When some years ago I had asked: "Why Roundup?" I was told: IT USED TO BE FOR CATTLE; NOW IT IS FOR PEOPLE. So be it, then.

PART II

Some Basics

Vision vs. Imagination

To discern between vision and imagination is not an easy endeavor, not only in uninitiated circles, but also in what at one time I might have called the circle of initiates. In this I count the entire spectrum of New Age organizers and programs. Rarely have I encountered anyone who had learned to differentiate his or her own fantasy and creatively effective imagination from the complex subtle energies of the visionary experience. Even more rarely did I find this among those who traveled all across the country and taught these things. To speak of this here is, for me, therefore of special concern. I feel the urgency of a careful schooling to handle these psychic openings and energies responsibly. I am also concerned about the mammoth events of American "New-Age Missionaries" not only in the US, but also in Germany, who do not exercise the necessary care and thus create and foster considerable confusion through sciolism and their methods to enthuse people——similar to cheerleading on football fields——and by their own still smoldering illusions. As is often the case, here, too, the well-being of people seems to come after the interest in professional fame, personal recognition, and financial success. This saddens but also angers me.

There is another point I wish to make. Many people have difficulties with the continuously evolving appearance of percipience and extrasensory perception. With growing consciousness and the opening of the chakras associated therewith, many more of us will become clairvoyant, supersensible, and develop preternatural hearing as well. Often those individuals doubt their experience and believe they are deceiving themselves, or they run the risk of considering visionary experiences as overloaded fantasies or even pathological symptoms, which sometimes is definitely true. That is why it is necessary that we learn to discern and deal with these things——not only for ourselves, but also for others in our surroundings who, perhaps due to lack of understanding, end up in psychiatric care. There, however, you rarely find anyone that is competent to discern extrasensory perception from hallucinations and projections. But let me get to the point.

Imagination and vision are like day and night——male (Yang – visible) and female (Yin – in the shadow). Both have merit but should not be confused. This necessitates that we familiarize ourselves with how they affect our lives, operate, and interact.

Imagination

Imagination is of the masculine——it is (our own) creative expression called forth by the collaboration of many factors. The masculine energy pattern is expression per se. It means exhaling, acting, and activity, and has nothing to do with a man or being male, as both men and women, that is, all human beings, are essentially both masculine and feminine. To this collaboration belong fantasy, our creative capabilities and skills, artistic ideas, our desires, and our longing for change and creation (divine spark) that formulate into a creative expression. Through imagination we are, for example, in a position to develop advertising flyers, draw plans for a new house, furnish a room, or implement other ideas.

Also, in our imagination our wishful thinking appears——in answer to our repressed suffering and lack of trust. Thus, we are tempted to imagine a different world than the one we live in and experience. Many children enter this world of fantasy to make their being on Earth bearable. They dream up ——just to name an example——a new mother and father and imagine them to behave very differently towards them than their actual parents. You even may have been one of these children and concocted a mystical, "rescuing" world, in order to *survive*. But by that you did not learn to live, did you? Here, also, the lone adult appears who tries to think positively and imagines a "beloved" being coming to her/his rescue with flowers in hand, or riding on a horse as a prince/princess, ending up making love. Imagination knows no boundaries.

There are a number of much sought after, one could say famous, New Age programs that advise us to use our mental capacity and potential for such applications. They recommend methods of "protection" for example, sending beings "into the light" (which often *only* means to send them packing, but "spiritually"), and advise us to disassociate and separate from all and everything of which we are afraid or that is uncomfortable. They propagandize that we can make use of our minds to create our own reality in order to become rich, prosperous, happy, and successful. This is reduced mainly to material goods and money, but also includes partnerships and health. It is suggested to us that we use the mind to manifest our desirous addictions because, it is said, the wealth of God's kingdom is available and ours to take.

Truth is thus unconsciously twisted and abused. Of course, the mind is the creative force; and of course, we are able to create and are responsible for what we create and manifest in our lives. But we have to become aware of how and for what purpose we use it in thoughts, actions, or non-actions! We have to become aware that our mind *already* created what we are stuck in! Only the uncovering of our fallacy and the *gleaming* truth beyond it will change our reality and will free us. Life is not about this kind of homemade success or self-created happiness. It is about: "Seek ye first the kingdom of God and His righteousness, and all these things will be added to you" (Matt. 6:33). It does not say just take everything you want.

How then *can* we use imagination? How can it serve? In order to answer this question, I have to go a bit afield. Part of imagination, aside from what has been said above, is also the inner pictures that——due to *your* imaginary world and *your* inner condition——can appear before your inner eyes. These are the pictures that reflect your conscious thoughts and perceptions.

If I say, for example, "Close your eyes and look inside at your dad," you will see him as you picture him and not how he actually was/is or as someone else would perhaps "picture" him. It is *your* world that shows itself thus, not a universal one; it is your personal, current truth. These inner pictures are important and valuable if you use them to become aware of your preferences and antipathies, your prejudices and conflicts, and to make room for love and compassion. Becoming aware opens the possibility of experiencing imagination for your own growth, unfolding, and liberation from illusions and addictions.

Thus, imagination has its place on the spiritual journey as long as it is not being used to escape circumstances and conditions. This may become clearer after I have said more about the quality of the visionary. Imagination is the necessary gift that reconciles us with vision and assists in fulfilling it. That is why the ability to interpret and understand the vision is an important aspect of imagination. It only becomes useless and sometimes dangerous when we *interpret* the given vision according to our own images, wishes and illusions. I will come back to this later.

Vision

Vision is of the feminine. Similar to imagination, it is formed and provided often——but not only——due to our longing for change, relief, and deliverance. Often it is given for the selfless purpose of serving. As a major difference from imagination, it contains the element of surprise, of the unexpected, and, therefore, it is hardly ever equal to our ideas and wishes. And yet it comes to meet us in a way we would never experience if we sought to self-gratify our own needs. Vision arrives from another, higher, more encompassing, and complex order to which most of us have no direct or continuous access——and is consistent with it. It is, therefore, ensouled by a quality of perfection and completeness; it is the ultimate response, clarity, and veracity that we, in our limited thinking, would never be able to create.

Vision can only be received, not "made." It is not a sign of know-how or religiousness and is independent of the intelligence quotient or education of the receiver. It is received by kings and paupers, atheists, and mystics alike. It can appear to the illiterate as well as to the intellectual, to the spiritually experienced and inexperienced, to the child and the adult. It could reach a heartless persecutor and murderer like Saul of Tarsus just as easily as Hildegard von Bingen, nun and abbess. It is of the Spirit that blows where it wills.

Imagination and vision are complementary, as imagination serves vision and assists in its implementation——never the other way around. Imagination, though divinely granted, is not (yet) resting on a higher spiritual plane or consciousness. It has created most of what humanity suffers from today—— internally as well as externally. Our temptation to continue thus will not be hindered by a new age with its evolving consciousness for our divine essence. On the contrary, the new age asks us to be more vigilant for this danger and to command the powers within with more responsibility and respect. That requires practice. How one may learn to distinguish Imagination from Vision I would like to show by two examples.

First example (a small exercise)

Imagine a house. You can see the house, and I ask you to enter it. Look around you and find a hallway with doors. There is one interior door behind which you will find an empty room. Open the door. This room is completely available for you to furnish. You have ideas——things, colors——that you favor, and their presence will please you. So, you design your room in your fantasy: paint the walls, put furniture in, perhaps add a carpet, hang up pictures, move a window somewhere else, make the room larger, etc. It looks like a vision, but it is your imagination that created the room in accordance with your desires.

Now leave this room and cross the hallway. There is another door that you will open, but before you do, you must know this room is *not* empty. Become also aware of your feelings before you face the unexpected After you open the door and look across the threshold, you may see some things in there, or at first, only darkness. If you cannot see anything but darkness, wait until your eyes have grown accustomed to the darkness (you know what happens when you do that, right?), and then look at what is revealed. What you see now corresponds already to the visionary level. You have not created it. It

172

has created itself and is there to tell you something. You may consider one or two things in that room. Perhaps you know them. Perhaps you know where they were before, or in whose possession, or what they remind you of, etc. Do not do the entire room unless you have assistance and a lot of time.

Second example

Imagine you are dreaming——a lion/a violent man follows you. You would never have created this dream, because you are afraid of lions and violent men and would not want to meet or be persecuted by either. The pictures appeared, and you were unable to ward them off. This would also be an experience that touches the visionary level. It comes to you and affects you without you having expected it.

Among the many kinds of dreams we have, there are also those that are called lucid, meaning you are aware that you are dreaming. In a lucid dream, you will find it possible to let the lion disappear or you can kill it. Imagination is at work here. If you consider it a vision, however, then you would open yourself up to wondering why the lion (or the violent man) is appearing at this point in time——because it had to, no matter how scary it is——and you would try to get to know the lion by refraining from running from its appearance, asking and allowing the truth behind it to surprise you

In summary, here once again are the discernible and respective aspects of imagination and vision:

Imagination	Vision
Will/wanting	Receiving
Wishes created by a sense of lack	Waiting
and neediness	Experiencing creation
Control over ways and means	Hear and see with empty mind
to fulfill the lack	without imagining
One's own artistic creation	Truth about desires to be fulfilled or not
Manipulation	Allowing to be given to
Breathing out	Breathing in
Doing	Inactivity
What one saw once and liked	Surprise
or disliked	Being part of an integral whole
Knowing what would be "good"	Expecting without thinking
Creative act – doing	Creative act – receiving
Action	not-knowing, not-planning, not-doing
Individual expression (separate I)	Being at the mercy of
Image (illusory)	Dream as experience
Interpretation and drawing conclusions	Being under authority
I pollinate	I am pollinated

174

Dream as idea	Being changed
Wielding power	Being subjected to

These two energy patterns appear to be two different poles keeping each other in balance. In an integrated, conscious, and competent use, this is true. But unfortunately, most people cannot even discern between them, much less deal with them consciously. When you study the aspects of imagination, you will discern differences between those that are unbiased and not filled with your want and those that are. Be vigilant about such imprints for they are part of our individual (separate) will, the mechanisms that let us separate and consequently let us believe in and feel being separated. They are part of addiction, our forlornness, and fallacies.

You may have realized by now that imagination is an *active* position, either follows its own idea or takes from the visionary. In turn it draws conclusions as to how visions are to be implemented/applied. Your self-consciousness plays a big part in this, and so does what you think is "you." For we tend to consider ourselves to be makers (bosses) and experts. Yet the *passive* position corresponds more with the visionary, whereby the word "passive" does not equal to mean enduring everything but is rather an expecting and wakeful alertness that allows us to engage with what we do not control. It is imperative that we practice this expecting and wakeful alertness.

Why do I emphasize this so much? An answer may be a message that was given to our community during a morning meditation.

"HOW DARE YOU BOAST ABOUT YOUR ACTIONS? WHY IS IT YOU SEEK FAME AND RECOGNITION? IS IT NOT I WHO GAVE YOU THE IDEA? IS IT NOT I WHO GAVE YOU STRENGTH TO IMPLEMENT IT?"

The Chakras

The term "chakra"——meaning wheel——appears in the oldest texts of the Vedas (1500 BC to 500 AD) and Upanishads (Hindu teachings) and can also be found in Buddhism; it belongs to all Eastern religious traditions. Though it means "wheel," we in the West come closest to its meaning with "window of the soul." For the chakras are the connection points of the soul with its temple, the body. More simply said: By way of the chakras, the soul has access and expresses itself to the external world, but by the way of the chakras, it is also being impressed upon. This happens via and through the various ethereal bodies, upon which I will expand a bit later.

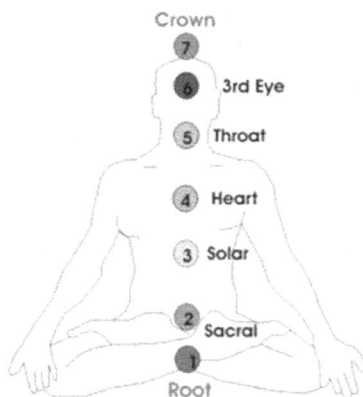

(Figure 12)

The chakras open to the front of the body but have their connection points to the source/soul in the spine and work through the endocrine gland system corresponding to its glands (see table following). They are separated in name only. In truth, they are interactive areas of varying energy density that are under the control of the central nervous system. The endocrine glands that correspond to the chakras are primary hormone-producing glands that keep

176

us viable, as well as balance and harmonize our state (mood) via the autonomic (vegetative) nervous system.

As long as the chakras themselves are *not* in a healthy and balanced state, they impair our experienced state of health and lead to distinct and major disturbances of either a physical or an emotional/mental nature. That is why I deem the healing work with the chakras and the connected ethereal energy bodies to be especially important, if not essential. On their opening and balance depend not only consciousness and health, but also a fulfilled and well-rounded life expression.

All old and new experiences are collected and present in the chakras, and thereby also in the energy bodies currently more or less developed and transformed, mostly rather less. Unfortunately, all too often experiences are unredeemed/unsolved issues and manifest as a disorder or blockage of a chakra and are on their way to express in the physical body as pathological symptoms or physical changes. Only when they are transformed and integrated can these experiences become wisdom and spiritual consciousness in the chakras. This consciousness lives and proclaims "in Heaven as in Earth" the kingdom of GOD——free, without attachment, without judgment, in love, perfect.

There are many possibilities and means to discover and heal old memories in the chakras, among them are the various forms of meditation, affirmations, past-life therapies, and any balancing of energies through body therapies, like bioenergetics, tai chi, acupuncture, massage, and inner awareness work. No matter which path you choose, walking it will require the desire for and the seeking of truth, be it of a personal or transpersonal nature.

It is not by chance that the chakras have been given special attention in the meditation practices of Eastern traditions, but I am surprised how little people are aware of their dynamics and consider chakra cleansing rather a mirror polishing than a catharsis. If you have catharsis in mind, a deep cleansing and transformative change, then it is not only advisable but essential that you keep your attention "back-bodied" (focused on and in the spine) and oriented towards the root chakra while relaxing *downward*. You may ask: "Why down?" It helps to balance the chakras, it "grounds" them, and it makes you receptive for what may be given to you during this time of silence. When you feel receptive, you no longer want to go anywhere (not even "up" or to GOD), and you endeavor to receive GOD, here and now, and to allow HIM to dwell in you.

It is possible to sense the source of each chakra in the spine, even though it may require some practice. I recommend that everyone who meditates and everyone who desires to live consciously become aware of the chakras and the presence of life within his/her own body——not by thinking, having ideas, reading about it, or any other mental acrobatics but by actual inner experience. For this inner experience, it becomes necessary that you relax———laying down or sitting——and feel the spine between the back of your head and your tailbone; make yourself aware of it. As soon as your attention is connected to it——that is, as soon as you can feel the flow of energy in the spine——you will be able to locate the chakras. You will also be able to ascertain whether your spine is passable, blocked, or painful in any area.

To make it easier for you to sense the chakras, I will tell you their approximate root positions in the spine and reflect on some things you may encounter as disturbances or sensations as well as their possible causes. You alone can and must find the exact points where you experience your own chakras.

First Chakra (also called root chakra)

You find this chakra at the bottom end of your spine, the so-called coccyx. You may find it *opening down and out*——the energy floods the pelvis and leaves through body openings there——or *opening up*——the energy flows from the pelvic floor into the abdomen. In this chakra lies the exact meeting point where the "heavenly" energy (breathing in) awakens the "earthly" energy (breathing out) and invites it to respond. At the same time, this chakra is the seat of the Kundalini, the energy often depicted as one arising from the base of the spine as a snake. In many Eastern traditions the flow of the Kundalini is considered a vertically streaming force, whereas in consciousness it is a circle. Kundalini is the name of the energy and also its energetic circuit, which is both giving **and** receiving: "Heaven" gives and "Earth" receives and incorporates; then the "Earth" responds and "Heaven" accepts. In this is contained all joy——not in a reversed sequence as is so commonly believed (I give and then I am rewarded, or I give in order to be rewarded).

This may not be very easy to understand, and yet it complies with the creative laws in which we take part and share. These we can easily observe in nature, for example in plants, in their growing and evolving toward the light only *after* the light, the sun, has called them forth from below the ground and nourished them. If only we could do the same! For we are invited to stand up, to unfold, and to bloom. Thinking has made our life quite complicated! Or don't you believe so? Would it matter to a rose that it could think it is a rose——*or is it enough to be a rose?*

A person whose root chakra is totally blocked does not really live, and usually has a very narrow, gray aura. He survives or exists to himself without bringing anything into the world. He lives mainly off the life of others, becomes alive with *their* energy, and his expressions are always reactive. There is no joy, no strength, no interest in life. He cannot let go, cannot surrender, cannot walk into life. Much of what life entails he judges or burdens with moral concepts——both inside and externally. In his tiredness he considers himself a victim of circumstances and hopes that someone will get him out of the hole.

Is the root chakra open, the entire abdomen feels warm and wide, sometimes hot. If it's locked or congested, we will find numbness, pain, or a burning. The burning may be a sign that it is on the verge or in the process of opening. Causally, the congestion of the root chakra comes from a total denial of the desire for relief from needs and the refusal to feel or fulfill them—— resulting in great inner suffering. Relief is not found——the possible fulfillment of needs is compensated by various measures, including, and rather predominantly, by sexuality, *if it*——even though lived in a relationship——serves only self-gratification.

That is why the opening of the root chakra leads at first to the *awareness* and feeling of deep despair and unredeemed, often very old, sorrows——

provided the emotional body is fully integrated. Eventually——and still during the healing process——the primal energy begins to flow freely and genuinely. Once this happens, we begin to accept ourselves where we are and let go of where we believed we were or wanted to be.

Second Chakra (sacral chakra)

This chakra sits about one hand-width below the waist; the energy flows from the spine to the abdominal front. In its root rests the connection to one of the ethereal bodies, called the emotional body. This body develops between the ages of seven to fourteen. During these years it forms, takes shape, and unfolds *as long as* there is an optimal and undisturbed environment. Unfortunately, this is rather rarely the case, for it requires great awareness and the ability to love impersonally from the parent as well as from the child. That is why this chakra is blocked in many if not most people (especially in the West), in men and women alike——even though we usually consider women to be more emotional/sentimental and thereby closer to their feelings than men. In this assumption, truth and misunderstanding are very close to each other.

The blockage of the second chakra inevitably leads to considerable problems in the lower back for which today many individuals are treated not only with painkillers, but also with surgical intervention. That, in my opinion, would in most cases not be necessary if the cause were not sought in the physical but rather in the disturbances or congestion of the emotional body and then recognized. I know individuals who circumvented operations by healing old sorrows through emotional work (one of my clients did this in two sessions) or doing yoga! More and more people have problems in that area while no one can detect any physical source or defect. If this was truly understood, people could be happy about it, as it can not only lead to healing, but actually heals.

Congestion in the second chakra also leads to general abdominal pains, problems with digestion, and painful menstruation disorders in women. These abdominal symptoms are probably easier to explain than those in the

180

back if you accept the hormonal correlation of the chakras. Whether the symptoms appear predominantly in the front or in the back of the body is quite important in the healing work when we seek the cause, but for now, I will leave it at that.

The opening of the second chakra depends on the permeability of the spine for the flow of energy in this area. When you focus there, you may be able to determine whether the energy flows here or jams, whether it is warm or cold, numb, or alive, or even painful. Very often, the connective tissue is knotted up in this area and the muscles are tight. Stretches (yoga) for the lower back can be of considerable help. If, for example, you declare your willingness by a loudly or silently voiced commitment to feel everything or to respect your feelings, this alone can actually take the pressure from this area and open the chakra. Of course, it has to be lived in order to fully heal.

Third Chakra (solar plexus chakra)

The root of this chakra is directly at your waistline, or sometimes a tiny bit above it. The energy pulsates through the front around the navel. In the root of this chakra, the mental body is connected, just like the emotional body, and imprinted during the formative, early years of childhood but will develop completely between the ages of fourteen to twenty-one. Unfortunately, this energy body is regularly more than over-fed with increasing mental, rational activity, such as reading, thinking, and arguing as well as with floods of external stimuli like TV, computers, cell phones, advertising, and other often rapidly changing impressions that cannot be sorted or digested quickly enough. This, while feelings, emotional expression, and experience are neglected.

By this, two especially noticeable disorders are created in the body. *Either* we close the solar plexus or we "cushion" ourselves with a belly ("the belt does not fit anymore" or such), still believing we are happy even though we no longer feel ourselves or others. *Or* we become too open in this area and——as a consequence——are constantly overwrought and exhausted from getting too much input while being disconnected from it (ADD is one of these effects). We may have backaches or pains/frustrations in the organs below the costal arch, the stomach, the liver, the gall bladder, the spleen, or the pancreas.

Here it is helpful to know: The solar plexus also has the task of absorbing all external impressions as gifts and "nourishment" that have to be "eaten," "digested" (quotation marks because this is not meant physically) and desired to be used for growth and development. But because here is not only the place of discernment but also that of judgment and narrow-mindedness (black-white thinking), everything absorbed falls right into one or the other pattern of perception. That is why we are immediately affected in this area and experience emotional reactions yet are not necessarily willing to express what we experience. But——remaining a moment with the helpful picture of the digestive process——elimination is also necessary; that is, expressing ourselves becomes necessary, or the expression gets stuck within us and causes problems, like stomach ulcers, gall bladder or liver congestion, or other such issues. Only absorbing is not healthy for anyone. Absorbing *and* eliminating, taking *and* giving, have to be in balance and complementing each other, even here. By the signs of an evolving pathology, and depending on the organs that are affected, we can determine——with some practice——what the specific problems are that caused the symptoms.

Judging plays quite a role in all disturbances and disorders in the solar plexus region, and it is only possible as long as we perceive dichotomously and think along polar patterns, in either/or, black/white, right/wrong, good/evil, but also in we/them——in opposites, that is. The complex difficulty of projection has its basis here. From here we recognize our "enemies," the "guilty," all the characteristics that we see in others but believe not to have in ourselves. Here we are being confronted by our shadow within our own shadow. For we not only judge "the other," but also ourselves. In fact, we do this so strongly that we no longer recognize ourselves but instead pretend to be not like that. Or——which is quite common——we place others on a pedestal, remove them far away from ourselves, and do not recognize *them* within ourselves either.

Fourth Chakra (heart chakra)

The heart chakra holds a special place among the seven main chakras: It is the center, the middle, the midpoint, and the hub between the three upper chakras and the three lower ones. Since it has its place between "Heaven and Earth," so to speak, it must be recognized as the bridge and mediator.

Contrary to some traditions and some opinions of those who have written or spoken about chakras, I know that CHRIST consciousness dwells here, and here I also dwell in IT. Here GOD becomes MAN; here happen impression and expression of loving, true/sincere encounters and fellowship. In this sense, the significance of the heart chakra becomes even more discernible and transparent in the visions described in the chapters **Divine Manifestation, The Nine-branched Menorah,** and **Exodus.**

The root of this chakra is midway between both shoulder blades and opens through the sternum or breastbone. Because the qualities of love, truth, freedom from judgment, and wakeful presence are situated here, a blocked or congested heart chakra is a problem beyond problems. It makes effectively opening and healing the other chakras very difficult, if not impossible——for when this chakra is not open, the willingness to face *and* accept one's own condition and truth is as good as nonexistent, despite any declaration of intention and internal pain. Since without the love of the heart even the relationship with GOD is only a relationship of separation, motivated by fear of punishment or a hunger for praise and recognition, any attempted healing process will be characterized by wanting to do, wanting to have, and wanting to get rid of. **This will not work!** Healing can only be received by grace, in loving trust and faith.

Disturbances in the area of the heart chakra manifest as pain in the upper back, stiffness in the spine in this particular area, or chest tightness and pressure. It may also affect the area of shoulder girdle and throat, and the neck muscles——whereby the throat often feels pressed shut when the heart chakra is blocked. However, you must keep in mind that all symptoms in the area of the shoulder girdle and throat/neck relate to the fifth chakra as well.

Should the problems of the heart chakra be ignored over a long time, disorders will eventually manifest in the physical heart. In my experience with people working on their problems, I saw a few times that individuals would show heart attack symptoms seconds before breaking through to the heart chakra. One of my clients had had a heart attack the year before and remembered the experience; he was very afraid as in his current session he once again had strong pains in his heart and left arm. As soon as his heart chakra opened and his deep sorrow dissolved in tears, all his physical pain and symptoms disappeared. This experience suggested to him that the earlier heart attack would not have been necessary had he done something previously for his own good. I had to agree.

The unconscious, inconsistent opening and closing of the heart chakra as a behavioral pattern appears as cardiac dysrhythmia, a rhythmic disorder, or other irregularities of the heart activity. The inconsistencies come from controlling the heart, and every individual must find the cause for that control. It will be fear . . . but fear of what?

This chakra is also in charge of the immune system. Its gland connection is the thymus, which, unfortunately, is totally underrated in medical circles, underestimated, and even ignored. It has been observed that it is common for the thymus to shrink during adolescence and, rather than considering this a sign or problem, it is interpreted as the thymus probably not being needed when physical growth is complete. However, this gland, among other functions, also produces the T-cells which——as you may know——are desperately low in HIV/AIDS patients. Why is there no greater interest in this gland? The thymus is even totally removed when a tumor occurs. God have mercy!

I am deeply troubled——and this I add into this translated version of the book——by a newly appearing diagnosis of sternum pain. It has a name, though the causes are assumed, and none that I found relate at all to the painful opening of the heart chakra. Ignorance is not always bliss. Sometimes it is downright foolish and neglectful. What troubles me most is that the "experts" say they are not sure with such assuredness, and then prescribe medication without having a clue. Then again——we are all responsible for what we believe and what we question.

184

Fifth Chakra (larynx or throat chakra)

The larynx or throat chakra has its seat around the first cervical vertebrae that protrudes right above the shoulder girdle and is often called the atlas. It opens into and through the lower front of the throat.

This chakra is, next to the second chakra, one of the most blocked chakras I have encountered in people. This may not be surprising when you look at the chakra table and see what is associated with it, for here the All-Will is in habitual conflict with the personal/individual will——if and as long as the latter is neither in accord nor wishes to be in accord with the former. Everything that wants to come out to be expressed by a human being as inner truth or gift to life and is not allowed to do so by self-censorship will be blocked here and held in the true sense of the word. This pertains to feelings and words, "good" and "bad". We block our expression to avoid being seen as we are, while at the same time wishing nothing more fervently than to finally be seen. Paradoxical, is it not? This suggests the realization: What we long for most, we fear most. Why do we do this to ourselves? It pays to pursue that question!

It may not be without reason that we rejoice, or at least become aware of what we did to ourselves and to life when our neck muscles ease that were painfully tense and constricted. That, of course, pertains to all other symptoms in the body that we may become aware of. But the neck has its place of importance because of our selfishly protective use of the will given us. We must understand that we ourselves are the suppressers!

Next to physical exercises, special massages, and relaxation techniques, we may find some affirmations helpful to open this area and unburden it. But the blockade will repeat itself here (as in other chakras) when there is no real change, and we do not recognize our willfulness, become aware of our lifestyle, and do not respect life and feelings.

Sixth Chakra (third eye, forehead chakra)

The root of the third eye is at the back of the head, directly where the spine enters the head. It,opens on the forehead close to and above the nose bridge.

Disorders in the area of the third eye appear mostly as what are normally considered headaches, but also as migraines or various forms of vertigo. The aches appear particularly in the area of forehead and temples. A headache under the top of the skull does *not* belong to the symptoms of the third eye but to the seventh chakra. A blocked third eye allows only to a very limited extent, if at all, the ability to form images and make creative use of them in the mind; that is, to recognize, understand them as an inner picture, and perhaps express/implement them.

People with this predicament can hardly engage in anything that has to do with the past. When they close their eyes, they may see photos but not images of themselves, and they neither relate to anyone in a photo nor remember the details of how they lived when that photo was taken. Though most of them can gently be led there.

The blocked third eye often indicates that the person with this condition considers it dangerous to look at things more squarely. A close look could rob him of many of his illusions about himself and others, might necessitate an unwelcome confrontation with a partner, or destroy his dream of having had a nice childhood with loving parents who had no problems of their own (or the total opposite). That's why migraines can be found here. However, this disorder is also closely related to the second chakra.

A special problem exists regarding the third eye that personally impacted me——visual disturbances of the physical eyes. When seven years old, I received my first glasses for nearsightedness, of minus 2.5 diopters. In addition, I had been born with corneal curvature. It took years for me to finally understand that my nearsightedness could be linked to my reluctance to look at myself honestly, and that pertained not only to my personality aspects, but also to my spiritual being. Even more years passed until I realized that I had lived and struggled in a continuous conflict between my third eye and my physical eyes, the inner world and the exterior world, my

186

clairvoyance, and my perception of physical reality, between self and personality. Again and again, I experienced painful disturbances of my physical eyes that dissolved when I experienced awareness through the third eye. All visually impaired should, therefore, not just be busy with their physical eyes and compensate for their impairment with glasses, but also seek awareness of what they need to learn about what their eyes are telling them and what they perhaps do not wish to see.

I will give you an example: One day I decided to take my glasses/contact lenses off and go without (by then, one of my eyes had scars on the main vision field due to burst vessels and the other was at minus 11 diopters). I did this for half a year. During this time, I gardened and nailed tarpaper on a roof, but I also had to travel to Europe to lead retreats. I left glasses and contact lenses behind. Because I saw everything in a fog, I constantly had to ask people for help. They often looked at me as though I was fooling them, since nothing about me suggested I was vision impaired. I habitually needed to say, I cannot see this, I cannot read the train timetable or the boarding schedules at the airport, etc. But people helped me all the time! It was an amazing experience. I felt such gratitude and an increasing humility for someone who had previously always been so self-sufficient. If you wear glasses and believe you cannot be without, try it (not while driving, of course).

Seventh Chakra (crown/apex chakra)

The crown chakra opens in the center of the head. Its root is directly connected with the pituitary gland [11] that holds a special place in the endocrine gland system as the function of all other glands depends on it. In colorful depictions of chakras in the body, we often find a lotus flower there instead of the crown chakra wheel. It is——at least this is how I understood it——supposed to represent blooming enlightenment or completeness, maybe even a completed realization of GOD. Perhaps that is why some meditation paths direct their followers to orient themselves from the bottom to the top, while opening their chakras/energies in a corresponding sequence. I consider this more than questionable, especially since I have learned and understood that it is not about getting away from earth——not even into "enlightenment"——but to be on earth, to remember here that I was never separated, and to be *permeable for the Divine Presence here*. That means having the lotus in the heart chakra or having lotus blossoms in all of them. Nevertheless, the crown chakra has its special place in the chakra "network", which may be easier to recognize by looking at the disorders that may occur.

A blocked crown chakra may be held responsible for headaches and pressure discomforts in the cranial vault under the parietal bones——that is right under the top of the head. He who suffers from this should at first try to find out whether the pressure seems to come from outside and above (as though someone is pressing on the head) or comes from inside and below (as if something wanted to get up and out). Either one is possible and each has its own meaning:

• If the pressure comes from inside, this may mean you have ignored your needs and worries. shrugged them off instead of expressing them. This pressure is often found in people who make an extra effort to avoid a problem, to ignore conflicts, or to move too quickly to GOD, that is, they try especially hard to flee the earth, their current responsibilities, and their own humanness, by whatever means. The basis for such efforts is a strong longing to leave body and earth behind. Deep down, this longing is rather a longing for prayer and dialogue with GOD than for escape. The pressure announces the need for speaking out, to let go, and to surrender——like a drowning man's need for air, one dying from thirst for water. Alone the willingness to turn to GOD with laments of the heart relieves many of these headaches.

• The pressure from outside reflects a need for meditation and receiving/letting in through the head chakra, grounding, withdrawing, and surrender of one's own energy——like a tree in winter whose earthly energy withdraws, moves back into the roots, and waits until the spring sun awakens it and calls forth the energy again to respond to the sun. Accepting what cannot be changed has to be practiced: allow GOD to love you and allow HIM to fill you (right through the head——and as though water and its surface were slowly sinking inside). In the chapter about meditation, you can find some more information.

The Fear Belt

There is one area in the body——between the solar plexus and the heart, in front and back under the rib cage——to which I would like to draw your special attention. I have named it the fear belt. Here fear can acutely be felt when something wants to come up into heart and mouth and is deliberately blocked. When you push two fingers right under the lower end of the sternum, you may feel pain there. Hold your fingers in place for a while and breathe. Ask what it is you fear.

Chakras	Glands	Color	Quality	Religion	Lord's Prayer[1]
7th chakra (1)[2]	Pituitary[3]	violet white[4]	seeker	Judaism	You are
6th Chakra (2)	Pineal	light blue	imagination vision	Buddhism	Holy is Thy name
5th Chakra (3)	Thyroid	Indigo	will communication	Islam	Your will is being done
4th Chakra (4) (All-Ein)	Thymus	green	Love Relationship receiving/giving	Christ	You are redeeming us from evil
3rd Chakra (3)	Adrenal (+. Leydig cells)[5]	yellow (orange)	judgment discernment	Confucianism	You are forgiving us our trespasses
2nd Chakra (2)	Leydig cells (+ Gonads)	orange (red)	feelings/emotions	Hinduism	You are not leading us into temptation
1st Chakra (1)	Gonads (+ Leydig cells)	red (orange)	power	Taoism	You are giving us our daily bread

This information comes not only but mainly from Edgar Cayce (s. Glossary) material. The qualities have been proven and confirmed by my own experiences and that of others.

It is yours to find a relationship of these correlations with yourself, your experiences, and the chakras within you—to work with/reflect the possible meaning or consequences of such correlations. You may have become curious and will look for additional information elsewhere.

---

[1] The Aramaic language in which the original prayer is assumed to have been spoken, knows no future or past tense. Such the prayer becomes one of remembering what is now
[2] the numbers in parentheses correspond to the figures in chapter 1
[3] some authors associate the Pineal gland with this chakra
[4] white and/or violet
[5] the Leydig cells are responsible for male hormones (secondary characteristic)

190

The Ethereal Bodies

At first, this may not make any sense. Why do I give the subject of ethereal bodies——also called energy bodies——so much space? But my own liberation was directly connected to becoming aware of, transforming, and healing my emotional body. The many years of suppressing my feelings had not only made me half-dead, seeming barely alive, but also had led to the frustration and irritation of all my inner organs. Gall bladder, liver, and both digestive and excretory systems were more than stressed and signaled trouble consistently. My blood pressure had been extremely low for as long as I could remember until I turned forty. The here-described processes led not only to *emotional healing* by recognizing truth, but also to the fact that my blood pressure normalized, that my gall bladder and liver are as good as inconspicuous, and that my general physical well-being improved noticeably. Life had forced me to care for my feelings, respect them, and to view any symptoms in my body as signals of unawareness. Some results of my observations and experiences are included in the following.

The term *ethereal bodies* is used to describe certain bodies of energy and patterns that are available to the soul. The soul uses them to walk through and cope with its own learning and maturing process on Earth, to overcome fallacies and to become aware again of its oneness with the Source. All these bodies also interact with those of other individuals. Clairvoyants and aura-readers are able to see or feel these bodies in or around other individuals and some sentient beings can perceive them differentiated from but through their own bodies.

I discern as energy bodies the etheric or causal body, the emotional body, the mental body, and the spiritual body, all of which interpenetrate the physical body more or less, depending on its permeability. They mold, influence, support, or hinder one another interactively and play an important part in transformation for each of us. Every one of these bodies, or every energy pattern, has its own specific task and purpose, but also its specific problems.

191

The Etheric or Causal Body

This body provides life energy per se to the physical body, its organs and their functions, and to maintain them. It will uphold life long after any of the other ethereal bodies have withdrawn for whatever reasons——for example, when in a coma or during certain out-of-body experiences. Still, this body, too, will be affected by disorders in the mental and/or emotional bodies and it supports the manifestation of these disorders in the physical body. It carries and endures everything that designs, forms, and builds the physical expression, and eventually appears fully integrated in the body. With its energy, it takes part in the chronification of pathologies, degenerative processes of the cells, and deforming processes of the body etc., but also in the process of healing and recovery. However, it is not cause, and cause cannot be found there.

The Emotional Body

Through the emotional body, as the name already implies, we are enabled to experience feelings; it is also burdened with them and harbors them. At this point it is important to discern between feelings and "maudlin sentimentality". Although all sentimental conditions, even self-pity, belong to the emotional body, and although all of them can also move us to tears and laughter, they have only a very limited influence on the emotional body; they cannot heal, redeem, or integrate it (see also The Mental Body). That makes it difficult for many to understand what I mean when speaking of their blocked feelings. They may still consider themselves, as did I for a long time, to be emotional and sympathizing.

How can we discern these varying qualities of feeling? Perhaps I can best exemplify this with the example of self-pity. When someone cries from self-pity, he can continue to do this for his entire life, without any change within himself or in his life. When the Self cries, it is from becoming conscious of truth, and that will always lead immediately to healing and change.

How can I discern whether I cry **about** myself or whether it is **me** crying? Listen to the following sentences (its best to say them aloud):

"I don't feel good; no one can help me."

"I am sad; I would like to live, but don't know how."

Do you notice something? The voice of your sorrow has its own *I-am*, and this should always be allowed to express itself. Do not speak or cry about your feeling but BE the feeling.

The emotional body seems to be the greatest challenge to all of those who seek truth; the healing and transformation attempts in this body vacillate between the wish to silence it (deaden it) on one hand and assuming an attitude of "anything goes" on the other. Up to now, I have met only a few individuals (the Dalai Lama was among them) who have a healed, stable, and matured emotional body while I have met many, including some internationally renowned Hindu gurus and other masters, self-proclaimed or otherwise, that have successfully suppressed their emotional body, have made it invisible and impalpable. There seem to be so many misunderstandings. It needs to be understood——having an emotional body that has been well-aligned does not mean you cannot live or show your feelings, but rather that the entire spectrum of feelings is subordinate to Divine Will, is embedded in IT, and available to IT. Striving for enlightenment and the mastering of feelings in connection with it all too often leads to their oppression/inhibition and renunciation, and thus to a great lack of compassion and an even greater lack of an ability to relate to others.

It is obviously not an easy task to recognize the temptation of self-gratification in the process of self-realization and not to succumb to it, but rather to surrender to GOD so entirely that HE can live me and die me, use me and my entire humanness in HIS Love for HIS purpose. That means HE will become true "Man" (Mensch), meaning "only begotten son," in me (the witness). Here, specifically, it is essential to be aware and not to throw the baby out with the bathwater——the emotional body, just like all the other ethereal bodies, must be transformed and integrated but not, by any means, negated.

193

As already mentioned above, the emotional body stores all emotionally captured experiences. This includes those that were judgmentally charged and consequently attached to fallacies, which——as long as they have not been overcome, lovingly recognized, transformed, and integrated——will eventually cause pathological symptoms and inadequate or inappropriate behavior. Those, in turn, will burden if not disturb and ruin our relationships. Here, the space that we allow our fears to fill plays a prominent role, for initially it is the fear of punishment and guilt (see also Adam, Eve, and fig leaves) that misleads us to divide things into good and evil and judge or interpret accordingly. It is fear, again, that induces us to hide our true feelings so that we are not seen as we are——forget about seeing ourselves.

In many people the emotional body splits off from all other bodies and is projected to the outside. At times I perceive an emotional body walking right next to the physical one it belongs to or I become aware of some that have——
——for whatever reason——been projected out (appear as hallucinations but ought not to be confused with such) or were stopped in their development at certain ages (did not mature), perhaps due to trauma. Often it only requires the expression of the deep-felt truth to draw the person's attention to his suppressed emotional condition, and it can be reintegrated. If I ask individuals about their experiences at such a time, and if they finally express their feelings from that time, not only rarely but always is the condition revealed and totally solved.

Here is an example. A woman came to see me because for years she suffered from asthma. She wanted to know why she was afflicted with asthma and what had caused it. I asked inside and was shown her being at the age of 13. So, I asked the woman what had happened when she was 13. She said: "Oh! That's when the asthma started!" But she could not think of anything that may have caused it at the time. But Spirit insisted: age 13. So, I insisted as well. She pondered and suddenly stared at me with big eyes. Then she blurted out: "That's when we fled from the Russians!" (WW II) and cried and cried.

Without help, any individual in such a condition can no longer feel her condition but is still able to perceive more or less consciously the emotional conditions of others, which remind her of her own unconscious condition. Due to this dilemma, she is often motivated to pity-induced——instead of

194

compassion-induced——action while trying to avoid by any means to feel her own suffering.

In extreme cases, the projection appears in hallucinatory experiences, as in forms of schizophrenia and paranoia, when one's own shadow is perceived as existing externally even though it seems invisible as not physical to others. Here I would like to share another experience.

I was asked to see an AIDS patient who had been transferred back and forth between the general hospital (AIDS) and a psychiatric clinic because of his "hallucinations." When the man was brought to me by a psychiatric worker, he told me of two men who had been chasing him at home for quite some time, seeking contact——or that is what he assumed. He wanted to be freed of them. I saw he had split off parts of himself and that it was not a matter of other beings or external powers——I have learned to discern their energies. But I kept this to myself. In his ensuing inner work, I invited him to meet the two men and get to know them——and not to be afraid as I was with him—— and we gave them our attention. Soon he said: "Is it possible that that is me?" and became aware of his disconnected deep, internal suffering. While going through the pain (experiencing it), he was able to reconnect and integrate the parts, which contributed greatly not only to his mental but also to his physical health.

The emotional body is, as you may recognize by now, co-influenced by the mental body, for it is our thoughts and their patterns (attitude, comparison, appraisal) that let us evaluate and interpret our experiences. That is why the mental body has to be involved in the healing of the emotional body and the reciprocal conditionality be kept in view. For not only are our feelings influenced and suppressed by our thinking, but also our unresolved feelings react to and influence our thinking, and thereby the mental body.

Conclusively, I would like to draw your attention to some experiences in my work and the insights acquired so far. I observe an increasing sensitivity in people for the repressed feelings of sorrow and agony *in others.* Most of the time, this is not a conscious occurrence, but it is also not about finding someone to blame for the experiences or believing someone should not be subjected to these. This sensitivity, however, is an aspect of the emotional body, and we may consider it a gift or a burden, depending on one's degree of consciousness. Without becoming aware of such occurrences and without a differentiated approach, the feelings of others will be absorbed, can tremendously burden, and may lead to all kinds of symptoms, disturbances, and various states of exhaustion.

Consequently, I experience a great urgency and necessity for us all to learn to deal lovingly and *appropriately* with such experiences and conditions. Since there is nothing in life that does not have its meaning——ITS meaning——it is ours to find out why something happens and what its purpose is. It stands to reason, as is always the case with things that challenge us, that love is to be expressed so that it becomes the healing element. That is why I practice—— and I advise you and all who have such sensitivity to do the same—— becoming the bridge between the one who does not feel his own feelings and his feelings that are accessible to me. I feel them while he cannot express his feelings or is not even conscious of them. I can articulate what is not (yet) possible for him. What an opportunity to pave the way!

Once you begin to do this, the first imperative will be: *Be careful with your words!* For as long as you cannot discern between your own feelings and those of the person in question, you have to ascertain by *asking* whether you are "in line"——in other words, rather than stating things you may suggest them. It is also well advised to first inquire about his condition before you beat him around the head with what you seem to know. That requires instinct and tact (not to be confused with manipulation!): Love is capable of both. You will, however, also experience that some individuals——perhaps even most of whom you encounter——do not want their feelings, not even if you could help. That is a difficult lesson and hurts profoundly. Often, and for the moment, it is necessary that you first express your own sorrow about this or even cry the tears the other person is not crying (not necessarily in his presence). Both are helpful.

Even more helpful is dissolving all suppressed feelings of others within yourself; that is, feeling and recognizing their truth, finding their words, and expressing them. You will recognize them also as yours, and, with this truth, a shadow (and projection) of your own will be redeemed that held sameness inside and outside in image as well as in feeling. You then both heal.

The Mental Body

Herein lies our ability to think——here are, therefore, all of our current thought patterns as well as what we have gathered during our life as mental property, like learning languages, for example, balancing a check book etc. We usually declare this mental area our "head," even though much more than our head or brain is involved—— our solar plexus is also closely connected. Unfortunately, the intellect is given a place in the so-called developed countries that it does not deserve. The ability to think is considered disproportionately higher-ranking than the ability to feel, is cherished accordingly, and given honors and glory. As a matter of fact, our entire educational system rests on this mindset, with some alternative institutions being the exception. Not only in institutionalized education has this mindset taken root, but also in the entire social fabric, in families, and in workplaces. How often are we asked to be reasonable or to let our intellect rule us, even if it is against better knowledge, against inner certainty, and against our conscience? That is why the term "practical constraints"——often used not only in economics and politics but also in daily life——is an expression of an imbalanced demand on and use of our thinking. It is frequently misused to exclude our at least equal feelings and intuitions, leaving them out.

The various patterns stored in the mental body can create all kinds of imbalances and disturbances in our lives. At one time, this must have brought forth the advocates of positive thinking that served a great purpose in making us generally aware of thought patterns and their consequences. But always and from time immemorial, scientists and philosophers have occupied themselves with thinking and its ramifications. Edgar Cayce, the great American psychic, once said in a trance-reading: "That what man eats and what he thinks, that he is" (Reading 288-32). He cared greatly about drawing people's attention to what they would take in as sustenance and what they would identify themselves with. In scripture we read, "Speculation has led many people astray" (Sirach 3:24), and we are reprimanded to watch over our thoughts.

Any overestimation of thinking and intellect, be it positive or negative in expression, leads to either arrogance or lack of self-esteem. Either one thinks one knows and has all the answers (mostly read in books), or one believes oneself stupid and inadequate in comparison with those that one considers erudite in the classical sense.

It is, therefore, not only necessary that we watch over our thinking and become aware of it, but also that we realize thinking alone is not enough. A change in thinking is not transformation. Admittedly, it is an important and needed step in the right direction, which is toward transformation, but changes in our lives are not entirely due to a change in thinking. No matter how often we repeat during the day, "My life is lovely like a rainbow," such mental acrobatics may only contribute to belying our true condition, which we refuse to face. Only awakening and healing stabilize a change in thinking.

In those individuals that have either hidden or split off their emotional body, a conflict may arise in the mental body, which then assumes a compensatory function. This means that the mental body tries to represent feelings in sentimental/emotional expressions. In the manifestation of this pseudo-emotional body, it becomes apparent that an individual has practiced reactive emotional expressions, largely supported by the psychology of the me-generation that encouraged: "I have to react and defend myself, or I go to pieces." This expression, however, covers up the true feeling and with that, also the possible liberation of the self/soul.

The mental body, meaning thought forms, may use the feelings in its own interest. Instead of liberating the feelings, it tries to protect and defend the self to the outside world, which neither needs protection nor defense. In this instance, there are emotions that suppress the inner condition and do not allow it to be felt (see also Exodus, there Pharaoh), much less allow the being to be IT at the time.

The Spiritual Body

The spiritual body is often called the soul, or high or highest self. This is accurate, even though the spiritual bodies of soul or higher self can be differentiated. I recognize the soul as an aspect of the high self but not identical with it, as it determines itself still as a personal spiritual identity (for more see Exodus).

The soul as spiritual body has very specific learning and expressing tasks which, when crowned with success, are integrated and become part of the high self. At a specific point during the development of consciousness, the high self will take over leadership on the path; it may still be in a maturing stage, but it will now permeate all ethereal bodies depending on the degree of their permeability. In every respect it is one with GOD and comes out of GOD. The goal of our transformation and development can therefore only be that this high self——or GOD in HIS individual momentary expression—— fills the given space to the fullest (immanence).

In its being, the spiritual body is innocent, whole, healthy, and perfect. That does not mean, however, that fluctuating conditions cannot be recognized there as well. It appears to clairvoyant individuals in many forms. For example, it can be malnourished due to the person disregarding spiritual nourishment that could uplift or strengthen it. It can in some way appear as "blown up," and thereby in no way in proportion to the other bodies. That is the fact, for example, when a spiritual Being with great spiritual knowledge comes to Earth and represents this knowledge——sometimes even supplements it——in a theoretical-philosophical way only, without having gained wisdom with which it would be able to interrelate knowledge, experience, and action. This Being knows what being is (or thinks it does), but he himself is not. In many cases, there is a deep-seated rejection of being on Earth, a derogative denial and aversion towards Earth and all its manifestations in form, as well as a certain spiritual arrogance, such as was found in Atlantis and Egypt.

All our earthly experiences serve to develop and express the gifts of the Spirit and bring them to expansion, completion, and finally, full integration—

—via our spiritual body and high self, or one could also say by our divine essence——into Earth. Everything we recognize, everything we learn, such as truth, patience, capacity for love, compassion, and abandonment in devotion, is absorbed by the spiritual body, unfolds and perfects it. Not that we feign them, but we *become* truth, patience, love, compassion, and devotion, and in the end, we *ARE*.

Considering all of the above, what remains to be said is this: the spiritual body cannot ever be hurt in its essence, but it can hunger and thirst, be hindered, denied, judged, and used for blown-up egos. In the case of drug abuse, a specific problem arises as an exception. The User of mind-altering drugs has experiences that he is not prepared for in any of the other bodies and the consciousness therein. This creates great confusion and chaos for the spiritual body, as well as the high self, as they develop in accordance with our growing awareness and correspond to the level of consciousness gained. The discrepancy created by the drug-abuse-experience creates chaotic conditions that are not easily put back into order and balance by therapy. The drug addict also often displays a high level of spiritual consciousness and experience that he does not know how to integrate or implement. At the same time, he shows self-destructive wishes and actions to a high degree, which may lead to suicide (and I do not mean only a physical suicide).

Reincarnation

The idea of reincarnation has in the past not only been the subject matter in Eastern thought and religions, but also in early Christendom, where people certainly had something to say about it, albeit records and writers were later suppressed and prohibited by the decisions of various Church synods and councils. We can call ourselves lucky that some of the early texts and transcripts have survived censorship *and* the councils of the Church. As the suppression was also recorded historically, it became comprehensible what actually happened to those texts.

Contemporary researchers and authors have taken the subject of reincarnation in Christian history under their wings with meticulousness and courage. I say "courage" because the Christian church seems to consider itself still unable to openly grapple with the subject matter. Their representatives appear to champion the traditional strategies of disassociation from and denial of this issue.

Among the brave ones, I count Geddes MacGregor. I recommend his book *Reincarnation in Christianity*[12] to any skeptic within the Christian tradition. It is enlightening.

Essentially, the teaching highlights the idea (already studied by researchers[16]) that our personal life on Earth is not the only life upon which we look back, but that we have been to Earth more than once, possibly as man or woman, in other social and cultural circumstances, within other religions, and among other races. It declares individual differences in living conditions that we find on Earth necessary and appropriate. Every place of life and its conditions provides the inherent opportunity for the individual to experience what is needed for the development of his consciousness and to find and deal with the way to the "Father's house" (prodigal son). For me, every life harbors the chance to learn the needed inevitable lessons and to fulfill the challenge of the place on Earth with the tasks given. More than ever, I am convinced that this is also each individual's participation in the homecoming *of humanity as a whole.*

Closely connected with reincarnation is the karmic law, without which reincarnation would lose its essence: It is the law of cause and effect——"a man reaps what he sows" (Gal. 6:7)——as though we did not know that already from everything in nature. This law makes our attitudes, our fallacies, and the consequential actions tangible. That is, we are constantly confronted by the harvest of our own seeds. Once we understand the inherent value of the law (if not the law itself), we find it easier to come to terms with ——that is, understand and accept more easily——the seeming injustices of life prevailing in the world. It offers a new perspective on our own experiences, but it does not release us from our responsibility for good or bad experiences or our actions based on attitudes. Once one has effectively accepted this law as working in one's life, there will be no one left to blame for any of the suffered pains and humiliations, not even GOD. The only thing remaining is to become aware of our illusions and fallacies and be at least startled if nothing else.

There is a hidden danger of using the law for one's own relief from the responsibility for the well-being of others. For if we are all responsible for ourselves, why should I be "my brother's keeper"? (Genesis 4:8) It is a different kind of responsibility to which this refers. In our oneness with CHRIST, our brother is a part of us, who——to remain with the concept of reincarnation——may have a more difficult task. We cannot take anything from him or off him, but we can stand by him in compassion or even cry with him. We can offer our hand, if he wants it, or if he can use what we can give. Our refusal to help when the tacit or declared call for help reaches us would be the seed we might not want to harvest. How this help will look cannot be explained by rules. It can only conform to the respective inner truth.

For those of you who meet with experiences and memories of past lives it will become an unquestionable certainty that reincarnation exists. It will also be clear that it is a helpfully creative provision on our path to GOD, even though the experiences that may come up in our memories are mostly not very easy to take, for our straying is immense and so are our pride, our fear, and our resistance.

Unfortunately, most of us do not especially care to courageously look at these experiences from the past and be confronted by their revealing truth. We are not aware how greatly this unresolved past harries, influences, and tempts us constantly to hope for a better future——whereby the present day becomes an unbearable experience. In the therapeutic approach that incorporates the possibility of reincarnation, old and new pathological patterns, unconscious fears, and physical symptoms dissolve. Their cancellation does not only lead to healing of body, mind, and soul, but also leads to a changed attitude towards life and often a new lifestyle. Those, again, lead to new and changed interpersonal relationships and to a different relationship with oneself.

I happen to have had very early karmic memories, even though at that time I had them only in my nightly dreams. As a child, I was between six and seven,

I had a recurring dream, a short moment in time: I am a woman, late twenties, and come down a long, narrow staircase, kind of a stair path. The narrow stairs go down along a very bright rounded house wall, which is of stone but has no joints. After a few steps, it curves and then follows quite a few more steps down along the wall. In my hand I carry a large clay jug; I am on my way to fetch water. I am wearing a black, full-length garment that also covers my head. It is around noon, the sun is high in the sky, and it is very, very hot. The landscape upon which I look is arid and barren. When I am about halfway down the stairs, I wake up. I dream this again and again until I am about thirteen years old——going down the same stairs, waking up in the same spot.

I knew even then that I am that young woman and that I am in another, earlier life, but there was no one to talk to about it. Later on, as an adult and having searched for answers to my many questions about the meaning of life and having——to my great relief——found books and texts about reincarnation, I started wondering about the place where I had possibly lived in that life. Years passed.

Meanwhile, I had emigrated to the US and after seven years returned to Germany, when the dreams came back to my memory during various travels: sometimes because of a stairway, the heat, the aridness of a landscape, some other times because of the smells, the old stones, or an arch way. That was in Tuscany, in the mountains of the Riviera, western Turkey——but nowhere was it "right".

In 1992——I was then forty-nine years old——I traveled for the first time with friends to Cappadocia in Central Turkey. We were travelling by public transportation, a bus. When someone said we were approaching the city of Nevşehir, our destination, I was suddenly and unexpectedly overcome by a terrible nausea. There was no plausible reason, but I knew without a doubt that something was brewing and coming my way. What it was about I learned the next day during our hike into the Göreme Valley. Stunned, I recognized the rock formations, the sandstone towers that fill the entire valley, and I knew the narrow paths that meandered through the dry and barren landscape. I was familiar with the cave dwellings cut out of the sandstone that we visited, and everywhere I saw pieces of stairs along the walls of the towers.

The walls were very bright sandstone, without joints. I was absolutely certain I had been there.

I spent time acquainting myself with more local history, for I had already learned that early Christians had sought refuge here, fleeing from their persecutors. I looked around, separated from the travelling group, and eventually entered one tower, inside of which I found a path going down underground to another level. There was what seemed to be a small chapel, with benches and an altar cut from the rock. Memory pieces flooded in rapidly like small puzzle pieces and began falling together. It was as though my dream of long ago, my actual memory, and my present being there, all merged, somehow becoming one.

I also got in touch with a latent, agonizing sorrow. Life then had not been easy; had been filled with fear and hope, and I could still feel being filled with a distressing sense of responsibility for keeping the community together under such circumstances, even though——and this took me by surprise—— I had not been given that task. I recognized, though, that our Christian belief had been only a belief, a hope-religion, no internalized CHRIST.

So many tears, so many agonizing tears had to be cried right there and then. Yet all the horror and all the despair from that time dissolved with them. Simultaneously, I began to comprehend the many fears I had had in my current life that had not made any sense up to that point——one of them my especially long-lasting fear of persecution.

From my experiences with people that ask for my help, I know that many people are closer to their past life memories than they would like to acknowledge. It is a sign of our times that these memories come more and more to the surface of our consciousness so that they may be recognized, redeemed, and let go. We have entered into an era of new awareness, and this era will and must fulfill itself. But often such memories mix in with current realities and change or influence those. Can we even trust our perception? We probably can if we accept it with nothing else but love.

Here I would like to point once again to the indescribable love and grace that manifest in the redemption of our illusions, revealed in the recognition and experience of truth. In retrospect, I am deeply grateful that the at first horrible

204

experiences eventually led me closer and closer to home, closer and closer to freedom, to true essence. Their redemption not only left me greatly relieved, but also with great amazement about the actual lightness of being.

But past-life memories are not only burdensome. There are also those that connect us in wondrous ways to old knowledge and wisdom, experienced love, and once-developed gifts of the Spirit that we already implemented in former lives. Much that I use today in my healing work came from memories of experiences in other lives that suddenly erupted when needed. This happened when a young girl was brought to me with a congenital skin disease. During the session——I always ask GOD to be guided——I had the feeling that I needed to bring her to sweat, but I did not know how other than with hard physical exercise, which would have defeated working with the ethereal bodies. Looking for a way, I suddenly received detailed knowledge about initiation rites in Egypt that were equal to some Native-American rites that I was familiar with from other experiences. I used some of the old knowledge and the girl started to sweat profusely. Her mother later told me that her health practitioner had also recommended that the girl be brought to sweat. Her skin healed.

However, first and foremost, I had to deal with the more difficult experiences, for they had covered up the joyful ones and not given them room. There was an interesting though painful observation I made during my own healing process through past lives and while doing reincarnation therapy with others. These karmic lives all had various common denominators at the time.

- No awareness of the personal life situation
- No confrontation with truth and reality of that life or phases of that life
- No acceptance of life and circumstance, but subtle resistance, resentment, rebellion, and denial
- Extension and repetition of the personal human dilemma through this rejection
- Oscillation between two extreme poles: one life full of denial of sexuality, the next life in uncontrolled promiscuity——in one life

one's own extensive brutality, the next life experiencing brutality by others (and again denial of one's own)

What shocked me was how long I had been on the road to just learning and understanding a few things——and those barely. Some had needed a number of full lifetimes! But I also became aware how much Life, GOD, loves and lets me be without judging. It is our own fright and guilt (see also the chapter on Adam) that keep us in the loop. Were we honest, and could we feel remorse instead of guilt, or even humble acceptance, we would experience grace presently and assuredly. I know now what I did not know then in my recovery: Time on Earth means nothing. Waking up brings one beyond time.

It is necessary to move out of this karmic cycle and its oscillating repetitions, but only if we live the law, that is, fulfill it, can we overcome our bondage and enter grace. Only in accepting our experiences and in the grace received by this can we find the answer to the old law and its fulfillment. "Eye for an eye, tooth for a tooth" (Exodus 21:23) gives way to loving and giving.

PART III

Epilogue

How much I desire that you can make use of my experiences! How great is the wish in me that a longing may emerge in you, to hear the voice of GOD or ITS Spirit directly and personally inside of you and to open in their presence the prison doors you still may hold onto——to live, to learn, to heal, and to find complete expression. I know something of the longing of your heart for truth and love and for finally arriving at home. This longing is, in the end, that which lets each of us seek, which drives us, and leaves us in the restlessness of our heart until we finally hear, listen, and become willing to follow.

I, too, was a seeker like you. I carried this longing inside of me like you, and I was afraid like you. For a long time, my fear was bigger than my courage and for a long time it was bigger than my longing for freedom. I was very well aware of my inner prison, and yet for a long time I preferred to remain there: I tried to make it more livable, more likable, making a virtue out of a vice, or trying to, while admittedly still hoping that something may happen or someone may come who would get me out of there——a husband, perhaps a prince on a horse, or GOD. The journey of the heart seemed enormous and full of risks. It seemed impossible, or only limitedly possible, to walk it. I did not want to be a Moses; the trials and tribulations of my thoughts and the hypotheses of my fears continuously tried to convince me to leave my dreams of freedom, my trust in life, and my longing buried, and to be something like a *normal* human being, or become one, as everyone else seemed to be. It was a constant struggle.

"Can't you be happy with a normal, ordinary life like other people?" That was a question I often heard from my family and some of my friends. I never really knew what that meant. But however it had been intended, the **normal life** of others did not convince me. Yes, it was true, I could not content myself with that. It was not enough, it was not "my peace". My peace did not come that way. I also no longer believed that those who settled for this were really satisfied.

You may have become aware that my path was not wide and smooth and that I was not spared——I had to walk through many a deep valley filled with darkness and tears. But you will also have read and recognized that a new day always followed the nights of my soul, just like there is daylight visible at the end of each tunnel. There is not only light again once we have gone through, but there is a new world, a different world——a new life, a different life. You have to remember: After each tunnel, you will never find the same world that you left behind before you entered the tunnel.

I have shared many adventures and experiences with you. They were experiences that stood in a temporal connection to important personal steps of growth, that constantly required new decisions, that changed my external way of life, and that made my task on Earth more and more apparent. I recognized with amazement when people came to see me at various times that they seemed to *need* me at exactly this point of my own development and that I could let them partake directly in the newly won awareness, sometimes won just hours before.

In the beginning, the visions were followed by experiences and other visionary appearances that helped me to deepen my understanding while consciousness made further progress. There was a dynamic present in those pictures and experiences, perfectly attuned to my then-current realm of living and the state of my growth. My life never stood still again; never again did I have a feeling of stagnation or meaninglessness. So now, my life finally feels like life——**alive**! It seems as though I have been brought into a much more comprehensive context and am embedded in it. In my daily life I have an increasing sense of not knowing anything, but I no longer experience this not-knowing as daunting insecurity——rather as relief.

It is especially important to me to assure you with this book and the recounting of my experiences of GOD's nearness to all of us——to you, too, and how alive HIS signs and encounters are with us. But it requires intensive training and the practice of wakefulness/mindfulness to recognize the spirited and by all accounts perfect movement of life, and the love and grace therein contained, to receive, accept, and be in it. All too often we are tangled up in our own ideas and plans, hope for a change and deepening of life, but get in the way with our fear, run in circles due to our own "thought salad"——as one of our community members so adequately called that mess.

To avoid such a standstill, we tend to look for changes we ourselves can bring into our lives *without* having developed an awareness about what got us into this tight spot in the first place. We do like to be *in charge*. So, we may change our workplace, change partners, or renounce life altogether, only to realize after a while: This whole effort did not do anything except finding ourselves at the same point with the same frustration. We only changed messengers, but the message remained the same. What has to happen that we start to seriously consider things? What has to happen that we pause, wake up, see and hear the message, and change direction?

Well, I hear some say: I have to live here. I have to earn money, pay the electrical bill, rent. My debts, my health insurance, and I have a husband, children, or I am by myself . . . What does any of this have to do with what I said? What does life have to do with any of these external things, people? I ask this question with the deepest seriousness, for I believe that in our fear anyone and anything can serve as argument and justification for our denial and rejection. Do I wish to say at the end of my life, I did not live because I built a house, because I had to pay off so many debts, because I had children, because I was unable, because I was alone, because . . . because . . . because? To whom will I say this; whom will I convince? Myself?

Apart from this, no one has to do anything. In reality, there is nothing that could hinder you from opening yourself to life and seeking truth, not even if you ended up in a jail cell. But there are consequences! You may not want to risk not having a roof over your head. You may not want to risk losing a partner, or the love of your children for whom you believe you sacrifice so much. You may not wish to let go of your dreams of security. Not even for the consequences of your own irresponsible, predatory exploitation of body and soul may you be willing to pay——you may prefer to pay for various kinds of insurance that are to help you when *the time comes*. You may not want to experience how it could be if you lived differently. Or do you? Yet you, too, admire all and anyone who does.

The price of freedom may be foregoing a few things, who knows! Perhaps not! As long as we refuse to feel our true dependency on life/GOD, our helplessness, we will never know. Of course, we do not want anyone to feel hurt——as if that was possible! So, we try to remain predictable for others and to make others predictable for us. Or do you believe it is not so for you? Is it not the most frequent goal of our arguments in relationships? Believe me, these expected predictabilities are the true walls of our prisons. We create the constriction and lovelessness in ourselves and in our relationships.

Yet creation is unpredictable, within us *and* in others. That is why we needn't have to make a fuss over anything in life. Cause for excitement occurs only when our expectations and ideas are confronted by the otherness of current life experience or when we rub against it.

Perhaps it would be more appropriate to say: It is time that we become seriously willing *to be amazed.* For if we surrender to creation and its Spirit with an attitude that says, childlike: "Let's see what happens! Let's see what life brings and why!" and if we walk with this, we will have interesting experiences. One thing is certain; it will not be boring, and it will never be like being dead again. Of course, we will be confronted by our fears, ideas, and plans with which we like to control life that we cannot just drop so easily. But if we will deal with them differently, we can. We will not be children but will be *like children* (Luke 18:17). Joy will arrive and leave, pain will arrive and leave——we will learn and understand, falling and getting up again.

If we do not take this chance, we will find ourselves more often than not at the end of our tether experiencing one disillusionment after another as we nurse, rebuild, and maintain our illusions like roly-poly dolls and we will do everything to not have them taken from us. We will enlarge the circle of the perpetually frustrated, the "always-getting-a-raw-deal" people.

So, let me invite you. Arise! Shine! Become the "salt of the Earth" (Matthew. 5:13) and be it. You have been called and appointed. That is your task! This becoming is the path as a continuum of being——the path of being is the becoming.

Prayer and meditation belong to this path as bread and water belong to our physical sustenance. Sometimes I encounter individuals that wish to be free and healed but do not want to know anything of GOD or the power of Life over their life. I have no idea how they believe this can happen. That someone can actually believe he could live or be life without dedicating himself respectfully and surrendering to IT, without gratitude and devotion, without practicing prayer or meditation in any one way, seems absurd and megalomaniacal to me.

How many fallacies do we have to encounter on this path until we find willingness? I just remembered a man who visited me years ago in Virginia Beach. He told me he had overcome his ego in a strict school of Zen and no longer had one (how can one be without ego?). While speaking he was sitting on a bench, his breath short and halting, his arms tightly crossed over his chest, his legs crossed over his knees and twisted again at his ankles. He looked like the utmost prisoner (of his ego), and yet he considered himself liberated. He hopefully found a different way.

I am also thinking of the close to two hundred people who, under the leadership of a New Age teacher, famous for her many books, enthusiastically jumped up and down at the beach shouting: "I am god!" Some of them looked very ill; others were popping pills against whatever. Some could not even master a headache without medication, not to speak of having enough trust to live. I asked myself: What would God want with painkillers? What does this mean, "I am god"? Such trials and tribulations of a searching soul! What an enormous misunderstanding of truth! It looks as though some live in the penthouse of a skyscraper (just an analogy!) that has not been built on any foundation and where the lower floors don't even exist. That is why I have to say more about prayer and meditation, for I think them the foundation of my spiritual relationship, and it is through them that I experience this relationship.

Prayer

For some people, it will be necessary, at first, to come up with a new attitude toward prayer itself, or at least to practice a willingness to question old ideas about it and, where applicable, let them go. Many grievous experiences with the dogmas of a heady and judging Church with only a limited understanding are often standing in the way of prayer. Obligatory prayers in worship services, or the heartless reading of liturgical prayers, have not encouraged us to seek anything in a prayer or to practice it. But prayer itself is the language of the heart and is not bound to any form or religion or membership in a church. It is also irrelevant in what circumstances we live, in which culture, whether we have learned to pray or not. Our soul knows about prayer and its language, even though we may not have given her permission to articulate it when at times she lacks the words.

Perhaps your own suffering, your resignation, have muted you; but even in such circumstances, your prayer can begin. Try it. It may be your very first prayer, ever. A prayer of mine that I would like to share with you may assist you.

I have become mute

about all my experiences

on this Earth, GOD.

Now I no longer know

how to talk to YOU.

But perhaps you are also angry with GOD and would like to scream at him. You may believe that HE has brought you here without your consent and then left you. Shout at HIM all you desire and speak your truth at the moment——whatever it looks like. Fling it at HIM (it may be at yourself). Covered up by your rage is the entire ballast of pain and forlornness, the

212

sorrow over everything in the world where you believe GOD has not been present, all that you have hidden from yourself and others since time immemorial. Do not worry; it does not harm GOD if you throw everything at HIM or at his feet. The sun will continue to shine upon you.

If you have only an inkling that your life may have been recorded, that is, that you are writing your life and all your thoughts, your feelings, your actions in the Book of Life (Akashic record)[13] and that they are visible, then you have to surmise that every truth of yours is already known before you yourself may recognize it. You do not have to look far to better understand this; you can recognize this in simple, if not always pleasant, experiences with your fellow human beings. How often is something visible to you in someone else but the person himself seems to be oblivious, something that he tries to hide from you and from himself——such as anger or pain? He does not like to be seen, but he is seen. Okay, then: if you are already seen anyway, why not recognize the entire truth inside of you and accept it? Why would you still pretend and beat about the bush?

Prayer serves to make us more honest towards ourselves, towards GOD, but also towards others. In prayer we practice admitting to ourselves what we have become aware of——and put it into words. Sometimes we will only catch it when we hear ourselves formulating it How often this happened to me! Frequently, this realization is filled with pain and shame or feelings of uncertainty and vulnerability. Once the pain is felt, however, or shame has been experienced and overcome, it is no longer difficult to show ourselves "naked" (vulnerable) to others, to admit and to stand by our truth. Prayer is given to us so that we may relate in sincerity to our essential Beingness. It is like a bridge by the Word[14] that opens the possibility of loving devotion and commitment. Yet, this bridge, too, will have to be pursued, and pursuing it will have to be learned and practiced.

True prayer does not spare us, it relieves. In it, confession may be contained in its pure, natural invitation. It is a handrail giving us orientation. But it would be a misunderstanding to believe that we could speak to GOD as to an errand boy that fulfills our desires and delivers what we order or think we need. "Do not be deceived: God cannot be mocked. Whatever man sows, he will reap in return," writes Paul to the Galatians (Gal. 6:7).

213

It reminds us that even the pictures that we make and have made of GOD have to be questioned. How do we see HIM; as what? How do you see HIM? Is HE the judge in front of whose chair you admit your transgressions——after you have already judged and convicted yourself according to your own standards——or of whom you desire that he is not angry? Have you by chance transferred experiences with your physical parents unto GOD and believe now that HE, just like them, desires to press you into some form? Or is HE your friend, your lover, to whom you can show yourself in all your weakness and helplessness, whose eternal life and love you have faith in, no matter where you find yourself in your process? Is HE the one whom you trust to give all you need, is already giving all you need——who heals you? Is it HIS presence you would like to experience within and whom you could ask to reveal HIMSELF to you? Accordingly will be your prayer and your prayer experiences.

Speak to GOD in your own words; no style of speech is needed, nor will it be censored. Speak from your own current point of being, describing and expressing your current truth. Lay at HIS feet (internally) with your concern, your distress; lift your hands in worship and veneration. Remember HIM and return into HIS presence over and over again as it is alive in you. Feel yourself in the experience and remind yourself in awareness. Do not let any day pass in which you do not pray. "Pray without ceasing" (1 Thess. 5:17) is the message: That means to be in constant prayer, to let the moment be the prayer, become the prayer itself in thought, word, and action.

In our learning and living community in Virginia Beach[17] we exercised a shared prayer. Here we practiced praying with one another and in front of each other. This way, we often experienced that the prayer of one in our midst was also our own; for your GOD is my GOD——there are no other gods. Personal divine experiences exist, but there is no "private" GOD whom we ought to hide or keep away from others. There is nothing else in us, either, that others would not know of themselves, that we would need to keep hidden.

Look for people *with* whom you can pray. Once we have overcome our initial shyness, we will find quickly how beautiful and beneficial it is to share in prayer and meditation with others. In our community, we experienced our shared prayers as a great healing force, and we were often deeply affected by the grace in our experiences. Grace ever more strengthened our desire to become receptive for all that is given. For this, meditation is necessary and important.

Meditation

Contrary to prayer, in which we speak to GOD, open ourselves, share, and express, meditation can and should be the space for silence that allows us to *listen* and *receive*. We sit in silence and wait for GOD's encounter with us; we step aside, let HIM move in, and let HIM love. We practice letting go of our pictures, our thoughts, our ideas, and our codifications so we become empty for IT that desires to reveal ITSELF in its own way. Here we practice mindful attention with all our senses, without hooking into or expecting something specific. Yet we are in expectancy.

In order to sit in silence, you need to acquire a relaxed body posture. You may lie on the floor or sit. I personally prefer the sitting position, as it keeps me from disappearing into daydreaming or falling asleep. For sitting, I suggest you use a firm meditation pillow instead of sitting flat on the floor. The pelvis and the end of the spine should preferably be above your knees. If sitting on the floor with a pillow is uncomfortable, then chose an upright chair instead of an armchair, as an upright chair without arm rests allows for a straighter back and upright sitting. Here, too, pay attention that sitting height and seating surface allow the pelvis to be above the knees——if necessary, use a pillow under you. Legs and feet ought not to be crossed, but rather flat on the floor, comfortably apart. Arms hang quietly at the side of your body with your hands relaxing in your lap. Instead of placing your hands open on your knees, as is common in some meditation practices, unite both hands, folded and fingers entwined, loosely in your lap during meditation, as it helps you to focus and bring all energies into a closed circle.

To get started in meditation, breathing exercises and the awareness of breath are not only a great help, but are essential. Thereby we *practice* seeing with the heart instead of our eyes. The non-judgmental observation of the breath, as it comes in and leaves again, without us having to fetch or release it, opens our body past the lungs and allows us to accept ourselves in our bodies and let go of tension. More than that, the breath is the connection to life itself, just as IT currently lives in us in ITS own rhythm.

Breath makes us aware of our equal participation in life without discrimination and without preliminary achievement of any kind. It gives us a sense of being sustained and wanted, even if we sense at the same time that we reject life. In observing and being aware of our breath, we may also notice during the intake and exhalation of breath, our desire for control over life/breath (as tension) in our bodies. If we do not jerk around to get rid of or avoid the tension that we observe, we may sense and recognize the kind of control we exert and with what intention.

Under the term "meditation", we discover many possibilities or paths of gathering ourselves. To these belong various paths of yoga and practices of Zen, but also forms of guided meditation and contemplation. Some of these paths have a more receptive, awaiting, observing "color," whereas others come from movement, and yet others use active methods of the mind and body, such as Hatha yoga, Tai Chi, guided visual "travels"——or in contemplations that follow words, pictures, or sounds. In my view, it is important and good to get to know the various paths in depth in order to be able to use and integrate them according to your own life rhythm as our constantly changing inner conditions and outer circumstances may require a differing, yet adequate, approach.

However, in this book I will elaborate only on three paths. One is the practice of silence; the others are chakra and picture meditations.

It is most important to me to point to the necessity of **silence**. The therein-contained practice of receiving, of learning to see and listen (a feminine energy pattern), I consider most needed and vital in our times. Only a very few people are not out of balance. Seeing and listening with a receptive mindset is something entirely different from what most people understand as seeing and hearing. Only in true receiving can what has been seen or heard fall into place inside like a seed onto the field, germinate, grow, and bear fruit.

When ***practicing silence***, do not give up when you find yourself constantly everywhere with your thoughts and awareness——all over the place just not in silence. Everyone who practices silent meditation experiences this. It is possible that all your good intentions are not enough to keep you from suddenly remembering what you wanted to get for your mother's birthday or that you are still raving mad at your boss, whom you should have finally told where things stand. These thoughts only remind us of our delayed decisions and unexpressed feelings, which like to trot to the surface just when we settle down. Simply admit it and promise yourself to take time later to attend to your mother's gift or you conflict with your boss. In other words, be forbearing and kind to yourself.

For me, it was of great help one day to listen to the excited voices in me who would not calm down for anything and explain to them that right now, I wanted to be with GOD and that I wanted everything else to wait. It often felt to me as though I was raising children inside of me——kindly, but also strictly——not ignoring their cases, but also without giving them priority. They stopped. I had practiced hard to set my own priority, collect myself (these voice children), pay attention, and learn to listen, not to them but to GOD. In such moments, it often happened that I got answers or clues to things I had just tried to accomplish with my mind. Or I experienced liberating redemption of the pain that lay beneath the anger that I had not been able to let go.

It is important that we become single-minded within (i.e., of one mind and focused). Your thoughts and what I may call their voices can harry you as soon as everything is quiet around you and as soon as you try to focus on your inner being. Meditation does not spare you to eventually become aware of all these voices, their meaning, and quality. If you do not want to be mastered by something over which you ought to be master yourself, you will have to work on it. You also will have to learn, as we all do, to discern your inner dialogues and debates from the voice of your heart and the inner voice of truth. Meditation exercises will greatly contribute and help you so that you understand and recognize them more clearly.

217

In order to center yourself, it will be helpful, for example, if you count while your breath comes in and goes out, or if you take a word, a picture, or a sound into your silence. You can always call yourself back to these aids from your wandering and hassling thoughts or feelings. They can give you support and remind you of your intention. It will thus be easier to return to the quiet and settle in more deeply. Just make sure they do not become your crutch against having to feel during silence.

The *picture meditations* follow a somewhat different intent. I have already mentioned a few things in the chapter *Imagination vs. Vision*. While counseling people, I learned that deeply hidden and often totally forgotten painful experiences could be opened and healed by the use of guided meditations. It has always been a special wish of mine to teach people how to use and interpret those experiences so that they could assist each other with the aid of such meditations.

This is especially beneficial in a group. Whenever I have led a group through a guided meditation, every group member had experiences that were specific and personally relevant to their own place of being, and often differed from those of others drastically. One could almost believe I had led the meditation speaking of different things to each participant. But sometimes there were also overlaps, as a group often gathers in need of attention to a common theme. In any event, the gifts are manifold and full of magic when we learn to recognize and interpret them. At the end of this chapter, I offer some suggestions that you can do either by yourself or with others.

I am giving the *Chakra Meditation* some extra space as I consider it especially helpful for energy balance in the body, on which depends not only your physical but also your mental well- being. In inner work, energy balance is an essential requirement even though the inner work itself will also lead to it.

Lay down quietly and relaxed or sit on a meditation pillow so that the pelvis is higher than your knees. You may also sit on a straight-backed chair as long as you are mindful of the position of the pelvis. Take care that your spine is upright. In sitting, **sit *in front* of the two sitting bones** in your butt, not on them. Focus on the two endpoints of your spine and feel the energy connection between them by going very slowly up and down.

You will have to discover whether you need to start working from top to bottom with the chakras or the other way around. It depends on how the main energy flow is directed as observed in the spine. If it is your impression that the flow goes up, you will go from up to down, reversing the flow, in other words: do the opposite of what currently seems to be happening. If you notice anything odd in your spine, such as temperature variations, a tautness, or blockage that does not allow the energy to flow, the following exercises or affirmations may help. Observe the energy reactions in your body while you speak them aloud.

Seventh Chakra

Find your own words for what wants to be said to GOD; or the words "I withdraw so that you, GOD, may take room within" (let HIM in).

Sixth Chakra (forehead and back of head)

"I desire to see and recognize truthfully."

Or, once you have admitted that you do not want to see,

the question: "What is it I don't want to have to see?"

Fifth Chakra (throat and neck)

"Your will be done." (May need repeating.)

"I surrender."

"I am willing to express my feelings."

Fourth Chakra (chest and between shoulder blades)

"I open my heart."

"My heart is burdened." (By what? – Discern!)

"I love."

"I come out of GOD."

"I am... (fill in what is yours)!"

"I would like ... (fill in what you'd like!" ——Every expressed truth will open the heart more. Try it!)

Third Chakra (solar plexus and small of the back)

"I stop judging myself."

"I stop judging _____ (who or what?)"

"I am willing to receive and accept everything"

"I stop my desire to protect myself."

"I would like to know what I "swallowed.""

Second Chakra (abdomen and lower back)

"I accept all my feelings."

"I am willing to feel everything."

"I accept all my suffering."

"I accept all my sorrow."

"I am willing to face all my old, painful memories."

First Chakra (pelvis and coccyx)

"I want to live."

"I am angry."

"I am a passionate being."

"I am not who you think I am."

"I am not who I think I am."

"I want to have... (whatever)"

"Me, too – me, too!"

It's possible that these affirmations increase the blockage. If that is so, you will need to admit the opposite first. Always be aware of your breath during these exercises and while speaking any of these affirmations and/or truths. They address the blockages in the chakras and can dissolve them. *But please consider the opening of the heart chakra a priority.* The heart chakra is—— as mentioned before——the center between the upper and the lower chakras. It is the bridge between thinking and feeling, is the mediator between everything polar, controversial, and separated, the mediator between half-truths on either side.

The opening of the heart chakra is especially important when the solar plexus is opened too wide. For the expressions from outside are "digestible" only when the heart participates in receiving and transforming them. That is why I entreat you to always give your heart chakra special if not prior attention. In meditation, focus again and again on the back between your shoulder blades. Here resides the non-judgmental acceptance of yourself and the external world. Only here can you heal what went estray, "downwards" or "upwards". As the fox says in the story of *The Little Prince*[15]: "It is only with the heart that one can see rightly what is essential and is invisible to the eye," and I full-heartedly agree.

Additional Exercises

(Most of these are better done with someone who listens to you while you share what you see.)

Once you have practiced *feeling* your chakras, you can do various other exercises from which you may benefit, for example the ***rainbow meditation*** mentioned earlier. My own account of this meditation may not be very encouraging, but I hold the fundamental conviction that everything that happens or is experienced is for the best and serves the unfolding of our higher consciousness. Perhaps it will encourage you when you hear that all other participants of that particular group had only delightful experiences. The colors in themselves are healing and helping.

Another beautiful exercise is the **animal meditation**. It serves to reveal which animal (pattern) dwells predominantly in the respective chakras (the animal kingdom is also within us). You relax, breathe, and imagine each one of your chakras as a space in which lives an animal. Do not put an animal there, let it show up. Go slowly, observe each animal and its condition closely so that you can describe it before you go to the next chakra. Once you have seen all seven animals, ask them to gather in a conference and watch if or how they relate to each other. Perhaps there is an order of rank, a pecking order. If you study the animal kingdom a little, you may find what *you* associate with a respective animal, its way of being, its place in nature, and its behavior and characteristics. Then relate these to your own (possibly), and you may have great fun learning something about yourself. Write things down after each such meditation, for in time, the animals may change places.

Here follows an ***angel meditation with detailed guidance.*** This meditation can help you to meet the angel or spiritual being who walks with you. This is also better done in a group. Whether you are alone or in a group, <u>someone should guide you through it</u>. It will also be important and beneficial if all of you share your experiences afterwards. You will better understand what I said above about the gain in a group.

Preparation: Lie down on a mat or bed, covered with a blanket. Legs are uncrossed and comfortably placed apart. Your arms are loosely at your side. Close your eyes. Observe/feel your breath as it comes and goes. Feel all of your body the way it has been placed. Feel the ground under you as it supports your body.

To the Guide: speak very slowly with lots of pauses/be attentive to further remarks in parentheses: "Come with me to a large, green meadow. It is summer—— flowers are blooming——the sun is warm. If you listen carefully, you can hear the hum of insects and the song of the birds. Perhaps you also smell the scent of grass and flowers. Look to the sky above where various shapes of clouds move along like puffed cotton. Decide on one of the clouds and ask it to come down to the meadow. It will land in front of you, offering an opportunity to climb on. Do this. It carries you up, joins its cloud sisters, and sails across a vast landscape that you can easily follow as you watch from above. You see forests, fields, meadows, small villages, and rivers. From up here, Earth looks like a picture book.

After a while, the cloud you are on lands on another meadow, far away from where you started. This meadow is even more beautiful, more colorful. You step off, and you see in the near distance three big, flat stones on the ground, lying side by side in a row. Go there. You step onto the *first stone* to your left: Take off all your clothes, stand still. You now receive from above a lovely warm shower of light. Feel as it pearls like water over and through your entire body. It cleanses and prepares you for your divine encounter. Receive this gift in calmness and serenity and enjoy! (Leave time for the experience.)

Slowly the shower decreases to a slow trickling, and then stops altogether. Reflect for a moment on your experience and then step over onto the *center stone*. Here you are given new clothing. Look at what you were given and are wearing now. How does it feel? Look also at your feet, and whether you received something for them or remain barefooted. (Leave time.)

After a while you step onto the *third stone* to your right. Here you will meet an entity——your angel or guide. Ask the entity to please appear. Our spiritual companions wish to be asked. Our encounter is not a matter of course and should not be taken for granted. Wait and be attentive. (Leave time.)

When you realize a presence, be it as an image or an energy, greet it and observe. Now look into your hands. You have brought a gift of which you knew nothing until now. Look closely at the gift you hold but do not assess it in any way, and——most importantly——*do not judge or try to change it.* The entity will receive it from you. (Leave time.)

After this Being has accepted your gift, it hands over his/her gift for you. Accept it, consider it closely, and be aware of how it affects you. (Leave time.)

Express your gratitude for his/her coming, for the encounter and the gift, say goodbye, and let him/her go.

Take your gift with you, leave the stones, and walk over to the cloud that has been waiting. Climb onto the cloud again and settle. It takes you up into the air again and carries you over the Earth and its landscapes back to the meadow from where you started. Enjoy the ride and watch over the edge of the cloud what you see below. After landing, thank the cloud for its help and participation, thank the wind that carried the cloud, and release the cloud to the sky.

Now return to the room, into your body, and into the possible presence of others who also traveled. Bring your gift. Move arms, hands, legs, and feet, and slowly open your eyes. Write your experience down.

So? How was it? You can repeat this meditation any time——the experience will always be different and new. Never forget, you are not alone, there is always an accompanying presence whether you are aware of it or not, whether you can see it or not.

ADDENDUM

More Questions for Contemplation

1. The Human Dilemma

- Do you know this condition of being earth-bound?
- Can you recognize the dilemma you may be in? How does it relate to your dealing with your difficulties and your suffering?
- Do you try to help people that have no questions?
- To what degree are you willing to ask and then be open for what is being offered and given? How great is your willingness to accept it?
- With what do you quench your longing? Do you need what you take or buy?
- Would you like to learn to trust GOD's invitation and to rely on HIM?
- Are you willing to let go of all you believed to be, and follow HIM?
- Which small steps towards this goal are you willing to take?

2. Divine Manifestation

- Do you consider yourself to be God? Or is GOD allowed to live in you? What would be the difference?
- Can you see what it may possibly mean to walk the "Cross" instead of carrying it?

- What would it mean to you to realize CHRIST in relationship with others? What would this in effect look like?

3. Via Crucis

- Does the history of the crucifixion have any personal meaning? Is it new to you, or do you no longer want to hear anything about it?
- Do you recognize this Light Being and are you willing to accept the hand it offers? Would you even be willing to go beyond and receive it inside of you?
- Do you have the courage to set out——before you know where to——into a "land" that GOD will show you (like in the story of Abraham Genes.12:1) ? Or would that be too great a risk?
- Which of your goals, plans, and securities would be at stake? How important are they to you? Could you let them go?
- What do you think is meant by the self-denial that Jesus speaks of? (Matthew 16:24). Is it self-mortification or self-humiliation that we know from Christian religious history and also from other religions, or is it something else?

4. The Altar of GOD

- Do you entertain the idea that you may have lived more than once on Earth? Or is this a foreign and unacceptable thought to you?
- Do you remember times in your life when you actually lived bypassing yourself?
- Where do you still effort to be worthy or more worthy? Before GOD or before man?

- In what forms does your resistance appear against truth that pops up and reveals itself? Can you surrender the resistance?
- Can you utilize your realizations or is it hard for you to implement them? Do you tend to leave them laying around unused?

5. The Nine-Branched Menorah

- How is your bravery? How is your clenching of your teeth? In what way do you try to be a hero?
- Are you tempted to discipline yourself to not feel? In what way?
- Which screams did you not howl? What were the situations?
- What are the pictures of your self-image? What are the pictures others pin on you?
- What do you do so that those you are close to remain close? What do you do to rid yourself of those who are uncomfortable? At what cost?
- What tradition or what method means more to you than others? Is there one you consider absolute?
- What are your defense mechanisms to keep yourself from feeling?
- Are there heroes in your life whom you admire? What is their heroism?
- Do you know what is meant by abandonment (in the spiritual sense) or agape (Greek)? Are you open for it, willing? Completely or partially? Is partially possible?

6. GOD's Angels

- Do you also try to love your enemies——to generously forgive them?

- Do you know the feeling of being crucified? What happens to you? How would you prefer to act?

- Consider such a specific situation or even many different painful situations. Can you recognize the angels of GOD in them? Or do they remain enemies?

- Can you envision that such a new perception could shape your relationships fundamentally different?

- Do you believe that this analogy of angels could be applied to all perpetrators on Earth, or even may have to be? Or are there also some who do what remains "unforgivable"?

- What about Jesus's declaration: "Father, forgive them, for they do not know what they do" (Luke 23:34)? What does that mean? Does it also apply to you?

7. The Son of GOD

- What do you fear most? The insults or verbal abuse from others or being alone?

- Do you remember any situations in which you betrayed yourself in order to not feel or be excluded?

- Whom or what would you have to let be if you lived honestly?

229

- How does it feel when the people around you reject what you are or can give? How do you deal with it? Do you try harder, or do you turn towards those that are willing to receive?

- How important is the appreciation of others to you? Or whose appreciation is important? Which of your notions would you like to see acknowledged by that person? What are the consequences of this for your life and your relationships?

- Do you truly believe that you are a child of GOD? To be of HIM? Or are you a child of your parents?

- If you have given birth to a child, do you believe it is *yours*?

- Are you aware of the many experiences of death and dying on the spiritual path? Which ones have you personally experienced?

- How and in what way do you cultivate your pride and defend your "shield"? Are you willing to give it up? Or do you believe a spiritual person ought to keep it?

- Do you grasp Jesus's surrender into His own death experience? Do you believe as I did that we could be spared?

8. Mother Earth

- To what degree did you surrender responsibility for your being and doing to your parents?

- Are you free of the ties to your father, your mother? If not, what consequences does this have for you?

- Have you recognized and accepted GOD as your true FATHER and MOTHER?

- What do you think: Can it be possible that Heaven could be earthly, Earth could be heavenly? And what would that imply?
- If you have birthed a child, what do you recognize in her/him? Do you believe you know her/him?

9. Renouncement

- What do you do with your needs? Do you suppress them or take notice of them?
- Do you know of the promise given us with the story of the lilies of the field (Matt. 6:28)? Does Jesus direct these words to you? Do you feel spoken to?
- Can you trust His words? Rely on them?

10. The Chakras of the Earth

- Are you willing to trust GOD and HIS laws (not that you have much of a choice)? Can you recognize HIS love in the circumstances of life?
- Is it possible for you to appear as a predator? To be seen as one? How hard is it, if so, and what do you do with being blamed, the finger-pointing?
- Are you willing to allow the old to be destroyed in you? Old habits, old attachments, old wishes?
- Are you willing to destroy and recognize it's happening through you in others?

- Where are you a judge? Who are the judges in your surroundings?
- Do you judge people and their actions or rather their attitudes in their action?
- How do you deal with the judge in you and in others?

11. Adam, Eve, and Fig Leaves

- Where and particularly how do you project the respective male or female externally? What does it look like? What can you tell about your own mirror in others?
- Where and when do you attempt to apportion blame to others? What is behind it?
- If you blame... What is difficult to admit?
- Close your eyes and see yourself in front of your inner eye. Where are your fig leaves? And what do they cover? Feel them.

12. "And" is Cooperation

- How does "as well as" differ from "and"?
- What can help you to cooperate? What can help the one you are with?
- What may hinder you from cooperating? What tempts you to compromise? Are you aware of the lifelessness and lovelessness of a compromise, the lowest common denominator?
- What are the situations in your life where you either were or are willing to compromise? What relationships are affected?

- Is it agreeable to you when you find your partner, boss, father, mother, or someone else compromising because of you? Even though they won't stand fully behind you and may someday hold it against you?
- Do you resent those who, in your eyes, press you to compromise?
- Do you believe that there are situations where one has to compromise? What are they?
- How important is "winning" to you?

13. The Bodhisattva

- Do you know conditions of sorrow that never seem to end? What experiences have you had with them?
- Is the Bodhisattva at all meaningful to you? Do his tasks and concerns speak to you?
- What would it mean for you to do your best, if you don't even know when, what, and why?

14. You are Spirit

- Do you yourself limit the space given to you to live? Why and how?
- Did you ever think after a disillusionment, that you would have preferred to continue your illusions instead of being disillusioned?
- Did you ever feel grateful when an illusion was taken?
- Or did you become bitter and throw the baby out with the bathwater?

- What does it mean to you to be Spirit and free? Do you understand the implication?
- What does it mean to be One with all? What consequences does that have for your life?

15. The Servant

- Do you recognize that everything in this creation is master as well as servant?
- Do you remember the words of another human being that still hurt? Try to listen again, more closely and separate from your interpretation at the time. Ask for help.
- Can you conceive to go into meditation with what has affected/hurt you and ask for revelation?
- Did you ever have the experience of knowing you have to do something and then just froze in fear? Or procrastinated?

16. The Thief on the Cross

- Are you aware that we are all interconnected? That there is nothing in human experience that you do not also carry inside?
- Did you ever experience something similar in your body to what is described in this chapter? How did you deal with it?
- Read the story of the two thieves, maybe again (Luke 23:32–43). Do you know the respective states they are in? Do you know them inside of you or do they seem foreign to you?

- Do you find it difficult, like it was for the one thief, to accept gratefully that which is and that which isn't? (Gratefully accepting does not mean just swallowing and pretending to have accepted!)
- Do you remember situations in your life for which you still have to find gratefulness? That you still haven't fully comprehended (and I don't mean explained to yourself)?
- Can you bear that I speak of these hurtful and humiliating experiences?
- Do you dare to allow yourself to loudly express your deep-seated resentment against life as it was for you——perhaps once and for all?
- Do you believe that GOD can take it when you attack HIM, let HIM know how you truly feel, and give HIM a tongue-lashing? Or do you believe no one should behave like this to GOD?

17. The Rosary

- Are you longing for such or similar experiences of divine intervention——or that you may also experience directly and unexpectedly such assistance?
- Do you believe that all your pleas are perceived?
- Can you see how wonderful life can be when we are open and permeable?
- Do you take the trouble to see your spirit companions, encounter them, and speak to them? Are you willing to do this?
- How stuck are you in the rules and rituals of the Church?
- How open are you for the living Word, the "living water," the living encounter with the living GOD? How open for the church IN YOU?

235

18. The Shack and the Palace

- Is there any difference between giving and being? Do you know one?
- Is it easier for you to speak about feelings, or are you able to be them?
- What happens when someone refuses to carry and nurture you? Do you look for someone else, or do you assume responsibility for your own life and your ability to relate?
- Are you aware that CHRIST in you is Bread and Water? Your sustenance? How can you be one with Him?

19. The Crucifier

- Can you see that all the crucifixion stories are pointing to the eternal essence of life?
- Can you see that you can't escape the "crucifiers", and that in your capacity as crucifier, you either crucify outside or inside?
- How great is your willingness to stop defending yourself?
- Can you bear to lose your reputation? That whatever you thought it was, is being killed?

20. The Cleansing of the Temple

- What excuses do you have for your temple dealings?

- Do you see that you can't eat the cake and have it, too? Or, as we say in German: you can't dance at two weddings (or serve two masters: Matt.6:24). What side will you be on?
- Do you know the language of your heart, its voice? Will you practice hearing and listening to it? Follow it?
- Do you have any idea how unpredictable life is, in every respect? Does that make you afraid or joyfully excited?

21. The Ghetto

- Here is room for all your own questions

22. Exodus

- Do you know the Pharaoh in yourself (perhaps it is a female Pharaoh or your mother)? Do you know *your* "people of Israel"?
- Do you feel encouraged to step in and contribute to healing?
- Do you already know something about the walk through the desert? Where are you now?
- Do you also desire to go back——to your Egypt so to speak—— whenever it gets difficult? For example, go back to your old miserable job when the new one turns out not much fun either? Or go back into an abusive relationship because being alone is worse?
- What would you rather not have to give up?
- Do you feel a Moses in you? An impartial voice? Will you support him?

May I be a bridge

from you to you

Christa Phillips
Living Spring Ranch
261 West Parrot Creek Road
Roundup, MT 59072 - USA

End Notes

[1] Three different versions of biblical translations. (Any text especially highlighted is the author's choice).

[2] I later learned by accident that this image represented the eye of God in early Egypt and depicted the human manifestation at the time (i.e., the condition of human evolution in relationship to God). Concurrently, I learned that this Egyptian epoch repeats itself in our age on a different level of consciousness, depicted by reversed triangles. With this information comes a warning: Today, humanity appears equally tempted to stray into the same trap as the Egyptians of that time; that is, deifying the human person, to deify a separate being instead of moving closer to GOD, to unite with and realize Him, to become a permeable vessel for the Creative Force, It's intent and order.

[3] Mainly from Edgar Cayce: *A Commentary Based on the Study of Twenty-four Psychic Discourses*——ARE Press, Virginia Beach. Also in the many readings of Edgar Cayce, catalogued, that are available.

[4] Gitta Mallasz: *Talking with Angels*, English Rendition by Robert Hinshaw, Daimon Verlag, Einsiedeln (publishers).

[5] There is a documentary about people who no longer eat: *In The Beginning there was Light.*

[6] Taizé CD titled *Bleibet hier* – in German only

[7] Gitanjali *Strong Mercy* by Rabindranath Tagore.

[8] Irina Tweedy. *Daughter of Fire*, Little Brown, Waltham: USA. 1976.

[9] *A Course in Miracles* – Textbook, Workbook for students, Manual for teachers – Foundation for Inner Peace, Mill Valley, CA 94942.

[10] The word "obedience" and its connotation are loaded and burdening to many people. Many are unreconciled with what life asks and requires of them – often under the auspices of religion, patriotism, parental love, and responsibility. I belonged to those and, in my defiance, had tossed out the baby with the bathwater. I was not spared, and had to face *my* error about obedience, was confronted by *my* misunderstandings, and had to surrender my rebellion in order to discern between bathwater and baby. That is why here I use the word "obedience" consciously, even though it may stimulate resistance and/or old, unhealed aches.

[11] There are authors who attribute this chakra to the Pineal gland.

[12] Geddes MacGregor: *Reincarnation and Karma im Christentum,* Book I and II, Aquamarin Verlag, Grafing 1990 (published in the US by Quest Books).

[13] Akashic records – akasha or akasa, the Sanskrit word for "sky", "space", "luminous", or "aether") are a compendium of thoughts, events, and emotion—some gifted psychics like Edgar Cayce et al. can access them

[14] Word – Man, Center, heart chakra – see menorah

[15] by Antoine de Saint-Exupéry - *The little Prince*

[16] *Twenty Cases Suggestive of Reincarnation*——by Ian Stevenson

[17] Community House in Virginia Beach, Virginia closed in 1999

www.ingramcontent.com/pod-product-compliance
Lightning Source LLC
Chambersburg PA
CBHW062050080426
42734CB00012B/2602